D1628403

The Scottish Parliament
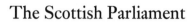

The Scottish Parliament
LAW AND PRACTICE

Mark Lazarowicz and Jean McFadden

EDINBURGH
University Press

Edinburgh University Press is one of the leading university presses in the UK. We publish academic books and journals in our selected subject areas across the humanities and social sciences, combining cutting-edge scholarship with high editorial and production values to produce academic works of lasting importance. For more information visit our website: edinburghuniversitypress.com

© Mark Lazarowicz and Jean McFadden, 2018

Edinburgh University Press Ltd
The Tun – Holyrood Road
12 (2f) Jackson's Entry
Edinburgh EH8 8PJ

Typeset in 11/13 Ehrhardt by
Servis Filmsetting Ltd, Stockport, Cheshire,
and printed and bound in Great Britain

A CIP record for this book is available from the British Library

ISBN 978 1 4744 3373 0 (hardback)
ISBN 978 1 4744 3374 7 (paperback)
ISBN 978 1 4744 3375 4 (webready PDF)
ISBN 978 1 4744 3376 1 (epub)

Contents

Table of Cases

Table of Statutes

Table of Statutory Instruments

Preface

It used to be said that what distinguished the British political system from those of practically every other country in the world was the absence of a written constitution. The extent to which that statement is true has become significantly smaller in the last forty-five years as a result of the United Kingdom joining the European Community, now the European Union, and becoming bound by the Treaty of Rome and its successors. Now the combined effect of the Human Rights Act 1998 and the Scotland Acts 1998, 2012 and 2106, when added to the European treaties, mean that, in Scotland, the rights of individuals and the powers of the state are to a considerable extent based on fundamental constitutional laws which, together, can truly be said to be the written constitution of Scotland.

This book aims to be a concise but comprehensive guide to that part of the Scottish constitution which is based on the Scotland Acts 1998 to 2016. It seeks to place the constitutional settlement which these Acts represent in its historical setting, as well as the internal context of the Scottish Parliament's relations with other public bodies, and the external context of its relations with the Westminster Parliament and Europe. The procedures and internal working arrangements of the Parliament are also considered.

This book draws substantially on the authors' previous work, *The Scottish Parliament: An Introduction*. This book takes account of the results of the fifth ordinary election to the Scottish Parliament and the forming of the new Scottish Administration in May 2016, and the decision of the UK Parliament to withdraw from the European Union following the referendum of 2016. It also brings the reader up to date on various other constitutional changes which have occurred since the Scottish Parliament was first established in 1999.

The authors wish to thank Drew Smith, Kenneth Campbell QC, David Johnston QC, Sarah Boyack and Roderick Campbell for helpful comments on the text. They would also like to thank Alan Barr, Baroness

Clark of Calton QC and Lord Davidson of Glen Clova QC for advice on some particular issues considered in the book. They are also grateful to the Parliament's Presiding Officer Ken McIntosh MSP for his helpful comments regarding possible reforms of the Parliament's procedure. Thanks are also due to the staff of the Scottish Parliament for helpful advice on a number of factual matters concerning the operation of the Parliament. Jean McFadden expresses her thanks to Tracey McKerlich and Elizabeth Stewart of the Legal Services Agency, Glasgow for secretarial assistance. Thanks, too, to Dr Andrew Mylne, Head of the Non-Government Bills Unit at the Scottish Parliament for helpful comments on Chapter 5. Tables 5.1 and 5.2 are reproduced by permission of the Scottish Parliament. Mark Lazarowicz would like to thank his son, Thomas, for assistance with tabular presentation of material. The authors, of course, accept full responsibility for any errors and omissions.

At the time of writing, a few of the provisions of the Scotland Act 2016 had not yet been brought into force. As it is expected, however, that all those provisions will become effective in the near future, the book assumes that all sections of that Act are in force. Otherwise, the law is stated as at 1 September 2017 unless the text indicates otherwise.

The Scottish Parliament is normally referred to in this book as 'the Parliament', and the UK counterpart as the 'UK Parliament'.

Jean McFadden
Mark Lazarowicz
September 2017

CHAPTER ONE

The Scottish Parliament:
The Background

INTRODUCTION

The Scotland Act 1998[1] was one of the most important constitutional
statutes passed by the United Kingdom Parliament in recent years, with
great significance for the rest of the United Kingdom as well as for
Scotland. In Scottish terms, it established a parliament which has the
powers to make laws for Scotland in a wide range of areas. In UK terms,
it was seen as an important element in a wider package of devolutionary or decentralising measures which have so far included a National
Assembly for Wales (originally with mainly administrative powers but
now with some legislative powers also) and an Assembly in Northern
Ireland with legislative powers from its inception. The establishment
of these institutions represents a significant transfer of power from the
United Kingdom Parliament and may in time lead to devolutionary
changes in England.

SCOTLAND AND THE UNION[2]

Prior to 1707, England and Scotland possessed separate constitutions
and parliaments. Scotland and England came together in a political
union in 1707 after the Parliaments of England and Scotland passed
individual Acts of Union whereby the separate Parliaments of the two
countries ceased to exist and were replaced by the Parliament of the
United Kingdom of Great Britain. Although the Scottish Parliament
was abolished in 1707, the Scots maintained a sense of national identity
owing, in part, to the fact that the Presbyterian Church and the Scottish
legal system were preserved by the terms of the Union. The union was
not warmly embraced by most Scots. Indeed, there was rioting on the
streets of Glasgow and Edinburgh when the terms were first made public.

However, the economic situation at the time was such that acceptance of the union was almost inevitable and it was largely tolerated.

The arrangements for the government of Scotland from London were, for much of the eighteenth and nineteenth centuries, in the hands of the Lord Advocate, a Law Officer appointed by the government. Interest in parliamentary affairs by Scots was minimal as their MPs were manipulated to dance to the government's tune. The electoral system was so corrupt and the number of people entitled to vote so tiny that not even the Scottish aristocracy, let alone the ordinary Scot, could hope to achieve influence. In 1823 it was estimated that fewer than three thousand men were entitled to vote. (Women were not to get the vote until 1918). However, demand for electoral reform grew and, in 1832, the male middle classes were enfranchised by the Representation of the People (Scotland) Act, followed by the Representation of the People Acts of 1867 and 1884 which extended the franchise to include all men aged twenty-one years or over. As more and more men were given the vote, discontent rose about the lack of interest shown by the Westminster Parliament in Scottish affairs.

THE ROAD TO DEVOLUTION

Demand grew for the appointment of a Scottish Secretary of State, a post which had been abolished in 1746. In 1885, the government passed the Secretary for Scotland Act which established the post of Secretary for Scotland and the Scottish Office, based in Dover House in London. In 1926, the post was upgraded to that of Secretary of State and, in 1939, the Scottish Office was moved to St Andrew's House in Edinburgh. The Secretary of State (or predecessor Secretary) for Scotland has had a seat in the Cabinet in peacetime since 1892.

A number of factors, including the rise of the Irish Home Rule movement in the nineteenth century, led to the emergence of a Scottish Home Rule Association in 1886. Scottish home rule was frequently discussed in the House of Commons although no bill reached the statute book to provide a parliament for Scotland similar to that which was provided for Northern Ireland by the Government of Ireland Act 1920. The National Party for Scotland was founded in 1928 and started to contest elections in the following year. In 1934, the National Party of Scotland merged with another home rule party, the Scottish Party, to form the Scottish National Party (SNP). The SNP won its first parliamentary seat in a by-election in Motherwell in 1945 but lost it in the general election later that year. The SNP made no more headway in terms of parliamentary seats for more than twenty years but gained an increasing number of votes, particularly in by-elections. In 1967, the SNP won the previously safe Labour seat of Hamilton in a by-election and, in the following year, won 30 per cent of the vote and 108 seats in the local government elections.

The Labour Government, concerned by the electoral success of the SNP and of the Welsh nationalist party, Plaid Cymru, which had won a Welsh by-election in 1966, appointed, in 1969, a Royal Commission (chaired by Lord Crowther and, after his death, by Lord Kilbrandon) to examine the constitution of the United Kingdom. The Commission reported in 1973.[3] It rejected separatism and federalism as solutions and recommended a directly elected assembly for Scotland, elected on the system of the single transferable vote. The response to the Commission's report by the Conservative and Labour Parties was lukewarm and neither party included devolution in their manifestos for the general election which was held in February 1974. However, the results of that election gave devolution a new lease of life as the SNP won seven seats and Plaid Cymru two seats in the Westminster Parliament.

The new Labour Government, which did not have an outright majority of seats in the House of Commons, was forced to make concessions to the nationalist parties and announced that it would bring forward proposals for consideration. In September 1974, a White Paper was published entitled Democracy and Devolution: Proposals for Scotland and Wales.[4] It proposed directly elected assemblies for Scotland and Wales, with the Scottish Assembly having legislative, but not tax-raising, powers and the Welsh Assembly having executive powers only.

A further general election was held in October 1974 at which the SNP won eleven seats. A second White Paper was published in November 1975 entitled Our Changing Democracy: Devolution to Scotland and Wales.[5] A Scotland and Wales Bill was published in November 1976 but the government, lacking a secure majority, was unable to get it through all the necessary stages in Parliament and the Bill was dropped. The following year, separate bills for Scotland and Wales were introduced. During the parliamentary process an amendment was introduced which made it necessary for 40 per cent of the electorates to vote 'Yes' in referenda before the Acts could be brought into operation. The Scotland and the Wales Acts received the Royal Assent in 1978 and the referenda were held in March 1979. Although the majority of Scots who did vote voted 'Yes', the 40 per cent threshold was not reached. The Welsh decisively voted 'No'. A motion of no confidence in the Labour Government was tabled, the government was defeated and a general election was held in May 1979 which was won by the Conservatives under Margaret Thatcher. The Scotland and the Wales Acts were repealed in the following month.

THE SCOTTISH CONSTITUTIONAL CONVENTION

The Conservative Government remained in power for eighteen years and was implacably opposed to devolution but the desire for some form of devolution in Scotland remained and a cross-party Campaign for a Scottish Assembly (CSA) was formed in 1980. Following the re-election of the Conservatives in 1983 and 1987, the CSA set up a committee of prominent Scots who produced The Claim of Right for Scotland in 1988 which advocated the establishment of a constitutional convention to draw up plans for Scottish self-government. The Scottish Constitutional Convention (SCC) was set up in March 1989 with the involvement of the Labour and Liberal Democrat Parties and several smaller parties but without the Conservatives and the SNP. Also in membership were most of the Scottish local authorities and representatives of a wide spectrum of Scottish life. The SCC published a number of documents culminating in Scotland's Parliament: Scotland's Right (November 1995) which advocated a Scottish Parliament elected partly by the traditional 'first past the post' system and partly by a form of proportional representation. The SCC recommended that the Parliament should have legislative powers over a wide range of domestic issues and the power to vary income tax by up to 3 pence in the pound.

THE 1997 GENERAL ELECTION AND THE REFERENDUMS ACT 1997

The Labour Party and the Liberal Democrat Party included a commitment to a Scottish Parliament, based on the proposals of the SCC, in their manifestos for the 1997 general election. The Labour Party won that election with a very large majority and, within three months, published a White Paper, Scotland's Parliament,[6] which detailed their plans for a devolved Parliament with legislative and limited tax-varying powers. Before introducing a bill to establish the Parliament, the government wanted the proposal to be endorsed by the Scottish people in a referendum. The Referendums (Scotland and Wales) Act 1997 was quickly passed by the United Kingdom Parliament and a referendum was held in September 1997. The electorate had to vote on two issues – on the principle of a Scottish Parliament, and on its tax-varying powers. The answers which the Scottish people gave to both questions were emphatically in the affirmative. On the issue of a Scottish Parliament, 74.3 per cent of those who did vote voted 'Yes' (a total of 1,775,045 voters). On the issue of tax-varying powers, 63.5 per cent voted 'Yes' (1,512,889 voters).

THE SCOTLAND ACT 1998

The government introduced the Scotland Bill into the House of Commons in December 1997. The Bill received the Royal Assent on 19 November 1998. It should be noted that the existence of the Scottish Parliament was not 'entrenched' in the 1998 Act. 'Entrenched' means protected from repeal by a future United Kingdom Parliament. However,the doctrine of the sovereignty of the UK Parliament means that it cannot bind a future UK Parliament as to what Acts it may pass or repeal. It may be considered as politically entrenched.

The first general election to the Scottish Parliament was held on 6 May 1999. The Parliament was formally opened by the Queen on 1 July 1999 and, on that date, the Parliament assumed its full powers. After extended negotiations following that general election, the Scottish Labour and Liberal Democrat Parties formed a coalition administration with the backing of seventy-three of the 129 members of the Parliament. That coalition continued in office until the second Scottish parliamentary general election on 1 May 2003 and resumed the administration thereafter (although this time with a slim combined overall majority of five seats as a result of a decline in support for the coalition's larger party, the Labour Party).

In the third general election, in 2007, the Labour Party lost more support and the Scottish National Party emerged as the largest party with forty-seven seats, just one more than the Labour Party. Unable to form a coalition, the SNP decided to form a minority administration. Alhough the electoral system used for elections to the Scottish Parliament (see Chapter 3) was designed to make it difficult for any one party to gain an outright majority, the general election held in 2011 unexpectedly produced a majority for the SNP. It formed the administration which lasted until 2016 when the fifth general election was held. In this election, the SNP lost its majority and formed another minority government.

THE CALMAN COMMISSION AND THE SCOTLAND ACT 2012

Since the establishment of the Scottish Parliament in 1999, there has been much discussion as to whether the powers of the Scottish Parliament should be enlarged. In 2007, when the first minority SNP government was formed, the opposition parties agreed to establish a Commission on Scottish Devolution.[7] This was supported by the UK Parliament. Sir Kenneth Calman was appointed chairman. All the main political parties were represented on the Commission apart from the SNP who declined to participate because the question of independence for Scotland was not included in the Commission's remit. The Commission was independent of any political party and reported to both the Scottish Parliament and the UK Parliament.

Its remit was:

> To review the provisions of the Scotland Act 1998 in the light of experience and to recommend any changes . . . that would enable the Scottish Parliament to serve the people of Scotland better, improve the financial accountability of the Scottish Parliament and to continue to secure the position of Scotland in the UK.

Its final report was published in 2009[8] and recommended that various powers should be devolved to the Scottish Parliament. These included:

- The administration of elections to the Scottish Parliament
- The regulation of airguns
- Responsibility for aspects of licensing and control of controlled substances
- Regulation of drink-driving limits
- The determination of the national speed limits in Scotland
- Giving more power to the Scottish Parliament to vary the rate of income tax paid by Scottish taxpayers
- Greater borrowing powers
- Control of various minor taxes including a new land and buildings tax, control over business rates, and a Scottish Landfill tax

A Scotland Bill to implement the Calman Commission's recommendations was introduced in the United Kingdom Parliament in 2010. An ad hoc committee was established in the Scottish Parliament to examine the Bill's provisions and the Scottish general election held in 2011, which resulted in a majority SNP government, strengthened their hand in negotiating with the UK Government. The Bill finally reached the statute book as the Scotland Act in May 2012.[9]

THE REFERENDUM ON INDEPENDENCE FOR SCOTLAND

When the Scottish National Party unexpectedly won an outright majority in the Scottish general election of 2011 its leader immediately announced that he had a mandate to pursue the party's goal of independence for Scotland. This led to protracted discussion with the UK Government because the union of Scotland and England is a matter reserved to the Parliament of the United Kingdom by Schedule 5 of the Scotland Act 1998, and the Scottish Parliament did not have the legal power to hold a referendum.

In October 2012, an agreement was signed between the Prime Minister and the First Minister (called the Edinburgh Agreement). It was agreed that the UK Parliament would make an order under section 30 of the Scotland Act 1998 which would give the Scottish Parliament the power to hold a referendum of the people living in Scotland on the question of independence. The section 30 order was made in January 2013. The Scottish Parliament then passed the Scottish Independence Referendum Act 2013 which enabled a referendum to be held and the Scottish Independence Referendum (Franchise) Act 2013 which gave the right to vote in the referendum to sixteen- and seventeen-year-olds.

The date for the referendum was set as 18 September 2014. The result of the referendum was 44.7 per cent in favour of independence and 55.3 per cent against.

FURTHER DEVOLUTION OF POWERS: THE SMITH COMMISSION

On 19 September 2014, the day the result of the independence referendum was announced, the UK Prime Minister at the time, David Cameron, and other leading party politicians, announced the establishment of a cross-party commission to be chaired by Lord Smith of Kelvin to examine and make recommendations for the devolution of further powers to the Scottish Parliament.

That commission was given the remit

to convene cross-party talks and facilitate an inclusive engagement process across Scotland to produce, by 30 November 2014, heads of agreement with recommendations for further devolution of powers to the Scottish Parliament . . . The recommendations will deliver more financial, welfare and taxation powers, strengthening the Scottish Parliament within the United Kingdom.

Lord Smith of Kelvin chaired this commission and, unlike previous commissions, its membership was deliberately chosen to be representative of the major Scottish political parties represented in the Parliament who all nominated members to what became known as the 'Smith Commission'. Within only ten weeks of the independence referendum, on 27 November 2014, the Smith Commission produced a report[10] recommending further substantial devolution of powers to the Scottish Parliament, including the following:

- The Scottish Parliament to have complete power to set the rates and bands of income tax.
- The Scottish Parliament to receive a proportion of the VAT raised in Scotland, amounting to the first ten percentage points of the standard rate.
- UK legislation to state that the Scottish Parliament and Scottish Government are permanent institutions.
- The Parliament will also be given powers to legislate over how it is elected and run.
- The Scottish Parliament to have power to extend the vote to 16- and 17-year-olds, allowing them to vote in the Scottish general election in 2016.
- The Scottish Parliament to have control over several welfare benefits, including the under-occupancy charge (popularly known as the bedroom tax).
- The Scottish Parliament to have new powers to make discretionary payments in any area of welfare without the need to obtain prior permission from the Department of Work and Pensions.
- The Scottish Parliament to have control over Air Passenger Duty charged on passengers flying from Scottish airports.
- Responsibility for the management of the Crown Estate's economic assets in Scotland, including the Crown Estate's seabed and mineral and fishing rights, and the revenue generated from these assets, to be transferred to the Scottish Parliament.
- The licensing of onshore oil and gas extraction underlying Scotland to be devolved to the Scottish Parliament.

- The block grant from the UK Government to Scotland to continue to be determined via the operation of the Barnett Formula. New rules to define how it will be adjusted at the point when powers are transferred. MPs representing constituencies across the whole of the UK to continue to decide the UK's budget, including income tax.
- The Scottish and UK Governments to draw up and agree a memorandum of understanding to ensure that devolution is not detrimental to UK-wide critical national infrastructure in relation to matters such as defence and security, oil and gas and energy.

SCOTLAND ACT 2016

The main object of the Scotland Act 2016[11] is the implementation of the recommendations of the Smith Commission. Almost all the recommendations of the Smith Commission mentioned above are incorporated in the Act with the addition of the management and operation of certain tribunals which are currently reserved to the UK, statutory consultation on the BBC's Charter and the power to vary the number of gaming machines in betting premises.

A politically important section is section 1:

s.1(1) The Scottish Parliament and the Scottish Government are a permanent part of the UK's constitutional arrangements . . .
s.1(3) In view of that commitment it is declared that the Scottish Parliament and the Scottish Government are not to be abolished except on the basis of a decision of the people of Scotland voting in a referendum.

This is an attempt to entrench the existence of the Scottish Parliament and the Scottish Government and is, of course, not legally binding because of the doctrine of parliamentary sovereignty. The end result is that the Scottish Parliament is now one of the most powerful devolved institutions in the world.

The following chapters deal with various aspects of the Scottish Parliament, including elections, the powers of the Parliament, and how it goes about its business. The Scottish Government and the powers of the First Minister and other Ministers are examined, as are relations with the UK Parliament and how legal disputes and challenges to the powers of the Parliament and Government are resolved. The vital area of financing the Scottish Government is also examined. Finally, there is discussion of the relationships between the Scottish Parliament and the UK Parliament and the European Union.

NOTES

1. The Scotland Act 1998 is normally referred to as the SA 1998 in this book. All references in this book to sections and schedules which do not specify the legislation concerned are references to the Scotland Act 1998.
2. See the list of 'Further Reading' at the end of this book for more details of the political and historical background.
3. Cmnd 5460.
4. Cmnd 5732.
5. Cmnd 6348.
6. Cm. 3658.
7. See Chapter 2, p. 15.
8. Commission on Scottish Devolution, Serving Scotland Better: Scotland and the UK in the 21st Century, June 2009.
9. The Scotland Act 2012 is normally referred to as the SA 2012 in this book.
10. See Chapter 2, p. 15.
11. The Scotland Act 2016 is normally referred to as the SA 2016 in this book.

CHAPTER TWO

The Powers of the Parliament

INTRODUCTION

The form of government which the establishment of a Scottish Parliament brought to Scotland is known as legislative devolution. This means that the UK Parliament has voluntarily transferred a number of its law-making powers to the Scottish Parliament without relinquishing its own supreme authority or sovereignty. The Scottish Parliament is not independent. It is not free to make laws in any area which it chooses. Therefore, there has to be a framework that defines the areas in which it has the power to make laws (its legislative competence) and those areas where the UK Parliament has not relinquished its law-making power. In this chapter we examine how the UK Parliament has put in place that framework. We also consider the impact of the legal doctrine known as the sovereignty of Parliament.

THE DIVISION OF POWERS – TWO BASIC MODELS

In any system of government where powers are divided between two levels – central and regional, state or provincial – the possibility of one level of government encroaching into the legislative or executive territory of the other may arise. Therefore, the powers of each must be set out in a written document. In the vast majority of countries this document will be the constitution. Because, however, the United Kingdom does not have a constitution contained in one single document, the powers of the two levels of government are set out in an Act of Parliament. In the case of Scotland, the Act of Parliament is the Scotland Act 1998 (SA 1998). The powers of the Scottish level of government were substantially extended by two further Scotland Acts which became in law in 2012 and 2016. These changes were made in the form of amendments to the 1998

Act, so it is still that Act, in its amended form, that sets out the basic constitutional law of the devolved settlement of Scotland.

Broadly speaking, there are two basic models for the constitution or the Act of Parliament to follow:

- the central authority devolves all of its powers to the local or subordinate body except for certain powers which it specifically reserves to itself;
- the central authority devolves to the local or subordinate body certain specified powers while everything not so specified is, by implication, reserved to the centre.
- The former is called the retaining model, and the latter the transferring model. Put simply, the retaining model spells out what the subordinate or local body cannot do and it is implied that it can do everything not spelled out. The transferring model spells out what the local or subordinate body can do and it is implied that it cannot do anything which is not mentioned.

The American Constitution is an example of the retaining model. The powers of the United States Congress (the federal or central legislature) are set out in Article 1. The powers of the states, known as 'residuary' powers are set out in the Tenth Amendment to the Constitution as follows: 'The powers not delegated to the United States by the Constitution, nor prohibited by it to the States, are reserved to the States respectively or to the people'. The American model thus tilts the balance, at least in theory, against the centre, as everything not specified in the Constitution lies within the powers of the individual states.

The Canadian Constitution is an example of the transferring model and was designed to produce a strong central government. section 91 of the British North America Act 1867, now known as the Constitution Act 1867, allocates national powers to the central or federal Parliament, while section 92 allocates regional powers to the provincial legislatures. section 91, however, also gives the federal Parliament the power 'to make laws for the peace, order and good government of Canada in relation to all matters not coming within the classes of subjects assigned exclusively to the Provinces. . .'.

The Scotland Act 1978 (SA 1978), which was to have established a Scottish Assembly in 1979, was an example of the transferring model, specifying in great detail the legislative and executive powers that were to be devolved from Westminster. The SA 1978 was extremely complex, would have required frequent updating to take account of new and amended legislation, and would be likely to have led to many challenges in court as to whether the Assembly was acting outwith its powers (ultra vires).

Three pieces of legislation for Northern Ireland give examples of the retaining model: the Government of Ireland Act 1920, the Northern Ireland Constitution Act 1973, and the Northern Ireland Act 1998.

The Government of Ireland Act 1920, which established the Northern Ireland Parliament at Stormont, listed not the devolved powers but the powers reserved to Westminster. Section 4 of the Act provides that:

> Subject to the provisions of this Act . . . the Parliament of Northern Ireland shall . . . have powers to make laws for the peace, order and good government of Northern Ireland with the following limitations . . . that they shall not have powers to make laws in respect of the following matters in particular, namely . . .

There follows a list of fourteen areas reserved to Westminster including, among others, the Crown, the making of peace or war, and the armed forces.

The Northern Ireland Constitution Act 1973 established the short-lived Northern Ireland Assembly and the power-sharing executive (it lasted for the first five months of 1974). Section 4(1) of the Act states: 'Laws may be made for Northern Ireland by Measures of the Assembly'. Matters excepted from the law-making powers of the Assembly were listed in Schedule 2 to the Act and included, among others, the Crown, the armed forces, and international relations.

The Northern Ireland Act 1998 (NIA 1998) established the Northern Ireland Assembly following the Belfast 'Good Friday' agreement earlier that year. Once again, this gave the Assembly the power to make laws in all areas which were not specifically excluded from its competence. Schedule 2 to the NIA 1998 lists 'excepted matters' which are permanently outside the competence of the Assembly, and Schedule 3 to the Act lists 'reserved matters', over which the Assembly may legislate but only with the consent of the Secretary of State for Northern Ireland. Section 4(2) of the NIA 1998 also gives the Secretary of State the power to remove matters from the list of reserved matters so that the Assembly then has the power to legislate in such areas without his or her consent (and also to put matters concerning which legislation did not previously need his consent on to the list of reserved matters).

THE SCOTLAND ACT 1998

The Scottish Constitutional Convention, early on in its life, adopted the principle of the sovereignty of the Scottish people which led it to favour the retaining form of constitution. In its first report, *Towards a Scottish Parliament*, it declared that

> The type of statute which sits most easily with that principle is the retaining one; it reflects a constitutional settlement in which the Scottish people, being sovereign, agree to the exercise of specified powers by Westminster but retain their sovereignty over all other matters.[1]

The Constitution Unit examined the two forms and, in its report, Scotland's Parliament: Fundamentals for a New Scotland Act,[2] recommended strongly that the best method of ensuring legal clarity as to the scope of devolution was to specify the powers to be retained by Westminster and devolve the remainder. It rejected the view that this was, of necessity, a more generous approach. The method is neutral. It is the length and complexity of the list of retained powers that determine the level of generosity.

The Scottish Office had the benefit of the work of both the Scottish Constitutional Convention and the Constitution Unit in drawing up the White Paper, Scotland's Parliament, and the Scotland Bill. Specific reference is made in the White Paper to the Northern Ireland model, and the government opted for the retaining model in the Scotland Bill. All matters which are not specifically reserved to the UK Parliament are devolved to the Scottish Parliament.

THE SCOTLAND ACTS 2012 AND 2016

The scheme of devolution established by the Scotland Act 1998 operated with only minor changes for more than ten years. Its division of powers into reserved and devolved, though complex, was relatively straightforward and coherent. No doubt that was one of the reasons why there have been very few successful challenges to the competence of legislation passed by the Scottish Parliament.[3] From the beginning of its establishment, however, debate continued as to whether the powers of the Scottish Parliament should be extended. This debate became more concrete at two notable points in the Parliament's history. The first occasion was in 2007 when the Calman Commission was established, reporting in 2009 with recommendations that were eventually reflected in the SA 2012. The Calman Commission and its recommendations are discussed in more detail in the preceding chapter.[4] The second occasion was following the 2014 referendum on Scottish independence when the Smith Commission was established. That commission speedily produced a report later that year. One recommendation, namely that the Parliament be given the power to reduce the minimum voting age to sixteen for elections to the Parliament and for local government (together with the power to make the changes to electoral registration necessary for this to happen) was put into effect by order even more quickly so that the age reduction could be introduced in time for the 2016 Parliament elections.[5] The Scottish Parliament was quick to exercise these powers after they were transferred to it.[6] The remainder of the changes consequential upon the Smith Commission recommendations was put into legislation in the form of the Scotland Act 2016.[7] The Smith Commission and its recommendations are discussed in more detail in the preceding chapter.[8]

As a result of the changes introduced by SA 2012 and SA 2016, and also minor changes resulting from secondary legislation by the UK Parliament, substantial amendments have been made to the original Scotland Act of 1998 (SA 1998) and its original clarity has been substantially diluted. In this chapter (as in this work as a whole), references to the Scotland Act 1998 are to the Act in its current, amended form rather than to its original terms unless otherwise stated.

THE SCOTTISH PARLIAMENT AND THE SOVEREIGNTY OF THE UK PARLIAMENT

As far as law-making powers are concerned, the important parts of the SA 1998 are sections 28–30 and Schedule 5 which lists the powers that are retained by, or reserved to, the UK Parliament. Schedule 4, which sets out various enactments protected from modification by the Scottish Parliament, is also significant. Before we examine these, however, mention should be made of the UK constitutional doctrine of the sovereignty of Parliament. The sovereignty of the UK Parliament is perhaps the most important doctrine of constitutional law in the United Kingdom. In its absolute form, it means that the UK Parliament is the one supreme law-making body in the United Kingdom and can, in theory, pass any law that it wishes. Its laws cannot be declared invalid even by the highest court in the land, the Supreme Court. This is not the case in federal states such as the United States or Germany where there is a written constitution and a supreme court which can strike down a law as invalid if it is in conflict with the constitution. The sovereignty of the UK Parliament was undoubtedly modified by the UK's membership of the European Communities but, as far as domestic or national law is concerned, the doctrine remains in place. Thus, under that doctrine, any Parliament or Assembly created by the UK Parliament is a subordinate body. It is not independent nor is it co-ordinate with central government as in a federal system. It may not only be overruled by the UK Parliament, it may even be abolished by it.

It is true that, from its establishment, the UK Government has committed itself to the convention, the 'Sewel Convention', which is to the effect that the UK Parliament will not normally legislate with regard to devolved matters without the consent of the Scottish Parliament. That convention has been complied with ever since by UK governments of varying political complexions. That convention, however, is not legally binding on the UK Government and Parliament. Even though that convention was given formal recognition by the SA 2016 which states (section 2) that: 'it is recognised that the Parliament of the United Kingdom will not normally legislate with regard to devolved matters without the consent of the Scottish Parliament', that did not change the position. The position was confirmed when the Supreme Court considered the question of whether the UK Government had the authority, in the absence of Parliamentary approval, to issue a formal notification that the United Kingdom would leave the European Union. The status of the 'Sewel Convention' was raised in that case, the *Miller* case, and the court held that section 2 did not place any legal requirements upon the UK Government but, rather, had 'an important role in facilitating harmonious relationships between the UK Parliament and the devolved legislatures.[9]

Of course, even though this principle of the sovereignty of the UK Parliament is legal theory which has been confirmed by the *Miller* case, account has to be taken of practical politics. If the Scottish Parliament remains a relatively popular institution, it can be expected that governments at Westminster would be reluctant to incur the wrath of the Scottish electorate by interfering with the Scottish Parliament without good cause. That said, one of the consequences of the 'Brexit' referendum in June 2016 was to raise questions as to which areas of policy, currently undertaken by the EU, would transfer to the Scottish Parliament, and which would fall within the remit of the UK Parliament. The debate on this question raised acrimonious disputes as to whether the

UK Government was acting within the spirit and letter of the 'Sewel Convention' by appearing to suggest that some powers over devolved matters, currently resting with the EU, would be retained at Westminster rather than being transferred to Holyrood. This issue is considered in more detail in Chapter 11 below.[10]

THE LAW-MAKING POWERS OF THE PARLIAMENT

Bearing this in mind, let us examine the law-making powers of the Scottish Parliament. The powers are contained in the SA 1998, sections 28–30. Section 28 states that, subject to various exceptions in section 29, the Scottish Parliament has the power to make laws that will be known as Acts of the Scottish Parliament. Proposed Acts are known as bills, as at Westminster and, once bills have passed through the Parliamentary stages and received the Royal Assent, they become Acts. The final subsection of section 28 states, however, that the power of the Parliament of the UK to make laws for Scotland remains unaffected. This is an assertion of the sovereignty of the UK Parliament. The UK Parliament can, by passing an Act at Westminster, override or nullify any Act of the Scottish Parliament and, if the Scottish Parliament refuses to pass an Act that the government at Westminster wishes it to pass, the UK Parliament will simply pass one for it. So far, however, the UK Parliament has not needed to assert its sovereignty over the Scottish Parliament in this way even though the Scottish Parliament has had SNP administrations (both majority and minority) since 2007 and thus has been governed by a party with a fundamental disagreement with the parties in government at Westminster as to whether the UK Parliament should have ultimate sovereignty over the Scottish Parliament.

As it is in the retaining form, the SA 1998 does not list the areas in which the Scottish Parliament has the power to legislate. Instead, it lists the areas in which it cannot legislate, some of which are found in section 29 and the remainder in Schedules s 4 and 5. An innovation which was brought into effect by SA 2016 was to introduce[11] the concept of 'protected matters' where a two-thirds majority (of the total membership of the Scottish Parliament, not just those voting) is required for proposed legislation on those matters to be passed. These are matters concerning the franchise for the Scottish Parliament, the number of constituencies, regions, or other electoral area, and the number of MSPs for each of these, and its electoral system. The requirement to have a two-thirds majority is described in the SA 2016 as a 'super-majority', and is aimed at giving the Scottish Parliament legislative competence over the relevant matters but preventing that competence being exercised without the consent of more than just a simple majority vote of MSPs.

Section 29 sets out a number of areas where any attempt by the Scottish Parliament to make law would be invalid:

- it cannot pass a valid law any provision of which would form part of the law of any country or territory other than Scotland or confer or remove functions which are exercisable except in or as regards Scotland. While it is extremely unlikely that the Scottish Parliament would want to pass a law for, say, France or Indonesia, this is designed to prevent it legislating, presumably inadvertently, for any other part of the UK;
- it cannot pass a valid law any provision of which is incompatible with those parts of the European Convention on Human Rights which are given effect by the Human Rights Act 1998;
- it cannot currently pass a valid law any provision of which is incompatible with European Union law. Though relations with the European Union are reserved to the UK Parliament, the Scottish Parliament is responsible for observing and implementing the various obligations under Community law in relation to devolved matters. This provision will obviously need to be amended after the United Kingdom terminates its membership of the European Union but exactly how that is to be done is unclear;
- it cannot pass a valid law any provision of which would remove the Lord Advocate from his or her position as head of the systems of criminal prosecution and investigation of deaths in Scotland. This is one of various measures in the SA 1998 designed to protect the independence of the Scottish Law Officers;
- it cannot pass a valid law any provision of which relates to matters that are reserved to the UK Parliament. These provisions are listed in Schedule 5 and are dealt with below;
- it cannot pass a valid law any provision of which modifies any of the enactments listed in Schedule 4. These are also dealt with below.

Section 30 enables Schedules 4 and 5 to be modified by a parliamentary order known as an Order in Council. This enables the UK Parliament to make changes to the contents of these schedules without the necessity of passing another Act of Parliament. Such changes still require Parliamentary approval but that can be obtained in a much quicker and simpler fashion than is necessary for an Act of Parliament. Most changes made by the use of section 30 have been of a non-controversial nature but that is not always the case. The power given to the Scottish Government to hold an independence referendum on a one-off basis in 2014 was transferred by means of a section 30 order,[12] and the Scottish Government requested a similar section 30 order in 2017 to allow it to hold another independence referendum as a consequence of the decision of the UK electorate, as a whole, to vote in favour of the United Kingdom leaving the European Union.

SCHEDULE 5 — RESERVED MATTERS

The matters reserved to the UK Parliament are areas into which the Scottish Parliament may not trespass. Any attempt to make law in any of these areas would be invalid. The Scottish Constitutional Convention recommended that the primary matters which should be retained by the UK Parliament should be defence, foreign affairs, immigration, nationality, social security policy, and central economic and fiscal responsibilities. The White Paper, Scotland's Parliament, added to the list the constitution of the United Kingdom, common markets for UK goods and services, employment legislation, the regulation of certain professions, transport safety and regulation, and a miscellany of other matters including the regulatory framework for broadcasting, abortion, and equality legislation. The general justification was that there are many matters that can be more effectively and beneficially handled on a UK basis.[13] The extensions of devolved competence described elsewhere in this work, however, have led to many powers, which were originally reserved, being transferred to the legislative responsibility of the Scottish Parliament, and executive power over further areas being given to Scottish Ministers to exercise.[14]

When translated into the SA 1998, the reserved matters are set out in considerable detail in Schedule 5. The schedule is divided into three parts: Part I dealing with what are called General Reservations; Part II dealing with Specific Reservations; and Part III dealing with miscellaneous matters under General Provisions.

General Reservations Part I

1. Various aspects of the constitution of the United Kingdom are reserved. These are:

- the Crown, including succession to the Crown and a regency;
- the Union of the Kingdoms of Scotland and England;

- the Parliament of the United Kingdom;
- the continued existence of the High Court of Justiciary and the Court of Session.

Thus, it is not open to the Scottish Parliament to restore the Stuarts to the throne, and the eighteenth-century Acts relating to the Hanoverian Protestant succession will continue to apply to the succession to the throne unless the UK Parliament deems otherwise.[15] Nor will it be possible for the Scottish Parliament to declare Scotland independent even if a majority of MSPs supported that change because that would affect, among other things, the union of the kingdoms which took place in 1603. The continued existence of the Scottish Courts was guaranteed in the Acts of Union of 1707 and that is further confirmed by these reservations.

2. The aspects of foreign affairs which are reserved include:

- international relations with territories outside the UK, the European Union, and other international organisations;
- the regulation of international trade;
- international development assistance and co-operation.

The observation and implementation of various international obligations, including the Human Rights Convention and obligations under EU law, are not reserved. The Scottish Parliament is able and, in fact, may be required, therefore, to legislate for the purpose of giving effect to international obligations as far as they relate to devolved matters. In the case of EU obligations, the Scottish Ministers may be liable under EU law to the same penalties as UK Ministers. Assisting UK Ministers is not reserved and so Scottish Ministers are able to assist UK Ministers in the formulation, negotiation and implementation of policy relating to international obligations and are able to participate in European Council meetings and in meetings with partners in the European Union for as long as the United Kingdom remains a member.

3. The reservations relating to defence include:

- the defence of the realm;
- the army, navy and air force and reserve forces;
- visiting forces, international headquarters and defence organisations;
- trading with the enemy and enemy property.

Thus, all the matters for which the Ministry of Defence is responsible are covered by these reservations. Civil defence, however, is not reserved:

in particular, planning and organisation by civilian authorities and the provision of non-combative defence against hostile attacks. There is also a specific exemption relating to sea fishing. The Royal Navy's Fishery Protection Squadron carries out various enforcement duties on behalf of the Fisheries Department (now DEFRA: Department for Environment Food and Rural Affairs) and Scottish Ministers are able to confer powers on members of the armed forces to enable this to continue.

4. The other matters included in the general reservations in Part I are:

- the registration and funding of political parties, except for payments to political parties to assist MSPs in their Parliamentary duties;
- the civil service;
- treason.

Specific Reservations Part II

Part II sets out specific, subject-related reservations by sections grouped under eleven heads. The reservations can be and, in many cases are, qualified by 'exceptions to reservation'. This means that the subject matter of the exceptions is not reserved to the UK Parliament so that the Scottish Parliament does have competence over those excepted matters, notwithstanding the reservation set out in the relevant head. The heads are:

Head A – Financial and Economic Matters
These include the issue and circulation of money, taxes and excise duties, government borrowing and lending, the exchange rate, the Bank of England, and control over UK public expenditure. Specifically excepted are devolved taxes (including their collection and management),[16] local taxes which partially fund local government expenditure, currently the council tax and non-domestic rates. Devolved taxes are currently land transaction tax, landfill tax, air passenger duty, and aggregate tax, and the Scottish Parliament can therefore decide on the nature and extent of any such taxes in Scotland. The list of devolved taxes can be added to by Order in Council.[17] The reservation of public expenditure does not affect the Scottish Parliament's ability to allocate its own resources.

The Scottish Parliament also had powers since SA 2012 (extended by SA 2016) to set a Scottish rate of income tax.[18] This is done by the Scottish Parliament passing a 'Scottish rate resolution' rather than by separate Scottish tax legislation. This head also reserves the currency, financial services (except fixing the dates of bank holidays), financial markets, and money laundering.

Head B – Home Affairs
This head covers a miscellany of matters dealt with by the Home Office, including various aspects of the misuse of drugs: possession, production, supply, import and export, and trafficking. The Scottish Parliament, however, has powers in key areas such as education, health, social work, and criminal prosecution. Immigration, nationality, and extradition are reserved although certain executive powers of the Secretary of State are transferred to the Scottish Ministers. National security, official secrets, the interception of communications, and terrorism are reserved under this head, as are firearms (except for the regulation of air weapons),[19] data protection, and scientific procedures on live animals.

This head also reserves elections to the House of Common and the European Parliament but the Scottish Parliament has power to legislate for its own elections, and Scottish local government elections, with certain limited exceptions. These exceptions are the regulation of political parties, the power to allow Scottish Parliament elections to be held on the same day as other elections, and certain matters concerning the Electoral Commission and the Boundary Commission for Scotland which remain reserved. In addition, the Scottish Parliament's powers to legislate for its own elections (but not for local government) is subject to such legislation requiring a two-thirds 'super-majority' as described above.[20] Most of these powers over elections were transferred to the Scottish Parliament only by SA 2016 but the Scottish Parliament did have the power to legislate for all aspects of local government elections, except for the franchise, from its establishment in 1999. The Parliament can, therefore, change the electoral system for local council elections and, in 2004, did just that following the coalition partnership deal between Labour and the Liberal Democrats agreed after the 2003 elections. That took the shape of the introduction of the Single Transferable Vote system of proportional representation which has been in force for local council elections since 2007.[21]

Betting, gaming, lotteries, and various aspects of the classification of films and the distribution of video recordings are also mostly reserved, with the exception of certain powers to regulate the number of gaming machines on licensed betting premises.[22]

Head C – Trade and Industry

This head covers a large number of areas including the creation, operation, regulation, and dissolution of business associations. The phrase 'business associations' covers companies, partnerships, building societies, and various other bodies. The intention of the reservation is to ensure a level playing field for business within the UK. Charities and certain public bodies are excepted from this reservation. The reasoning behind the latter exception is to enable the Scottish Parliament to create and regulate public bodies which are business associations for devolved areas such as health, education, sport, urban regeneration, and the environment.

Import and export control are reserved to ensure a level playing field for UK business but, as agriculture, fisheries and food are devolved, the movement of food, animals, animal products, plants, animal feed, fertilisers, and pesticides is excepted from this reservation.

Insolvency, competition (except for certain practices in the Scottish legal profession), intellectual property, consumer protection (except for the provision of consumer advocacy and advice by or in agreement with a public body, and also in relation to food safety), product standards, safety, and liability (except in relation to agriculture, fisheries and food) are all reserved under this head. The regulation of sea fishing outside the Scottish zone except in relation to Scottish fishing boats is reserved, as are weights and measures, telecommunications, and postal services.

Head D – Energy

The generation, distribution and supply of electricity are reserved. Legislative responsibility for most aspects of oil and gas is reserved, including the ownership of, exploration for, and exploitation of, deposits of oil and natural gas. The manufacture of gas, however, is not reserved nor are the powers to provide assistance for onshore activities in support of offshore activities. The power to grant and regulate licences for the search and drilling of oil within the Scottish onshore area is also excepted from reservation. This exception therefore gives the Scottish Parliament the legislative power, among other things, to control onshore fracking.[23] Coal, including its ownership and exploitation, deep and open-cast coal mining and subsidence, are all reserved. The only exceptions to this reservation are certain environmental duties. Nuclear energy and installations, including nuclear safety and liability for nuclear occurrences, are all reserved. Duties, however, in relation to the keeping and use of radioactive material, the disposal or accumulation of radioactive waste, and the regulation of non-nuclear activities at nuclear installations are excepted from reservation. Energy conservation is reserved but the Scottish Parliament is specifically allowed to legislate for, and in general promote, energy efficiency, and also for the provision of consumer advocacy and advice on electricity and gas by, or by agreement with, a public body.

Head E – Transport

In the case of road transport, various aspects of road traffic regulation and road safety are reserved including the licensing of drivers, driving instruction, and the licensing and registration of vehicles. The prosecution and punishment of offenders for a range of road traffic offences are also reserved. The Scottish Parliament, however, is able to legislate on the promotion of road safety by local authorities, and also on certain aspects of speed limits, parking, and vehicle use. Scottish Ministers and UK Government Ministers are given concurrent powers in relation to road safety information and training.

The provision and regulation of railway services and rail transport security are in broad terms reserved as is (not surprisingly) the Channel Tunnel but substantial powers concerning rail transport are excepted from reservation. These include most powers for the making of grants relating to railway services, powers over the provision and regulation of rail services, the promotion and construction of railways wholly within Scotland, and railway policing.

In the case of transport by sea, marine safety, navigation rights, the regulation of the British merchant fleet and all matters relating to the employment of seafarers are reserved. The Scottish Parliament, however, has the power to pass legislation relating to ports, harbours and piers. It also has the power to deal with the regulation of works which may endanger or obstruct navigation. An important exception from reservation is financial assistance to bulk freight shipping services between the Highlands and Islands and locations outside Scotland which are necessary for the social and economic well-being of these remote communities.

The regulation of aviation and air transport, including air safety and security, is reserved as are arrangements to compensate and repatriate passengers when an air transport operator becomes insolvent. Exceptions from reservation relate mainly to the provision of airports and various airport controls. (As is noted above with reference to Head A, air passenger duty is also now excepted from reservation.)

Miscellaneous reservations under this head cover the transport of radioactive material, standards for public passenger transport for the disabled, and the carriage of dangerous goods.

Head F – Social Security
This head reserves social security schemes financed by central or local expenditure which provide benefits to individuals. Examples include National Insurance and the Social Fund. A substantial number of exceptions to this reservation were introduced by SA 2016, however, and, as a result, the Scottish Parliament has been given legislative power, with some qualifications, over a wide range of benefits.[24] These include:

- disability benefits;
- severe disablement benefits;
- industrial injuries benefits;
- carer's benefits;
- maternity benefits, funeral benefits, and cold-weather heating payments;
- the discretionary topping up of reserved benefits;
- discretionary housing payments;
- assistance for short-term needs (except where the need arises from the imposition of a benefit sanction);
- payments to people in need and services such as home help and residential nursing accommodation;
- welfare foods;
- the power to create new benefits where the subject matter is not connected with reserved matters.[25]

Various provisions for the maintenance of children are also excepted although the subject matter of the Child Support Acts 1991 and 1995, in general, is reserved. Scottish Ministers also now have powers to make regulations regarding the rent elements of universal credit.[26] Occupational, personal and war pensions are all reserved but the SA 1998 contains specific provision for the payment of pensions to former members and staff of the Scottish Parliament.

Head G – Regulation of the Professions
The professions reserved are architects, the health professions, and auditors. The health professions include doctors, dentists, opticians, pharmacists, nurses, midwives, and many others including veterinary surgeons. The Scottish Parliament, however, has the power to legislate on the vocational training of doctors and dentists.

Head H – Employment
Employment rights and duties and industrial relations are, for the most part, reserved. An exception to this is the setting of wages for Scottish

agricultural workers, which comes under the remit of the Scottish Agricultural Wages Board, but the Scottish Parliament cannot legislate for a Scottish minimum wage. Health and safety at work are reserved but public safety in devolved areas is not, thus allowing the Scottish Parliament to legislate on, for example, the safety of sports grounds. The Scottish Parliament also has legislative power over many aspects of the provision of job search and support schemes, including careers services and the duties that Scottish Enterprise and Highlands and Islands Enterprise have to assist people seeking work to obtain training are excepted. Careers services are also excepted.

Head J – Health and Medicine

Xenotransplantation,[27] embryology, surrogacy, and genetics are all reserved. The justification is that all of these raise major ethical issues and/or require expertise to be pooled at a UK level to allow them to be regulated satisfactorily. The Scottish Parliament is, however, able to legislate on all other matters of sexual health. Medicines, medical supplies, and poisons are reserved, as is the regulation of prices for medical supplies for the National Health Service in Scotland. The regulation of veterinary medicinal products, and specified animal food additives and animal feeding stuffs is also reserved.

Head K – Media and Culture

All regulatory responsibilities relating to television and radio broadcasting are reserved although some executive functions relating to the funding of Gaelic broadcasting are transferred to the Scottish Executive. The justification for the reservation is that the regulatory framework is an important aspect of the single market in the United Kingdom and that the management of the airwaves and of competition in the independent television sector needs to be carried out on a UK basis.

The Public Lending Right scheme, which provides payments to authors whose books are borrowed from public libraries, is reserved as is the scheme by which the government indemnifies lenders for the loss of or damage to works of art and other objects.

Head L – Miscellaneous

The determination of the salaries of judges of the Court of Session, sheriffs, members of the Scottish Lands Tribunal, and the Chairman of the Scottish Land Court are reserved but payment of the salaries is not. Payment will be made out of the Scottish Consolidated Fund and will not require the prior approval of the Scottish Parliament. This is in line with UK practice and is one of the measures designed to protect the independence of the judiciary.

Overall responsibility for equal opportunities is reserved but substantial powers on equal opportunities were excepted from this reservation by SA 2016. The Parliament now has a general power (except by prohibition or regulation) to encourage equal opportunities. Also excepted from reservation is the imposition of duties on office holders in the Scottish Administration, Scottish public bodies and cross-border public authorities, with a view to ensuring that their functions are carried out with due regard to the need to meet equal opportunity requirements. This exception includes certain powers to make provisions and issue guidance on equal opportunities matters. Equal opportunity is defined as the prevention, elimination, or regulation of discrimination between persons on the grounds of sex or marital status, on racial grounds, or on grounds of disability, age, sexual orientation, language, or social origin, or of other personal attributes, including beliefs or opinions, such as religious beliefs or political opinions.

Also under this head comes the control of nuclear, biological, chemical and any other weapons of mass destruction.[28]

Timescales, time zones, and the determination of summer time are reserved along with the date of Easter and the calendar generally. Excepted are the dates of bank, public and local holidays.

The Ordnance Survey is reserved as is the regulation of activities in outer space.

General Provisions (Part III)

This part of Schedule 5 safeguards from reservation Scottish public bodies with no reserved functions and those which have mixed functions, some reserved and some devolved. Local councils are a good example of the latter, having responsibility for devolved functions such as education, housing, and social work, and for some reserved functions such as the regulations of weights and measures and the administration of housing benefit. It also safeguards from reservation the giving of financial assistance to industry to promote or sustain economic development or employment. This part also reserves the constitution, assets, liabilities, funding, and receipts of all the bodies reserved by name in Part II and specifically the Commission for Racial Equality, the Equal Opportunities Commission, the Disability Rights Commission, the Commission for Equality and Human Rights, the Office of Communication, and the Gas and Electricity Markets Authority.[29] This part also allows transfers to

Scottish tribunals of functions that relate to reserved matters where they relate to Scottish cases.[30]

Thus it can be seen that, although the UK Government decided to use the retaining model for the division of responsibilities between the Scottish and the UK Parliaments, the list of reserved powers is very detailed. Substantial extensions of the legislative powers of the Scottish Parliament have been made by Acts of the UK Parliament, in particular by SA 2012 and SA 2016. In addition, the list may be modified from time to time by an Order in Council, and modification by such method has taken place on a number of occasions.[31] The reserved areas listed in Schedule 5 and section 29 have been significantly reduced and, though substantial powers are still reserved to the UK Parliament, the Scottish Parliament is now free to make laws in a wide range of areas of government activity affecting Scotland. Not only that, it has power to amend or repeal existing Acts of the UK Parliament which relate to devolved matters.

EXECUTIVE DEVOLUTION

In addition to those matters where the Parliament has been given the power to make laws, it should also be noted that the Scottish Ministers also have extensive powers to act in areas where the Parliament itself does not have legislative competence. Some of these powers were transferred to Scottish Ministers by specific provisions in one of the three Scotland Acts. Others were transferred by orders made under those Acts. A number of powers was transferred to Scottish Ministers in one of these ways at the beginning of the new arrangements for devolution. Many others have been transferred over the years since the Parliament was established. These powers are described as constituting 'executive devolution'. The extent of executive devolution is considered in more detail in Chapter 6.[32]

Though, strictly speaking, Scottish Ministers are not accountable to the Scottish Parliament when exercising powers derived in such ways, their actions in the exercise of such powers are scrutinised by the Parliament. This can be through MSPs putting questions to ministers or raising issues in debate, just as occurs when ministers are exercising powers within areas where the Parliament does have legislative competence. Furthermore, in most cases where Scottish Ministers have been given powers under executive devolution, their exercise normally requires the passage of secondary legislation by the Scottish Parliament, which therefore has a great measure of effective control over their use.

Even where Scottish Ministers are able to act without requiring secondary legislation, it is hard to see how a Scottish Government (or individual Minister), which used such powers against the wishes of a majority of the Parliament, could survive in office.

DEVOLVED MATTERS

Taking into account both these areas where the Parliament has the power to legislate, and those where the Scottish Ministers have been given powers to act under executive devolution, the devolved areas in broad terms comprise the following:

Central government taxation

- Devolved taxes – land transaction tax, landfill tax, aggregate tax, air passenger duty
- Scottish rate of income tax.

Benefits

- disability benefits, severe disablement benefits, industrial injuries benefits, carer's benefits, maternity benefits, funeral benefits, cold weather heating payments, welfare foods
- discretionary topping up of reserved benefits
- discretionary housing payments
- assistance for short-term needs; payments and services for people in need
- the power to create new benefits
- rent elements of universal credit.[33]

Health

- overall responsibility for the NHS in Scotland, including terms and conditions of service; public and mental health; education and training of health professionals; abortion.

Education and training

- pre-five, primary and secondary school education; teacher supply, training, and conditions of service; the functions of Her Majesty's Inspectorate of Schools
- further and higher education policy and funding, the functions of the Scottish Higher Education Funding Council; student support

- science and research funding in support of devolved matters
- training policy; vocational qualifications; careers advice and guidance; job search and support schemes.

Local government, social work, and housing

- local government finance and local taxes
- social work including children's hearings and the voluntary sector
- housing
- land-use planning; building control; area regeneration including the designation of enterprise zones.

Business, economic development, and transport

- the functions of Scottish Enterprise, Highlands and Islands Enterprise
- financial assistance to industry subject to UK guidelines; inward investment
- promotion of trade and exports
- powers to make references to the Competition and Markets Authority, jointly with the relevant UK Minister[34]
- certain powers regarding consumer advice and advocacy
- promotion of tourism including the functions of the Scottish Tourist Board (now known as Visit Scotland)
- passenger and road transport; the Scottish road network; road safety; bus policy and concessionary fares; taxis and minicabs; some powers on speed limits, parking, and vehicle use: some powers over rail grants, franchising, and the regulation, operation, and construction of railways in Scotland; the Strathclyde Passenger Transport Authority and Executive
- air and sea transport: covering ports, harbours and piers; freight shipping and ferry services; Highlands and Islands Airports Ltd; planning and environmental issues relating to airports
- inland waterways.

Law and home affairs

- criminal law and procedure except for statutory offences relating to reserved matters including drugs and firearms (except the regulation of air weapons which is devolved)
- civil law except in relation to reserved matters
- judicial appointments
- the criminal justice and prosecution system

- civil and criminal courts; tribunals concerned with devolved matters and the Scottish Council on Tribunals; legal aid
- parole, the release of life prisoners, and alleged miscarriages of justice
- prisons, the Scottish Prison Service; the treatment of offenders
- police and fire services; civil defence and emergency planning
- liquor licensing
- protection of animals (domestic, captive and wild); zoo licensing; the control of dangerous wild animals and game
- certain powers over gaming machines
- gender quotas for public bodies in Scotland
- promoting equality of socio-economic rights in devolved areas.

Elections

- Scottish Parliament and local government elections.

Environment and energy

- environmental protection; air, land and water pollution, and the functions of the Scottish Environmental Protection Agency; water supplies and sewerage; sustainable development policies within a UK framework
- the natural heritage, countryside issues, the functions of Scottish Natural Heritage
- the built heritage, and the functions of Historic Scotland
- flood prevention, coast protection, and the safety of reservoirs
- fuel poverty support schemes[35]
- energy company obligations regarding carbon emissions and reduction of home-heating costs[36]
- powers in relation to the licensing and regulation of onshore oil (including fracking)[37]
- the functions of the Crown Estate in Scotland.[38]

Agriculture, forestry, and fishing

- domestic agriculture including crofting; animal and plant health and animal welfare within a UK framework; implementation of measures under the Common Agricultural Policy
- food standards
- forestry including the Forestry Commission
- domestic fisheries including inshore sea, salmon and freshwater fisheries and aquaculture; implementation of measures under the Common Fisheries Policy.

Sport and the arts

- sport and the functions of SportScotland
- the arts and the functions of the National Library, National Museums, and National Galleries of Scotland; Museums Galleries Scotland; Creative Scotland; and support for Gaelic.

Miscellaneous

- statistics, public registers and records including the responsibilities of the Keeper of the Records, the Keeper of the Registers and the Registrar General for Scotland.

THE POWER TO AMEND ACTS OF THE UK PARLIAMENT AND SCHEDULE 4

The Scottish Parliament has the power to amend or repeal Acts of the UK Parliament which relate to devolved matters. There are, however, limits placed on this power. These are detailed in the SA 1998, Schedule 4 which is entitled 'Enactments etc. protected from modification'.

The Scottish Parliament cannot modify Articles 4 and 6 of the Acts of Union of 1706–07 in so far as they relate to freedom of trade. Nor can it modify various sections of the European Communities Act 1972, the Act by means of which the UK joined the European Communities. The Human Rights Act 1998, which incorporates much of the European Convention on Human Rights, is protected in its entirety from modification by the Scottish Parliament. The law on reserved matters cannot be modified by the Scottish Parliament and 'law' is defined as including not only Acts and subordinate legislation of the UK Parliament but also any rule of law which is not contained in an enactment the subject matter of which is a reserved matter. This protects common law rules relating to reserved matters.

Significantly, SA 1998 with limited exceptions is protected from amendment. Most of the exceptions are relatively minor but they also include section 70, which deals with accounts and audit, and section 91, which deals with the investigation of complaints of maladministration. The Scottish Parliament is also able to amend those sections of the SA 1998 relating to elections over which it was given powers by the SA 2016 subject to the requirement for such changes requiring a two-thirds 'super-majority' as described above.

THE FUTURE

The powers given to the Scottish Parliament by the original Scotland Act of 1998 were already extensive, and the further devolution introduced by the Scotland Acts 2012 and 2016 have extended those powers substantially. That might not be the end of the story, however. If Scotland were ever to become independent, clearly the Scottish Parliament would obtain sovereign powers over all matters affecting Scotland. Even without independence, however, the case for the UK to become a fully federal state continues to be advanced in some quarters. It also seems likely that, in any constitutional arrangements for the United Kingdom after departure from the European Union, the Scottish Parliament would acquire further devolved powers which are currently with the European Union although there is some controversy as to how far such further devolution would extend. These questions are considered further in Chapters 11 and 12 below.

NOTES

1. Towards a Scottish Parliament, Scottish Constitutional Convention (1989) p. 36.
2. At p. 17 of https://www.ucl.ac.uk/political-science/publications/unit-publications/13.pdf (last accessed 4 April 2017).
3. This question is considered in detail in Chapter 9 below.
4. See p. 6.
5. By the Scotland Act 1998 (Modification of Schedules 4 and 5) Order 2015/1764.
6. These powers were transferred by the Modification of Schedules 4 and 5 Order 2015/1764 and put into effect by the Scottish Elections (Reduction of Voting Age) Act 2015.
7. At the time of writing, some of the extended devolved powers provided for by SA 2016 are not yet in force but it is expected that all the new powers will be put into effect without any substantial delay. Accordingly, this work assumes that all the provisions of SA 2016 have been put into effect unless the text indicates otherwise.
8. See p. 7.
9. R. (on the application of Miller and another) v. Secretary of State for Exiting the European Union, [2017] UKSC 5, para. 151.
10. See p. 242.
11. By provisions in Section 31(2A), (4), (5), and Section 31A of SA 1998.
12. See above.

13. Scottish Office, *Scotland's Parliament* (1997), Cm 3658, paragraph 3.2.
14. See p. 28.
15. Certain changes to the provisions regarding succession to the throne were, in fact, made by the UK Parliament by the Succession to the Crown Act 2013. These included the abolition of the rule that gave male children preference over females in the line of the succession to the throne. It also removed the rule disqualifying from the line of succession anyone who married a Roman Catholic although the rule requiring the monarch to be a Protestant remains.
16. See Chapter 10, p. 210 for more detail on devolved taxes.
17. See Part 4A of SA 1998 for details of the devolved taxes.
18. Section 80C, SA 1998. See p. 206 for further details of the Scottish income tax rate
19. Certain powers regarding the regulation of air weapons remain reserved to the UK Secretary of State.
20. See p. 17.
21. The new electoral system was introduced by the Local Governance (Scotland) Act 2004.
22. See Section 52, SA 2016
23. Section 47, SA 2016.
24. It should be noted that the Scottish Government has decided that it will take over responsibility for welfare benefits transferred to it by SA 2016 on a phased basis.
25. See SPICe (Scottish Parliamentary Information Centre) briefing 16/88, p. 9 on the transfer of welfare benefit powers to the Scottish Government. http://www.parliament.scot/ResearchBriefingsAndFactsheets/S5/ SB_16-88_The_Fiscal_Framework.pdf (last accessed 9 April 2017)
26. These powers were acquired as a result of the provisions of Sections 29–30 of SA 2016.
27. The transfer of organs and tissue between different species.
28. SA 2012 also added the reservation of regulation of activities in Antarctica. This is a rare example of power being removed from devolved competence and transferred back to UK competence. Presumably, powers over this matter were overlooked by the drafters of SA 1998.
29. Known better by their operational names Ofcom and Ofgen respectively.
30. See Section 39 SA 2016 for full details of the power and for definitions.
31. Most of these have been fairly minor but a few have been more substantial, in particular the transfer of certain powers in relation to rail transport. Many of these modifications were prompted by changes to the law relating to reserved matters made by the UK Parliament: for example, the substitution of a reference to the Regulatory of Investigatory Powers Act 2000 in place of the Telecommunications Act 1984; some make minor additions to reserved matters such as the addition of the Arts and Humanities Research Council, established by the Higher Education Act 2004, to the list

of research councils in Section C12; some added new exceptions from reservation, such as the making of payments to political parties for the purpose of assisting MSPs in the performance of their parliamentary duties.

32. See p. 133.
33. As a result of the provisions of Sections 29–30 of SA 2016.
34. SA 2016, Section 63.
35. SA 2016, Section 58.
36. See SA 2016, Sections 59 and 60.
37. SA 2016, Sections 48 and 49.
38. Subject to a scheme to be drawn up by the Treasury.

CHAPTER THREE

Elections and Members

THE ELECTORAL SYSTEM

The Scotland Act 1998 (SA 1998) established the Scottish Parliament with 129 members elected by the form of proportional representation known as the additional member system.[1] This combines the relative majority system, commonly known as 'first past the post', involving single-member constituencies, with an additional element which 'tops up' the political parties' representation from registered party lists by allocating regional seats on the basis of a second vote cast not for an individual but for a political party. The party lists contain up to twelve names and are known as 'closed lists' which means that each political party has decided the order in which persons on its list are to be elected. The voter thus votes for the party and not for any individual on the list. It is also possible for individuals without any political affiliation to stand as candidates. Thus, there are 'constituency members' and 'regional members'. The SA 1998 refers to them simply as 'members' but the term 'MSP' has become the normal way in which they are described and, in law, the status of constituency and regional members is the same.

THE NUMBER OF MSPS

At a general election to the Scottish Parliament, seventy-three constituency members and fifty-six regional members are elected, the latter divided equally among eight regions. The SA 1998 specifies that the Orkney Islands and the Shetland Islands are to form separate constituencies. (These two island groups are combined to form a single constituency for the purposes of elections to the House of Commons.) Until 2005, the other constituencies for the Scottish Parliament were identical to the constituencies used for elections to the House of Commons. So there were seventy-two constituencies at Westminster and seventy-three in the Scottish Parliament.

However, the SA 1998 as originally enacted contained provisions which would have led to a reduction in the number of both constituency and of regional MSPs. The reason for this is that SA 1998 linked the number of seats in the Scottish Parliament to the number of constituencies in the House of Commons and further required the ratio of regional seats to the number of constituency seats to be fifty-six to seventy-three so far was is reasonably practicable.[2] Another provision of the SA 1998 required the number of constituencies at Westminster to be reduced from seventy-two.[3] The way the Act did this is as follows. The Parliamentary Constituencies Act 1986 (PCA 1986) contained, until 1998, a provision that the number of constituencies in Scotland should not be less than seventy-one. This resulted in the average number of electors (the electoral quota) in Scottish constituencies being significantly lower than the average number of electors in an English constituency.[4] In other words, Scotland had more MPs per head of population than England. As a concession to the feeling that such relative overrepresentation at Westminster could no longer be justified once the Scottish Parliament had been established, the SA 1998 amended the PCA 1986 by removing that minimum of seventy-one. In addition, it laid down that, for the first review of parliamentary boundaries after the passing of the SA 1998, the electoral quota for England had to be used to determine the appropriate number of Scottish seats at Westminster.[5] This would have meant that the number of Scottish constituencies would fall to about fifty-seven rather than seventy-two.

The task of reviewing Parliamentary constituency boundaries in Scotland is allocated to the Boundary Commission for Scotland and it is statutorily bound to conduct a general review between eight and twelve years from the date of the report of its last general review. As a report was submitted to the Secretary of State for Scotland in 1994, the Commission's next report had to be made between 2002 and 2006. The Commission published its draft proposals in February 2002. As the Commission is able to take into account special geographical considerations which allow them to depart from the strict application of the electoral quota, its provisional recommendations provided for fifty-nine constituencies for Scotland rather than fifty-seven.

As the SA 1998 tied the number of constituencies for the Scottish Parliament to the number of constituencies at Westminster (with special provision for the Orkney and Shetland Islands), the number of constituency MSPs would have been reduced to sixty and, as the ratio of regional seats to constituency seats should be, as far as practicable, the same as in the original arrangement, that is fifty-six to seventy-three, the number of regional members would have been reduced to around forty-four, between five or six per region.

These provisions in the SA 1998 were extremely controversial. It was argued by many MSPs and by the Presiding Officer that the work of the Scottish Parliament would be undermined by a reduction in the number of members. However, during the passage of the Scotland Bill through the UK Parliament in 1998, government Ministers had made it clear that they would consider representations to amend the SA 1998 at some time in the future so as to remove the link between the number of Scottish constituencies in the House of Commons and the number of members of the Scottish Parliament. The Secretary of State for Scotland reiterated that view in September 2000 and, in 2001, a consultation exercise was launched to ascertain the views of the public. The overwhelming response was that, in the interests of stability, the Scottish Parliament should continue to operate with 129 MSPs. It was also argued that a reduction in the number of regional members would reduce the proportional element of the electoral system. On the other hand, some argued that difficulties would arise if the boundaries of the UK and Scottish Parliamentary constituencies were not coterminous.

In December 2002, the then Secretary of State for Scotland announced in the House of Commons that, in the interests of the Scottish Parliament's stability, she would seek to have the SA 1998 amended. The Scottish Parliament (Constituencies) Act 2004 was duly passed by the UK Parliament. The Act substitutes a new Schedule 1 to the Scotland Act which retains the seventy-three constituencies and eight regions of the original Schedule.

Thus, the number of MSPs looks likely to remain at 129 for the foreseeable future although the boundaries of the constituencies and regions are subject to periodical review by the Boundary Commission for Scotland, the most recent of which took place in 2011. That review made several adjustments to the constituency and regional boundaries but made no change to their numbers.

THE WEST LOTHIAN QUESTION

However, it should be said that the way in which the SA 1998 sought to deal with the issue of Scottish representation at Westminster did not guarantee that such overrepresentation might not arise again in the future. Furthermore, although the reduction in the number of MPs for Scottish constituencies at Westminster addresses one apparent anomaly produced by devolution in the constitutional arrangement of the UK as a whole, it does not meet the central issue raised by the 'West Lothian Question',[6] namely the question as to whether it is acceptable for the MPs for Scottish constituencies at Westminster to make laws for England on certain subjects on which they are unable to make laws for Scotland as such subjects now fall within the remit of the Scottish Parliament.[7] The powers subsequently devolved to the Scottish Parliament by the Scotland Act 2012 and the Scotland Act 2016 have increased that problem. That question has led to increasing debate about the implications of devolution to Scotland and Wales for constitutional arrangements for England in which numerous proposals have been put forward, including regional government for England, the establishment of an English Grand Committee, statutes affecting only England to be passed only by MPs representing constituencies in England (known as EVEL, English Votes for English Laws) and the setting up of a fully fledged parliament for England. Chapter 12 below considers in more detail the question of the impact of Scottish devolution on England.

CONSTITUENCY AND REGIONAL MEMBERS

In the single-member constituencies, the successful candidate is the one who receives the most votes on the straightforward 'first past the post' basis which currently applies in elections to the UK Parliament. Such constituency members are essentially elected as individuals although, in practice, most stand as candidates of political parties. In the first general election to the Scottish Parliament, in May 1999, seventy-two of the seventy-three constituency members elected were candidates of political parties.[8] In the second general election in May 2003, seventy-one of the constituency members elected were candidates of political parties. One independent was elected in each of the 2007 and 2012 general elections. In the general election of 2016 all members elected were candidates of political parties.

Seven regional members are elected in each of eight Scottish regions. In the first general election, the boundaries of each region were the same as the 1996 boundaries for European Parliamentary constituencies. However, the choice of the European constituency as the basis for a region for the election of the regional members of the Scottish Parliament was purely a matter of administrative convenience; there was no link between the MSPs and the European constituency. Any link would have become superfluous with the abolition of constituencies for individual members of the European Parliament which took effect in 1999.

In each region a registered political party[9] may submit a list of candidates for election as regional members. Each list may have up to twelve names on it (this allows for the filling of any vacancies that may arise from time to time). In addition, an individual without a party political affiliation may stand as an individual candidate for election as a regional member. The list system gives small political parties and individuals an enhanced opportunity to gain seats. The number of candidates on the lists rose from 500 in the 1999 election to 605 in 2003. A large number of parties put forward candidates for election via the regional list. In 2003, candidates from a broad spectrum of political parties were elected, including from the Scottish Green Party (which won seven seats), the Scottish Socialist Party (which won six seats), and the Scottish Senior Citizens Unity Party (which won one seat). Other parties which put forward lists of candidates (unsuccessfully) included, among many others, the Communist Party, the Monster Raving Loony Party, the Humanist Party, the Pro-Life Party, and the Natural Law Party. In addition, a number of individuals stood as regional candidates on a single-issue basis, such as opposition to local hospital closures and the preservation of the Scottish fishing industry.

Over the years since then, the number of smaller parties successfully fielding candidates has declined. In the 2007 election the smaller parties were squeezed by the rise of the Scottish National Party. The Green Party's representation was reduced to two and the Scottish Socialist Party and the Scottish Senior Citizens Unity Party lost all their seats. None of the other small parties won seats and only one independent was elected. In the 2011 election the one independent was re-elected and, in the 2016 Scottish general election, no independents were elected. None of the smaller parties won seats, apart from the Green Party, despite fielding a large number of candidates. However, the Scottish Green Party succeeded in increasing its representation to six seats in the 2016 election.

The SA 1998 permits a person to stand for election both as a constituency member (in only one constituency) and as a regional member provided that the constituency lies within the region concerned. The political parties initially used this as a fall-back mechanism to ensure that their leaders were elected. In the first Scottish general election in 1999, Donald Dewar, the then leader of the Labour Party in Scotland, stood as the Labour candidate in the Anniesland constituency in Glasgow. He was also at the top of the Labour Party's regional list for Glasgow to ensure that he was elected to the Parliament even if defeated in the Anniesland constituency. (The official party reason normally given for putting the leader of the party at the top of the regional list, as well as having him stand as a constituency member, was to maximise the regional vote for the party by having a well-known name at the top of the party list.)The leaders of the Scottish Conservative Party, the Scottish National Party, and the Scottish Socialist Party adopted the same belt-and-braces approach in the 1999, 2003, and 2007 elections, and the leader of the Scottish Liberal Democrats did so in the 2007 elections; the leader of the Scottish Green Party stood only as a regional member. Now all the major political parties appear to follow this practice. In the 2016 elections, the leaders of both the Scottish Labour and Scottish Green Parties stood in constituencies but were unsuccessful and had to rely on their places as the lead candidates in their respective parties' regional lists for their areas. The leaders of the SNP, Scottish Liberal Democrats, and the Scottish Conservatives were all elected from constituencies although they were all placed on their respective parties' regional lists as an insurance against failure to win a constituency seat. (The Scottish Liberal Democrat and Scottish Conservative leaders had been elected as regional list members in 2011 but both gained constituency seats at the expense of the SNP.)

Although it is unlikely that anyone would be nominated by more than one political party or stand both as a party candidate and as an individual candidate, there are provisions in SA 1998 to ensure that this is not possible.[10]

At a general election for the Scottish Parliament, each voter has two votes. One vote is cast to choose a named candidate from those standing in that voter's constituency to be the constituency member. The other vote is cast to elect regional members. It may be cast either for the list submitted in that region by a registered political party or for an individual who is standing for election as a regional member. However, the voter cannot choose to vote for a particular candidate on a party list; if he or she wishes to vote for the party list, he or she must do so en bloc. This type of list is known as a 'closed' list.

In an attempt to avoid confusion, the ballot papers for the constituency seats are a different colour from the ballot papers for the regional seats. In 2007, the constituency and regional ballots were combined on one ballot paper with the regional ballot peach and the constituency ballot lilac. Combining the ballot papers was a result of the introduction of electronic counting of votes. However, massive voter confusion occurred as the Scottish Parliament and the local council elections were held on the same day. A total of 146,099 ballot papers were rejected as invalid either because the ballot paper had been left blank or because the voter's intention was uncertain: 60,455 (2.8 per cent) regional; 85,644 (4.07 per cent) constituency votes were rejected. Various reasons were advanced for this situation. One was the single ballot paper combining the regional and the constituency candidates for election, albeit in separate columns and on differently coloured paper. Another was that the instructions to voters were not entirely clear. A further reason suggested was that a new electoral system, the Single Transferable Vote, was being used for the local government elections while the Scottish Parliament electoral system is the Additional Member System.

As a result of the confusion, the Scottish Parliament passed the Scottish Local Government (Elections) Act 2009 which has 'decoupled' the Scottish local government elections from the Scottish Parliament general elections so that they are no longer held on the same day.

THE RIGHT TO VOTE AND TO STAND FOR ELECTION

The right to vote in elections to the Scottish Parliament is based on similar principles to the right to vote in elections to the UK Parliament. However, it is extended to those who are entitled to vote in local government elections. The effect of this is to extend the right to vote to members of the House of Lords and to citizens of the member states of the European Union. There is no requirement in law to be a registered elector in Scotland. At the time of writing, it is not clear whether EU citizens resident in Scotland will retain the right to vote if the United Kingdom leaves the European Union. Under EU law EU citizens have a right to vote in local government elections in Scotland. However, that right to vote is given to them in Scotland under domestic UK legislation. For that reason, leaving the European Union will not automatically take away their right to vote in local government elections nor for elections to the Scottish Parliament. It would require specific legislation to do that. As the franchise for Scottish local government elections and Scottish Parliament elections is devolved to the Parliament by the SA 2016, it will be up to it to decide whether to make any changes to EU citizens' right to vote (unless the UK Government decides to do so as part of its legislation taking the United Kingdom out of the EU).[11]

The right to vote in most elections in the UK was extended to those aged eighteen or over on the day of the relevant election as long ago as

1969. However, the SNP Government decided that it would be politic to extend the right to vote in the referendum on independence for Scotland in 2014 to those aged sixteen or over. This was done by the Scottish Independence Referendum (Franchise) Act 2013. The Parliament gave sixteen- and seventeen-year-olds the right to vote in local elections and in Scottish general elections by passing the Scottish Elections (Reduction of Voting Age) Act 2015. Sixteen- and seventeen-year-olds were therefore able to vote in a Scottish general election for the first time in the election held in May 2016.

QUALIFICATIONS AND DISQUALIFICATIONS FOR STANDING FOR ELECTION

To be eligible to stand for election a person must be:

- eighteen years or over and a British, Commonwealth, Irish or EU citizen resident in the UK
- NOT subject to any legal disqualification (see below).

The rules relating to disqualification from membership of the Scottish Parliament are similar to those for the House of Commons and are set out in sections 15 and 16 of the SA 1998. Thus, judges, civil servants (including the staff of the Scottish Parliament and its agencies), members of the armed forces, members of police forces, and members of foreign legislatures are disqualified. Holders of certain public offices – for example, members of Scottish Enterprise, the Scottish Environmental Protection Agency, the Scottish Qualifications Authority, and the Crofters Commission – are also disqualified. However, members of the House of Lords who are disqualified from membership of the House of Commons are not ineligible to be MSPs merely because of their membership of the House of Lords. Three members of the House of Lords were elected as MSPs in the first general election in 1999, two in 2003 and one in 2007.[12]

Aliens are also disqualified. An alien is a person who is not a British citizen, a Commonwealth citizen, a citizen of the Irish Republic or a citizen of the European Union. A citizen of the European Union must, however, be resident in the United Kingdom to be eligible to stand. Until 2006 persons under the age of twenty-one were disqualified but now people aged eighteen are eligible to stand for election under the Electoral Administration Act 2006. Undischarged bankrupts, certain persons suffering from mental illness who are detained in hospital, convicted prisoners serving a sentence of more than one year, and persons guilty of corrupt or illegal election practices are also disqualified from standing. Senior local government officers who hold what are called 'politically restricted posts' are also ineligible to stand.

Persons who have been ordained or who are ministers of religion of any denomination, many of whom were, until 2001,[13] disqualified from standing for election to the House of Commons, are now eligible to stand for election to the Scottish Parliament.

THE ALLOCATION OF SEATS

The votes cast for the constituency candidates are counted first and the candidate who secures the majority of votes in each constituency is declared to be the MSP for that constituency. The names of successful candidates who are on regional lists are removed from the party lists.

The reason that the constituency seats are decided first is because the regional member seats are allocated on the basis of correcting imbalances brought about by the 'first past the post' system used in the constituency seats. If a party secures fewer constituency seats than its overall electoral support would suggest, it is allocated more of the regional seats to bring about a result in which the total number of seats won by any party is more proportional to the total number of votes cast for it in each region.

The calculation of the regional figures and the allocation of the regional seats is somewhat complex and the reader should refer to Table 3.2 at the end of the chapter for an example of the calculation. For each political party which has submitted a list of candidates, the total number of regional votes cast throughout the region is divided by the number of constituency seats won by that party plus one. The resulting figure is called the 'regional figure'. Parties which did not gain any constituency seats are also involved in this calculation. Each time a party gains a regional member seat, that party's regional figure is recalculated. The regional figure for individual candidates is the total number of votes cast for the individual in all the constituencies included in the region.

The first regional member seat is allocated to the party or individual with the highest regional figure. This will not necessarily be the party with the highest total of regional votes because account is taken of the number of constituency seats already won by the parties. The second and subsequent seats are then allocated on the basis of the recalculated regional figures. Seats are allocated to the persons on a party's list in the order in which they appear on the list, disregarding, of course, anyone who has already won a constituency seat.

Table 3.1   2016 election figures for Scotland (allocation of seats 2016)

Political Party	% constituency votes	% constituency seats	% regional votes	% regional seats	% total seats
SNP	47	81	42	7	48
Conservative	22	10	23	43	24
Labour	23	4	19	38	19
Green	1	0	7	11	5
Liberal Democrats	8	5	5	2	4

In calculating the allocation of regional seats, account is taken only of the number of votes cast for the regional lists. A party that received a total of votes in the election of constituency members which varied substantially from the total of the votes cast for their regional list would not have that difference taken into account in the allocation of the additional seats from the regional list.

The system for allocating seats does, in broad terms, result in an allocation of seats in proportion to the number of votes cast for the candidates on the regional lists. In the 2016 Scottish general election, the number of seats won by each party was as follows: SNP, sixty-three seats; Conservative, thirty-one seats, Labour, twenty-four seats; Green, six seats; Liberal Democrat, five seats. This result was relatively proportional to the votes cast on the regional list. However, the system does not result in complete proportionality as can be seen from Table 3.1 above.

ELECTIONS AND BY-ELECTIONS

Ordinary and Extraordinary General Elections

Members of the Scottish Parliament elected from constituencies and from regional lists are normally elected at the same time in a Scotland-wide general election. The first of these was held on 6 May 1999, and the subsequent ordinary general elections on the first Thursday of the month in 2003, 2007, 2011 and 2016. There is some flexibility provided in that an ordinary general election can be held within a period running from one month before until one month after the first Thursday in May. The term of office of an MSP begins on the day on which the member is declared to be returned and ends with the dissolution of the Parliament. The normal term is for four years but, if the Scottish ordinary general election is scheduled to be held on the same day as a general election for the UK Parliament or the European Parliament, the term is extended to five years. This happened in the 2011–16 session and will also be the case for the 2016–21 session (even though the next UK general election is now scheduled to take place in 2022).

Extraordinary general elections can take place earlier than four (or five) years after the previous election in two situations. The first situation in which an extraordinary general election must be held is where a majority of MSPs amounting to not less than two-thirds of the total number of members of the Parliament vote for an earlier election. The second set of circumstances is where, for some reason or other, the office of First Minister has been vacant for a period of (normally) twenty-eight days. The first situation would arise only if a clear majority of the political parties represented in the Parliament wanted to hold an earlier general election because, for example, government had become unworkable owing to a breakdown of a coalition or because a vote of no confidence in the Scottish Government had been passed. A two-thirds majority would probably require the support of three of the major political party groups. The requirement for such a majority thus makes it impossible for a government with a small majority to call an early general election at a time which it considers might suit its party political interests. This is in contrast to the situation in the UK Parliament which, until 2011,[14] did not have a fixed term and the Prime Minister could call a general election at a time that suited him or her.

In the second situation, the office of First Minister could be vacant for a variety of reasons. It could be that, after an ordinary general election, the MSPs fail to agree on a nomination for the post of First Minister because of a simple majority of MSPs voting against every nominee. If twenty-eight days elapse without a resolution of this impasse, an extraordinary general election would have to be held. If, after an extraordinary general election, held as a result of such a failure to agree on a nomination, there continued thereafter to be no agreement on the nomination of a First Minister, theoretically further extraordinary elections could continue to be held. In practice, however, this situation is very unlikely to arise as the political parties responsible for repeated elections would fear a backlash from the electorate.

The office of First Minister might become vacant as a result of the death of the incumbent. This happened in October 2000 when Donald Dewar, the first person elected as First Minister, died unexpectedly. The statutory twenty-eight-day period for filling the post caused the Labour Party some difficulty on that occasion. The period starts to run from the day on which the death occurred. Decency demanded that there should be a period of mourning and that campaigning by contenders to fill the vacancy should not begin at least until the funeral was over. This cut the period to about twenty-one days. The Labour Party's internal procedures for electing a party leader in Scotland from among the Labour MSPs (who would become the new First Minister) take a much longer time than that. In the event, Donald Dewar's successor, Henry McLeish, was elected by an electoral college consisting of all Labour MSPs and the Scottish Labour Party's Executive Committee ten days after Mr Dewar's death. Mr McLeish was duly nominated as First Minister by the Scottish Parliament five days later and was formally appointed to the post by the Queen on the following day. His formal endorsement as Leader of the Scottish Labour Party took place about six weeks later.

Another possibility is that the office of First Minister might become vacant as a result of the incumbent tendering his resignation. This happened in 2001 when Henry McLeish resigned having been First Minister for just over a year. Although there was no need for the delay necessary after a death, the twenty-eight-day period was again too short for the Scottish Labour Party to carry out its full procedures for the election of a new party leader and, to avoid the requirement of an extraordinary election, Jack McConnell was elected by the same truncated procedure described above, nominated by the Parliament, appointed by the Queen within the twenty-eight days, and formally endorsed as party leader by the members of the Scottish Labour Party some weeks later.

In 2007 the then First Minister, Alex Salmond, threatened to resign from office if his party's budget proposals were not passed by the Scottish Parliament. This threat was repeated in 2009 when the Scottish Government presented its second budget to the Scottish Parliament. The budget was passed and there was no need for Mr Salmond to carry out his threat. When Alex Salmond resigned in 2014, following the independence referendum, his successor Nicola Sturgeon was appointed First Minister without delay.

A First Minister might also choose to resign in order to seek a new electoral mandate from the Scottish electorate to demonstrate public support for a controversial policy. One example might be if the UK Government refused to make changes to the Scotland Act which were sought by the Scottish Government (for example, to give it the power to hold a second referendum on independence).

A further possibility, and one which has not yet occurred, is that the First Minister ceases to be an MSP (otherwise than as a result of the Parliament being dissolved for an election). This might happen by the First Minister simply deciding to resign from the Parliament altogether or by the First Minister being disqualified for some reason. Reasons for disqualification include bankruptcy, mental illness, and being convicted of an offence and sentenced to a term of imprisonment of more than a year. Again, the vacancy must be filled within twenty-eight days or an extraordinary general election will be triggered.

By-elections

In the case of a seat falling vacant between elections, different mechanisms apply depending on whether the seat was previously held by a constituency member or by a regional member. If the seat of a constituency member falls vacant for any reason, such as death or resignation, a by-election in the constituency will be held, normally within three months, to elect a replacement. However, if the latest date for holding the by-election would bring it within three months of the next ordinary election to the Parliament, the vacancy will remain unfilled until the next general election. This is to avoid the expense of the election process for the sake of filling the seat for only a few months.

It is possible for a person who has been elected as a regional member to resign and stand for election as a constituency member. This occurred in 2014 in the North East Scotland region when a sitting regional MSP resigned in order to contest the by-election in Donside caused by the death of the incumbent.

If the seat of a regional member falls vacant, different procedures apply depending on whether the seat was previously held by a member elected from a party list or a member who had been elected as an individual member. In the former case, the vacancy is filled by the next person on that party's list who is willing to serve and who is acceptable to the party concerned.[15] In the latter case, the vacancy remains unfilled until the next general election. This was the case when Margo MacDonald, elected as an independent candidate for the Lothian Region list, died in 2014. Her seat remained vacant until the Scottish general election in 2016.

The first by-election for the Parliament was brought about by the resignation, for family reasons, in December 1999, of the constituency member for Ayr. The by-election was held in March 2000 and was won by the Conservative candidate, thus giving the Conservatives their first constituency seat. This had no effect on the allocation of regional seats which remained fixed until the general election of 2003.

MISCELLANEOUS MATTERS

Administration of Elections

The date for the first general election on 6 May 1999 was set by the Secretary of State for Scotland and he or she continued to have the power to make rules for the conduct of elections, including rules on the procedure for electoral registration and on election expenses for candidates and for political parties. This power is exercised by the use of secondary legislation which, in this particular case, required the approval of both Houses of the Westminster Parliament[16.]Following the 2007 election when a large number of ballot papers were rejected, calls were made for the responsibility for the conduct of elections to be devolved to the Scottish Government and the Scottish Parliament. The Calman Commission recommended the transfer of some aspects of the conduct and administration of Scottish parliamentary elections to Scottish Ministers and this was effected by section 1 of the Scotland Act 2012 which transfers certain executive functions which had previously been exercised by the Secretary of State for Scotland. Further powers were transferred by section 4 of the Scotland Act 2016. These include the conduct of and questioning of irregularities, the registration of electors, the limitation of electoral expenses, and the combination of certain polls.

Male and Female Representation

The Labour and Liberal Democrat representatives on the Scottish Constitutional Convention[17] came to an informal agreement that, in the first election to the Parliament in 1999, they would attempt to field an equal number of male and female candidates in winnable seats. Although some wanted this requirement to be put into the SA 1998, this was not done on the ground that it might fall foul of anti-sex discrimination legislation in force at that time.[18] In their procedures for the selection of candidates for the constituency seats, the Labour Party 'twinned' pairs of constituencies in most of Scotland and instructed their members to select one man and one woman candidate for each pair. There was no challenge to this from within the Labour Party. However, despite the agreement the Liberal Democrats did not adopt such an approach as they were unable to get the party's agreement to the proposal.

The Labour Party's procedures resulted in twenty-eight men and twenty-eight women being elected as Labour MSPs in the first general election in 1999. Of the Liberal Democrat MSPs elected in that election, fifteen were men and only two were women. The comparable figures for the SNP were twenty men and fifteen women, and for the Conservatives, fifteen men and three women. For the second and third general elections, in 2003 and 2007, most of the sitting MSPs were readopted as candidates and thus there was no requirement for any artificial procedures on the part of the Labour Party. In 2003, this actually resulted in more women than men being elected as Labour MSPs. That election resulted in seventy-eight men and fifty-one women being elected: at 35.9 per cent this was one of the highest percentages of female representation in parliaments throughout the world. Only the Welsh Assembly (currently 41.7 per cent) and the Swedish Parliament have a higher proportion (currently 44 per cent). The world average is currently 22.7 per cent.

At the 2007 election, eighty-six men and forty-three women were elected. In 2011 forty-five women were elected and the same number in 2016 despite the parties fielding more female candidates. At the time of writing, women are leaders of three of the five parties represented in the Parliament.

The additional member system could ensure the election of ethnic minority candidates if the political parties put them at the top of their lists. For the 2007 election, the SNP put Bashir Ahmed at the top of its regional list for Glasgow. He was elected and became the Scottish Parliament's first Asian MSP. Unfortunately, he died suddenly in 2009. There are currently two ethnic minority MSPs, both of British Pakistani origin.

Dual mandates

Dual mandate is the term given to a situation where an individual is an elected member of two bodies and therefore has a mandate from two sets of electors. The SA 1998 does not prohibit dual mandates and thus it is possible for someone who is an MP in the UK Parliament, a Member of the European Parliament or a local councillor to be elected as a member of the Scottish Parliament. In the first election to the Parliament in 1999, fifteen serving MPs, one MEP and three councillors were elected and did not resign their seats at Westminster, in Europe or in their local councils[19]. In the 2003 election, it would appear that only one person, a councillor, had a dual mandate. In 2007, six MSPs were elected with dual mandates: one Member of the House of Commons (Alex Salmond, the Leader of the SNP) and five councillors. One of those councillors resigned as a MSP after only a few months to concentrate on his duties as a councillor in Edinburgh. Two others resigned as councillors in 2009 to concentrate on parliamentary duties. One member of the House of Lords, Lord Foulkes, who was elected as an MSP did not have a dual mandate because Members of the House of Lords are not elected.

There are, however, provisions which prevent an MSP who is also an MP or an MEP from drawing two full salaries,[20] and a person who holds ministerial office in the UK Government is not permitted to be a member of the Scottish Government.[21] MPs sitting in the UK Parliament, such as Donald Dewar and Henry McLeish, who held office in the UK Government as ministers in the Scottish Office at the time of the first election in 1999, resigned from these posts on election to the Scottish Parliament. The political parties came to an informal agreement that there would be no dual-mandate members of parliaments after the UK general election of 2001. As a result, at that election all but one of those members who held dual mandates in the Scottish and UK Parliaments opted not to stand again for the UK Parliament. The other, Alex Salmond, Leader of the SNP, opted to stand for election to the UK Parliament and resigned his seat in the Scottish Parliament. However, he stood again successfully for the Scottish Parliament in 2007 and announced that he would not stand for re-election to the Westminster Parliament at the next general election in 2010. However, he later changed his mind and successfully stood for election to the Westminster Parliament in 2015.

THE RIGHTS AND OBLIGATIONS OF MSPS

The Register of Interests and the Code of Conduct

Register of Interests
Members of the Scottish Parliament have certain obligations imposed on them to ensure that they do not act in an improper manner. They and their staff are subject to the Prevention of Corruption Acts 1889 to 1916, (now the Bribery Acts 2010 and 2012) which impose penalties for the corrupt making or acceptance of payments in money or in kind for activity in connection with the business of the Parliament.[22]

The SA 1998 also requires the Parliament to establish a register of members' interests, open to inspection by the public.[23] The initial rules relating to the Register were made for the first MSPs by a transitional order made by the Secretary of State for Scotland in May 1999. The requirements of the transitional order were temporary and have been superseded by the Interests of Members of the Scottish Parliament Act 2006, an Act of the Scottish Parliament.

Under the provisions of that Act, all MSPs, and also the Lord Advocate and the Solicitor General for Scotland, are required to register certain financial interests, including benefits in kind, and must declare any interest before taking part in proceedings of the Parliament which relate to that interest. The registrable interests include: remuneration, other than the salaries and expenses paid to MSPs; unremunerated directorships or partnerships; certain donations to election expenses; sponsorship; overseas visits; certain gifts, interests in heritable property and shareholdings.

Section 11 of the Act makes provision for publication and access to the Register of Interests and, since 2007, the register has also been published on the Scottish Parliament's website.

Code of Conduct

The Standing Orders of the Parliament require it to set up several committees which are called mandatory committees.[24] One of these is the Standards Committee (now called the Standards, Procedures and Public Appointments Committee) and this committee must be established within twenty-one sitting days of a general election. The original remit of the Standards Committee was to consider and report on the adoption, amendment and application of a Code of Conduct for MSPs and on whether the conduct of individual MSPs is in accordance with Standing Orders and with the Code of Conduct. The Standards Committee spent several months in the early days of the first Parliament in the drafting of a detailed Code of Conduct.

The rules relating to the registration and declaration of interests have been embodied in the Code of Conduct for Members of the Scottish Parliament. The terms of the code were agreed by the Parliament in February 2000 and came into force immediately. The code consists of four volumes which provide specific standards to cover most situations encountered by MSPs. Also included in the Code of Conduct are rules relating to the regulation of cross-party groups, engagement and liaison with constituents, and general conduct and conduct in the chamber and committees of the Parliament. The rules for MSPs are set out in Volume 2, section 5 and include rules about offers of hospitality, benefits and gifts.

The SA 1998 also contains provisions relating to paid advocacy. The code sets down detailed rules relating to paid advocacy which is defined as advocating or initiating any cause for any form of payment or benefit in kind, including hospitality.[25] Members of the Scottish Parliament who receive remuneration (other than their salaries and expenses as MSPs) are also prohibited from encouraging other MSPs to act on their behalf in an attempt to get around the rules against paid advocacy.

Also included in the Code of Conduct are rules relating to contacts with lobbyists. One of the first tasks of the Standards Committee was to investigate claims made in a Sunday newspaper that a firm of lobbyists could guarantee access to Scottish Ministers. This became known as the 'Lobbygate' affair. After interviewing various Ministers, their staff and members of the firm of lobbyists concerned, the members of the Standards Committee concluded that there was no truth in the allegations but an early priority for the committee became the regulation of the lobbying of MSPs and, in 2016, the Lobbying (Scotland) Act was passed. This sets up the concept of regulated lobbying and makes provision for a lobbying register, duties to register and a code of conduct for lobbyists.

Enforcement of the Code of Conduct

The Parliament established a Parliamentary Standards Commissioner in 2002 to investigate allegations of breaches of the code of conduct by MSPs.[26] This office has now been replaced by that of the Commissioner for Ethical Standards in Public Life in Scotland, established by the Scottish Parliamentary Commissions and Commissioners Act 2010. Certain complaints are outwith the commissioner's jurisdiction. These include complaints about an MSP's conduct at a meeting in the chamber and those relating to engagement with constituents which are referred to the Presiding Officer, while complaints about the use of allowances are referred to the Scottish Parliament Corporate Body.

Other complaints will be investigated by the commissioner who, if they are admissible, will report to the Standards Committee. After the Standards Committee has considered the commissioner's report, it in turn reports to the Parliament. If the Standards Committee has recommended the imposition of sanctions against the member, a decision on sanctions is made by the Parliament. Sanctions include restricting a member from participating in certain proceedings of the Parliament, excluding a member from all proceedings of the Parliament, the removal of all or part of the member's allowances, and the withdrawal of various rights and privileges. Certain breaches of the code in relation to the registration and declaration of interests and the paid advocacy rule may be criminal offences and a member found guilty is liable on summary conviction to a fine not exceeding level 5 on the standard scale (currently £5,000).

Members of the Scottish Parliament are protected by what is called 'absolute privilege' against any person seeking to take action against them on account of any statement made by them in proceedings of the Parliament. The publication of any statement made under the authority of the Parliament is similarly absolutely privileged.[27] As a result, MSPs cannot be made to pay damages if such a statement is defamatory, even if the statement is made maliciously. The justification for this is that it is in the public interest for MSPs to be able to debate and discuss matters freely without any fear of being sued. This freedom of speech is somewhat similar to the freedom of speech enjoyed by MPs at Westminster. However, unlike proceedings at Westminster, the proceedings of the Scottish Parliament are subject to the law of contempt of court, except in respect of publications made in proceedings of the Parliament in relation to a bill or subordinate legislation, or to the extent that a publication consists of a fair and accurate report of such proceedings made in good faith.[28] The Parliament's Standing Orders provide for a '*sub judice*' rule. This means that an MSP must not, in the proceedings of the Parliament, refer to any matter in relation to which legal proceedings are active, except to the extent permitted by the Presiding Officer; and, if an MSP does refer to such a matter, the Presiding Officer may order that member not to do so.[29] However, nothing in this rule is to prevent the Parliament from legislating on any matter.It should be noted that, in any legal proceedings against the Parliament, a court may not make an order for interdict (or similar order) against the Parliament but may make a declarator of the legal position instead.[30] The purpose of this is to afford the Parliament a measure of protection against attempts to interfere with its business through the use of legal proceedings. It is not yet clear what the consequences are for the Parliament of a declaratory order from a court.

Similarly, a court may not make an order for interdict (or similar order) against any MSP, the Presiding Officer or his deputies, or any member of staff of the Parliament in the Parliamentary corporation if the effect would be to give relief against the Parliament which could not have been given in proceedings against the Parliament. This provision is designed to prevent attempts to interfere with the business of the Parliament 'by the back door'. However, as a result of a decision of the Court of Session early in 2000 it is clear that, in certain circumstances, it is possible for a court to grant an interdict against an individual MSP.[31]

SALARIES

The Parliament is able to pay MSPs' salaries, allowances and pensions,[32] and the basic salary of each MSP, regardless of whether the member was elected as a constituency or a regional member, was set in the first year of the Parliament's existence at £40,092. By 2017, that amount had risen to £61,777.

The Scottish Parliament Salaries Scheme provided for an annual review of MSPs' salaries from April 2003 to maintain their salaries at 87.5 per cent of the salary payable to Members of the House of Commons. However, the link to MPs' salaries was abolished in 2015.

Ministers receive an additional amount depending on the level of seniority. The First Minister, for example, receives a ministerial allowance of £89,492 plus the basic salary of £61,777, giving him/her a total of £151,269.[33]

Cabinet Secretaries, that is senior Ministers, receive £46,426 plus the MSP's basic salary giving them a total of £108,293, while junior Ministers receive £26,026 plus the basic salary, a total of £87,803 (2017 figures).

If an MSP is also a member of the Westminster Parliament or of the European Parliament, he or she is entitled to receive the appropriate salary as well but the Scottish Parliament must ensure that the element of salary which derives from membership of the Scottish Parliament is reduced.[34] The Parliament decided that the amount of the reduction should be two-thirds of the MSP's basic salary. There is no reduction for MSPs who are also local authority councillors.Members of the Scottish Parliament also receive a Members' Support Allowance of around £70,000 per annum to enable the MSP to take on staff to assist the member in carrying out parliamentary duties, establish and run an office in his or her constituency or region, and meet constituents. There are various other allowances, such as travel allowances and Edinburgh accommodation allowances. There is also a 'winding up allowance' for members who cease to be MSPs.

The leaders of opposition parties which have at least fifteen MSPs, none of whom holds ministerial office, are entitled to an allowance to take account of their responsibilities as party leaders. In addition, political party groups within the Parliament are entitled to financial assistance to enable them to perform their parliamentary duties. To be eligible for this, the party must have no more than one fifth of their MSPs appointed as members of the Scottish Government or junior Ministers.

After every election each MSP is required to take the oath of allegiance to the Crown within a specified period (normally two months).

Until the oath is taken, he or she cannot participate in the proceedings of the Parliament or receive any payment of salary or allowances. If the oath is not taken within the specified period, the MSP concerned automatically loses his or her seat in the Parliament.[35] This provision concentrated the minds of various MSPs of a republican bent in both 1999 and 2003. They have all taken the oath of allegiance, albeit under protest. The Standing Orders of the Parliament allow members who do not wish to take an oath because of its religious connotations to make a solemn affirmation instead.[36] Both are of equal effect.

Table 3.2 Allocating seats on the regional list

1. In each region, the number of votes cast for each party in the 'second vote' for a regional list is totalled.
2. This total is then divided by the figure which equals one plus the number of constituency members elected for that party in that region.
3. The first regional seat is then allocated to the political party, or a candidate standing as an individual, having the highest figure after the calculation in Step 2 above has been carried out.
4. The total votes cast for each party in the region are then divided by the figure which equals one plus the number of constituency and regional members elected for that party in that region. Where the calculation results in a number which is not a whole number, that number may be rounded down to the nearest whole number by the exercise of the returning officer's discretion.
5. The next regional seat is then allocated to the political party, or candidate standing as an individual, now having the highest figure after the calculation in Step 4 above has been carried out.
6. This process of recalculation of the figure for each party is then carried out until all seven places for regional members have been allocated.
7. Seats on the regional list are allocated to candidates in the order in which the political parties have placed them on the list prior to the election.

The following example shows how the system of allocation of seats was carried out in Lothian in 2016. There are nine constituency seats and seven regional seats in Lothian.

1. The number of individual constituency members elected was as follows:

Scottish National Party	6
Scottish Conservative and Unionist Party	1
Scottish Labour Party	1
Scottish Liberal Democrats	1

Table 3.2 *continued*

2. The number of regional list votes cast was as follows: per cent

Scottish National Party (SNP):	118,546	36.2
Scottish Conservative and Unionist Party:	74,972	22.9
Scottish Labour Party:	67,991	20.8
Scottish Green Party:	34,551	10.6
Scottish Liberal Democrats:	18,479	5.6
UK Independence Party (UKIP):	5,802	1.8
Scottish Women's Equality Party:	3,877	1.2
RISE – Respect, Independence, Socialism and Environmentalism:	1,641	0.5
Solidarity – Scotland's Socialist Movement:	1,319	0.4

3. The first seat. The above totals were then divided by the figure of one plus the number of constituency members elected for each party to give the regional figure for each. As the Scottish National Party won six FPTP seats, its figure of 118,546 is divided by 7 (6+1) and, as the Scottish Conservative and Unionist Party, Scottish Labour Party, and the Scottish Liberal Democrats each won one seat, their respective figures are each divided by 2 (1+1). The other parties' figures are divided by 1 (0+1) and therefore their regional figures are the same as in the table above. Calculated figures are rounded down to the nearest whole number. The winning party is marked*:

Scottish National Party (SNP):	16,935
Scottish Conservative and Unionist Party:	37,486*
Scottish Labour Party:	33,995
Scottish Green Party:	34,551
Scottish Liberal Democrats:	9,239
UK Independence Party (UKIP):	5,802
Scottish Women's Equality Party:	3,877
RISE – Respect, Independence, Socialism and Environmentalism:	1,641
Solidarity – Scotland's Socialist Movement:	1,319

As a result of this calculation, the Scottish Conservative and Unionist Party had the highest regional figure so the top person on its regional list was elected. Thus, the total number of MSPs elected for each party at that stage was as follows:

Scottish National Party:	6
Scottish Conservative and Unionist Party:	2
Scottish Labour Party:	1
Scottish Liberal Democrats:	1
Others:	0

Table 3.2 *continued*

4. The second seat. Because the Scottish Conservative and Unionist Party had won the first seat, its regional figure was recalculated by dividing its original regional figure by 3 (2+1), giving the following:

Scottish National Party (SNP):	16,935
Scottish Conservative and Unionist Party:	24,990
Scottish Labour Party:	33,995
Scottish Green Party:	34,551[*]
Scottish Liberal Democrats:	9,239
UK Independence Party (UKIP):	5,802
Scottish Women's Equality Party:	3,877
RISE – Respect, Independence, Socialism and Environmentalism:	1,641
Solidarity – Scotland's Socialist Movement:	1,319

As a result of this calculation, the Scottish Green Party now had the highest regional figure, so the first person on its list was elected. The number of seats for the parties were then as follows:

Scottish National Party:	6
Scottish Conservative and Unionist Party:	2
Scottish Labour Party:	1
Scottish Liberal Democrats:	1
Scottish Green Party:	1
Others:	0

5. The third seat. Since the Scottish Green Party had won the second seat, its regional figure was recalculated by dividing its original regional figure by 2 (1+1), giving the following:

Scottish National Party (SNP):	16,935
Scottish Conservative and Unionist Party:	24,990
Scottish Labour Party:	33,995[*]
Scottish Green Party:	17,275
Scottish Liberal Democrats:	9,239
UK Independence Party (UKIP):	5,802
Scottish Women's Equality Party:	3,877
RISE – Respect, Independence, Socialism and Environmentalism:	1,641
Solidarity – Scotland's Socialist Movement:	1,319

As a result of this calculation, the Scottish Labour Party now had the highest regional figure, so the first person on its list was elected. The number of seats for the parties were then as follows:

Scottish National Party:	6
Scottish Conservative and Unionist Party:	2
Scottish Labour Party:	2
Scottish Liberal Democrats:	1
Scottish Green Party:	1
Others:	0

Table 3.2 *continued*

6. The fourth seat. Because the Scottish Labour Party had won the third seat, its regional figure was recalculated by dividing its original regional figure by 3 (2+1), giving the following:

Scottish National Party (SNP):	16,935
Scottish Conservative and Unionist Party:	24,990*
Scottish Labour Party:	22,663
Scottish Green Party:	17,275
Scottish Liberal Democrats:	9,239
UK Independence Party (UKIP):	5,802
Scottish Women's Equality Party:	3,877
RISE – Respect, Independence, Socialism and Environmentalism:	1,641
Solidarity – Scotland's Socialist Movement:	1,319

As a result of this calculation, the Scottish Conservative and Unionist Party now had the highest regional figure, so the second person on its list was elected. The number of seats for the parties were then as follows:

Scottish National Party:	6
Scottish Conservative and Unionist Party:	3
Scottish Labour Party:	2
Scottish Liberal Democrats:	1
Scottish Green Party:	1
Others:	0

7. The fifth seat. Because the Scottish Conservative and Unionist Party had won the fourth seat, its regional figure was recalculated by dividing its original regional figure by 4 (3+1), giving the following:

Scottish National Party (SNP):	16,935
Scottish Conservative and Unionist Party:	18,742
Scottish Labour Party:	22,663*
Scottish Green Party:	17,275
Scottish Liberal Democrats:	9,239
UK Independence Party (UKIP):	5,802
Scottish Women's Equality Party:	3,877
RISE – Respect, Independence, Socialism and Environmentalism:	1,641
Solidarity – Scotland's Socialist Movement:	1,319

As a result of this calculation, the Scottish Labour Party now had the highest regional figure, so the second person on its list was elected. The number of seats for the parties were then as follows:

Scottish National Party:	6
Scottish Conservative and Unionist Party:	3
Scottish Labour Party:	3
Scottish Liberal Democrats:	1
Scottish Green Party:	1
Others:	0

Table 3.2 *continued*

8. The sixth seat. The Scottish Labour Party's regional figure was recalculated. This time their original regional figure was divided by 4 (3+1). The following figures resulted:

Scottish National Party (SNP):	16,935
Scottish Conservative and Unionist Party:	18,742*
Scottish Labour Party:	16,997
Scottish Green Party:	17,275
Scottish Liberal Democrats:	9,239
UK Independence Party (UKIP):	5,802
Scottish Women's Equality Party:	3,877
RISE – Respect, Independence, Socialism and Environmentalism:	1,641
Solidarity – Scotland's Socialist Movement:	1,319

As a result of this calculation, the Scottish Conservative and Unionist Party now had the highest regional figure, so the third person on its list was elected. The number of seats for the parties were then as follows:

Scottish National Party:	6
Scottish Conservative and Unionist Party:	4
Scottish Labour Party:	3
Scottish Liberal Democrats:	1
Scottish Green Party:	1
Others:	0

9. The seventh seat. In this final calculation, the Scottish Conservative and Unionist Party's regional figure was recalculated. This time their original regional figure was divided by 5 (4+1). The following figures resulted:

Scottish National Party (SNP):	16,935
Scottish Conservative and Unionist Party:	14,993
Scottish Labour Party:	16,997
Scottish Green Party:	17,275*
Scottish Liberal Democrats:	9,239
UK Independence Party (UKIP):	5,802
Scottish Women's Equality Party:	3,877
RISE – Respect, Independence, Socialism and Environmentalism:	1,641
Solidarity – Scotland's Socialist Movement:	1,319

As a result of this calculation, the Scottish Green Party now had the highest regional figure, so the second person on its list was elected. The number of seats for the parties were then as follows:

Scottish National Party:	6
Scottish Conservative and Unionist Party:	4
Scottish Labour Party:	3
Scottish Liberal Democrats:	1
Scottish Green Party:	2
Others:	0

Table 3.3 Election Results for the Lothian Region (2016)

Party	Constituency (FPTP)			Regional List			Total	
	% of seats	% of votes	No. seats	% of seats	% of votes	No. seats	Total No.seats	% of total seats
Sc. Conservative	11	21	1	42	23	3	4	25
Sc. Labour	11	26	1	28	21	2	3	19
Sc. Lib Dems	11	9	1	0	6	0	1	6
SNP	66	42	6	0	36	0	6	38
Sc. Green	0	1	0	28	11	2	2	13
UKIP	0	+	0	0	2	0	0	0
Sc. Women's Eq	0	+	0	0	1	0	0	0
RISE	0	+	0	0	1	0	0	0
Solidarity	0	+	0	0	*	0	0	0
Others	0	*	0	0	0	0	0	0

(Note: * is shown where figure is less than 0.5%; + is shown where no candidates in that list)

NOTES

1. See sections 1–18 of SA 1998 for the provisions relating to MSPs and elections.
2. SA 1998, Schedule 1.
3. SA 1998, section 86.
4. In 1997, Scotland had an average of 55,339 electors per constituency while England had an average of 69,578 electors per constituency.
5. SA 1998, section 86.
6. Named after the Labour MP for West Lothian and later Linlithgow, Tam Dalyell, who frequently raised this issue after devolution for Scotland was proposed in the 1970s.
7. This issue flared up again in 2003 when John Reid, the Scottish MP for Hamilton North and Bellshill, became the Secretary of State for Health, dealing with English health matters while having no responsibility for health matters in Scotland because these are devolved to the Scottish Parliament. It was also a matter of contention in the House of Commons that the votes of Scottish MPs preserved the government's majorities in relation to the abolition of foxhunting in England and the establishment of foundation hospitals in England.
8. In 1999, Dennis Canavan, the Labour MP for Falkirk West at Westminster, was deemed by his party to be 'not good enough' to stand for the Scottish Parliament as an official Labour candidate. He stood as an independent in Falkirk West and won the seat with 54.98 per cent of the votes cast. He stood again as an independent in 2003, holding the seat this time with 55.69 per cent of the votes cast.

9. That is, registered in terms of the Political Parties, Elections and Referendums Act 2000.

10. SA 1998, section 5(7) and (8).

11. The fact that citizens of the European Union resident in Scotland were entitled to vote was misunderstood by some polling clerks in the first general election to the Scottish Parliament in 1999. As a result, several EU citizens were denied the vote to which they were entitled. For discussion of what might happen to the voting rights of EU citizens after Brexit, see: https://marklazarowicz.com/2017/02/28/the-right-of-eu-citizens-in-the-uk-to-vote-after-brexit/ (last accessed 9 April 2017).

12. Lord Steel (Liberal Democrat), Lord Watson (Labour), and Lord James Douglas-Hamilton (Conservative) in 1999, Lord Watson and Lord James Douglas-Hamilton in 2003, and Lord Foulkes in 2007.

13. The prohibition on persons who had been ordained standing for election to the House of Commons was removed by the House of Commons (Removal of Clergy Disqualification) Act 2001. This change in the law was hastened by the Labour Party in Greenock and Inverclyde selecting a person who had been ordained as a Roman Catholic priest as their candidate for the UK Parliamentary election in 2001.

14. The Fixed Term Parliaments Act 2011.

15. SA 1998, section 10(4)–(5A). This amendment was made to the Act when it was realised, belatedly, that a person on a party's list may have changed parties.

16. SA 1998, section 12 and Schedule 7.

17. For the Scottish Constitutional Convention, see Chapter 1, p. 4.

18. Prior to the 1997 general election, the Labour Party had attempted to increase the number of women MPs at Westminster by having all-women shortlists. This was successfully challenged before an industrial tribunal by two aspiring male candidates. See *Jepson and Dyas-Elliot* v. *The Labour Party* [1996] IRLR[116]. In response to this the UK Parliament passed the Sex Discrimination (Election Candidates) Act 2002, which amends the Sex Discrimination Act 1975, and makes all-women shortlists lawful for any Parliamentary and local government election.

19. Those members of the Scottish Parliament (especially those who were members of the Scottish Executive) who were also members of the UK Parliament found it difficult to attend meetings at Westminster and received some criticism from opposition parties for poor attendance at the time.

20. See p. 55 for salaries.

21. SA 1998, section 44.

22. SA 1998, section 43.

23. SA 1998, section 39.

24. For the committees of the Parliament generally, see p. 68.

25. For an interesting example of a legal challenge to an MSP, alleging breach of the advocacy rule and acceptance of benefits in kind, see *Whaley and*

Others v. *Lord Watson and the Scottish Parliamentary Corporate Body* 2000 SLT 475. Lord Watson MSP introduced a member's bill (the Protection of Wild Mammals Bill) the purpose of which was to ban foxhunting by dogs. He received legal and administrative assistance, including advice on drafting the bill, from the Scottish Campaign against Hunting with Dogs which the supporters of foxhunting considered to be benefits in kind. The Inner House of the Court of Session decided that it had no power to prevent MSPs from breaching the members' interests rules. The rules can be enforced only by retrospective sanctions which include a fine.

26. Scottish Parliamentary Standards Commissioner Act 2002.
27. SA 1998, section 41.
28. SA 1998, section 42.
29. Scottish Parliament's Standing Orders, Rule 7.5.
30. SA 1998, section 40(3), (4).
31. *Whaley and Others* v. *Lord Watson and the Scottish Parliamentary Corporate Body* 2000 SLT 475.
32. SA 1998, section 81.
33. As a result of his dual mandate, the first First Minister, Donald Dewar, was entitled to earn more per annum than the Prime Minister of the United Kingdom. He chose to forgo his entitlement to one-third of an MSP's salary.
34. SA 1998, section 82.
35. SA 1998, section 84.
36. Scottish Parliament Standing Orders, Rule 1.2.

CHAPTER FOUR

How the Parliament Works

INTRODUCTION

The supporters of the establishment of a Scottish Parliament frequently expressed the hope that such a body would be a new type of institution, with a new approach to the way in which the business of government is carried out.[1] This chapter looks at the way in which that hope has been reflected in the reality of the arrangements made for the way the Parliament works. It considers in some detail the role of the Parliament's committees. It also looks at the opportunities that are available to MSPs to hold the Scottish Government to account, and the way in which external individuals and organisations can influence the Parliament's work.

THE LEGISLATIVE FRAMEWORK

The Parliament is given a relatively free hand by the Scotland Act 1998 (SA 1998) in deciding how it should work. The Act does not set out detailed requirements for the Parliament's method of operation. It states that the proceedings of the Parliament will be regulated by standing orders.[2] Beyond that general requirement, there is only a small number of areas where the SA 1998 specifies what should be in the standing orders. These statutory requirements contain important provisions about the passage of legislation, including procedures to ensure that the Parliament cannot make legislation on matters which are outside the powers given to it. These provisions are explained in Chapter 5 below.

There is a number of other specific matters which the SA 1998 requires the Parliament to deal with in its standing orders, including rules to provide for the following:[3]

- The preservation of order in the Parliament's proceedings, including the prevention of criminal conduct or contempt of court during

proceedings, and the prevention of the discussion of matters which are *sub judice*
- The proceedings of the Parliament are to be held in public, except in certain specified circumstances
- The Presiding Officer and his or her deputies are not all to come from the same political party
- In the establishment of any committees and subcommittees, account must be taken of the balance of seats held by the different political parties in the Parliament.

The Standing Orders may also include rules allowing for the exclusion of MSPs from sittings of the Parliament and its committees and subcommittees, in certain circumstances.

It can be seen, therefore, that the SA 1998 lays only broad guidelines for the operation of the Parliament and, in particular, for how proposals for legislation should pass through the Parliament. The SA 1998 does not set out detailed guidelines for the way in which committees should operate or for the number of stages that proposed legislation should pass through in Parliament.

STANDING ORDERS

Although the statutory requirements to be observed by the Parliament in deciding how it should function are relatively few, the Parliament operates within the framework of a comprehensive set of Standing Orders. In order that the Parliament would have Standing Orders in place when it began operation, its first Standing Orders were made by the Secretary of State for Scotland,[4] using his powers to make transitional provisions for the Parliament. These transitional provisions were superseded in December 1999 when the Parliament adopted its own Standing Orders. The Parliament may, on a motion made by its Standards, Procedures and Public Appointments Committee, amend its Standing Orders if an absolute majority of MSPs so decide[5] and the Parliament has subsequently made a number of quite substantial amendments to its original Standing Orders, the most recent in 2017.

The Standing Orders are written in comparatively straightforward English and contain a glossary of terms, thus making them reasonably intelligible to members of the public. They cover such matters as meetings of the Parliament, elections to various posts within the Parliament and the Scottish Government, the management of business, committees, the conduct of meetings, procedures for passing various types of bills, subordinate legislation procedure, decisions and voting, statements and Parliamentary questions, the laying and publication of documents, public access, petitions, the reporting of Parliamentary proceedings, and miscellaneous matters.

The original Standing Orders were modelled largely, although not completely, on the proposals made by the Consultative Steering Group on the Scottish Parliament (the 'CSG'). The CSG was set up by the UK Government early in 1998 to make proposals as to how the Parliament should carry out its business. It drew together representatives of all the major political parties along with other leading constitutional experts, and published its final report, 'Shaping Scotland's Parliament', in January 1999.[6] Its broad recommendations were endorsed by all the major political parties.

Plenary Meetings

The Parliament meets in plenary session (that is, all 129 members) on Tuesday, Wednesday, and Thursday afternoons. These sessions are chaired by the Presiding Officer or one of the deputies. These sessions provide opportunities for the First Minister and other Ministers to be questioned, for the final consideration of proposed legislation, for general debates and statements by Ministers.[7]

THE PRESIDING OFFICER

It will be seen from other sections of this book that the Parliament's Presiding Officer plays an important part in its activities. Under the statutory provisions of the SA 1998, he or she has a very important part to play in the procedure whereby proposed legislation passes through the Parliament.[8] The Standing Orders give further important responsibilities to the Presiding Officer. These include the duty to:

- preside over plenary meetings of the Parliament
- convene and chair the Parliamentary Bureau
- interpret and apply the Standing Orders
- represent the Parliament in discussions and exchanges with any parliamentary, governmental, administrative or other body, whether within or outwith the UK.

The SA 1998 provides that the Parliament must elect a Presiding Officer and two deputies who should not all represent the same party. In the first session of the Parliament, the Presiding Officer was David Steel who had been elected as a Liberal Democrat; in the second session of the Parliament, elected in 2003, the Presiding Officer was George Reid, elected as an SNP member; in the third session of the Parliament, elected in 2007, the Presiding Officer was Alex Fergusson who was elected as a Conservative member. In 2011 Tricia Marwick, an SNP member was elected and, in 2016, Kenneth Macintosh from the Labour Party.

Once elected to the office, the Presiding Offer and his or her deputies[9] are expected to put aside party politics and act impartially on behalf of all the members of the Parliament. The Standing Orders further provide that the Presiding Officer and the Deputy Presiding Officers have casting votes in the event of a tie in a plenary meeting of the Parliament (except where there is a tie in a vote for First Minister, Presiding Officer and deputies, and members of the Parliament Corporation) or in a meeting of the Parliamentary Bureau. The Presiding Officer does not otherwise have a vote[10] but the deputies have normal voting rights except when actually presiding over Parliamentary business. To be appointed, each of the Presiding Officer and deputies must obtain an absolute majority of those MSPs actually voting in that election[11] but, once appointed, can be removed only by an absolute majority of all MSPs.[12] The Presiding Officer has a basic salary of £45,605, plus the MSP's salary of £60,685, while the Deputy Presiding Officers have a basic salary of £28,568 plus the MSP's salary (2016–17 figures).

The Standing Orders specifically require the Presiding Officer and deputies, when exercising their functions, to 'act impartially, taking account of the interests of all members equally'.[13] Nevertheless, the functions of the posts have the potential, particularly in the case of the Presiding Officer, to give their holders considerable influence over the business of the Parliament. The degree to which that proves to be the case no doubt depends on the personality of the person elected to the post and the political balance between the parties represented in the Parliament. Because the electoral system makes it difficult (but not impossible) for any one political party to win an outright majority and that, accordingly, there will be a greater role for inter-party bargaining, there is a reasonable possibility that the office of Presiding Officer is one that will have a public profile, and perhaps also a degree of political influence, that is greater than its counterpart in the UK Parliament, the Speaker.

THE PARLIAMENTARY BUREAU

A particularly important role in the management of the Parliament's business is played by its Parliamentary Bureau. The Bureau operates under special rules set out in the Standing Orders and, although clearly a committee of the Parliament, it is governed by different rules from those that apply to other committees.[14] The Bureau is made up of the Presiding Officer and one representative of each party with five or more MSPs (nominated by the Parliamentary leader of the party). In addition, members of parties with fewer than five MSPs, or independents, can combine together to form a group of five or more members for the purposes of appointing a representative to the Bureau. Members of the Bureau vote on a 'weighted basis' where they wield one vote for each MSP their party has in the full Parliament.

The main functions of the Parliamentary Bureau are to:

- recommend to the Parliament its business programme
- recommend the establishment remit, membership, and duration of any committee or subcommittee of the Parliament
- decide any issue as to whether a matter comes within the responsibility of a particular committee, and to decide which committee should be the 'lead committee' where an issue falls within the responsibility of more than one committee.

The Presiding Officer chairs meetings of the Bureau but has no vote unless there is a tie when he or she can use a casting vote. A Deputy Presiding Officer chairs the meeting in the absence of the Presiding Officer. Meetings of the Bureau are held in private although it can if it wishes invite other MSPs to participate in a meeting on a non-voting basis.

THE COMMITTEES OF THE PARLIAMENT

In most legislative assemblies, much of the detailed work is dealt with in committees rather than in a plenary session of all the body's members. The arrangements for an assembly's committee structure are therefore a key aspect of its method of operation. This is particularly so in the case of the Scottish Parliament where committees play a significant role in its activities because the Scottish Parliament is unicameral. This means that it does not have a second chamber, such as a senate or a House of Lords, which can revise proposed legislation. The CSG proposed a system of all-purpose 'subject' committees which combine the roles of both Public Bill and select committees found at Westminster with broad remits that cover the consideration and scrutiny of both policy and proposals for legislation. The Parliament accepted this proposal. Standing Orders provide that the Parliament may establish such committees as it thinks fit on a motion of the Parliamentary Bureau. Individual MSPs may also propose the establishment of subject committees. The CSG also recommended that certain 'mandatory' committees should be set up and, in the case of these, Standing Orders provide that the Parliament must establish them. In addition, whenever a Private Bill is introduced, the Parliament must establish a Private Bill Committee.[15] The Parliamentary Bureau proposes to the Parliament the establishment, membership, remit, and duration of subject committees.[16] In practice, subject committees are normally established for the whole of the Parliament's four- or five-year session.

Subject Committees

Eight subject committees were initially established by the Parliament in 1999 and were given broad remits. The committees were as follows:

- Education, Culture and Sport
- Enterprise and Lifelong Learning
- Health and Community Care
- Justice and Home Affairs
- Local Government
- Rural Affairs (later renamed Rural Development)
- Scottish Inclusion, Housing and the Voluntary Sector (later renamed Social Justice)
- Transport and the Environment.

The workload of the Justice and Home Affairs Committee soon became so heavy that it was necessary to establish a second committee with an identical remit, and the Committees were known as 'Justice 1' and 'Justice 2'.

After the 2016 election, the subject committee formed (and their remits), were as follows:

- Economy, Jobs and Fair Work: to consider and report on the Scottish economy, domestic and international investment; labour market strategy; business, industry and manufacturing; cities, energy including renewable energy and all other matters falling within the responsibility of the Cabinet Secretary for Economy,

Jobs and Fair Work, apart from those covered by the remits of the Transport, Infrastructure and Climate Change and the Local Government and Communities Committees

- Education and Skills: to consider and report on early years and childcare; schools and teaching; further and higher education, child protection and looked-after children; skills and other matters falling within the responsibility of the Cabinet Secretary for Education and Skills; and matters relating to culture and the arts falling within the responsibility of the Minister for Europe, External Affairs and Culture
- Environment, Climate Change and Land Reform Committee: to consider and report on the environment and land reform; water quality; climate change; national parks; Crown Estate; marine planning
- Health and Sport: to consider and report on public health; sport; physical health and well-being; the NHS in Scotland; primary care including GPs, dentists; optometry; acute services; health and social care integration and other matters failing within the responsibility of the Cabinet Secretary for Health and Sport
- Justice: to consider and report on the administration of criminal and civil justice, community safety, law reform and the legal profession, police, fire and rescue services, courts and tribunals; sentencing; prisoners and prisons; victims and witnesses; human rights and other matters falling within the responsibility of the Cabinet Secretary for Justice and the functions of the Lord Advocate, other than as head of the systems of criminal prosecution and investigation of deaths in Scotland
- Local Government and Communities: to consider and report on local government; community empowerment; community planning; devolution to communities and local government reform; regeneration; housing, building standards and planning; and other matters falling within the responsibility of the Minister for Communities
- Rural Economy and Connectivity: to consider and report on agriculture, forestry, fisheries, and aquaculture; food and drink; crafting; transport; digital connectivity; islands issues and other matters falling within the responsibility of the Cabinet Secretary for the Rural Economy and Connectivity
- Social Security Committee: to consider and report on new and existing Scottish social security powers; new and existing benefits; UK government welfare policy.

Mandatory Committees

Standing Orders prescribe the establishment, titles, and the remits of mandatory committees.[17] These are the Standards, Procedures and Public Appointments; Finance; Public Audit; European and External Relations; Equalities; Public Petitions; and the Delegated Powers and Law Reform committees. Standing Orders further lay down that the Standards, Procedures and Public Appointments and Finance Committees must be established within twenty-one sitting days of the general election, and the other mandatory committees within forty-two sitting days. Mandatory committees are established for the entire four- or five-year session of the Parliament.

It should be noted, however, that, in September 2016, a new Rule 6.1.5A was inserted into Standing Orders which enables additional matters to be added to the remit of a mandatory committee. The objective was to enable alignment of committee remits more closely with Cabinet Secretary portfolios. The rule change provides for flexibility in varying remits while protecting the mandatory aspects of mandatory committee remits. Utilising that new rule, the Parliament then proceeded to add matters to the remits of four of the mandatory committees, and also to rename those committees to reflect their increased responsibilities.

The names and remits of the mandatory committees are now the following:

Standards, Procedures and Public Appointments Committee

1. The remit of the Standards, Procedures and Public Appointments Committee is to consider and report on: (a) the practice and procedures of the Parliament in relation to its business; (b) whether a member's conduct is in accordance with these Rules and any Code of Conduct for members, matters relating to members interests, and any other matters relating to the conduct of members in carrying out their Parliamentary duties; (c) the adoption, amendment and application of any Code of Conduct for members; (d) matters relating to public appointments in Scotland; (e) matters relating to the regulation of lobbying.

Where the Committee considers it appropriate, it may by motion recommend that a member's rights and privileges be withdrawn to such extent and for such period as are specified in the motion.

Finance and Constitution Committee

1. The remit of the Finance Committee is to consider and report on: (a) any report or other document laid before the Parliament by members of

the Scottish Government containing proposals for, or budgets of, public revenue or expenditure or proposals for the making of a Scottish rate resolution, taking into account any report or recommendations concerning such documents made to them by any other committee with power to consider such documents or any part of them; (b) any report made by a committee setting out proposals concerning public revenue or expenditure; (c) Budget Bills; (d) any other matter relating to or affecting the revenue or expenditure of the Scottish Administration or other monies payable into or expenditure payable out of the Scottish Consolidated Fund.

2. The Committee may also consider and, where it sees fit, report to the Parliament on the timetable for the stages of Budget Bills and on the handling of financial business.

3. Constitutional matters falling within the responsibility of the Cabinet Secretary for Finance and the Constitution.

Public Audit and Post-legislative Scrutiny Committee

1. The remit of the Public Audit Committee is to consider and report on: (a) any accounts laid before the Parliament; (b) any report laid before or made to the Parliament by the Auditor General for Scotland; (c) any other document laid before the Parliament, or referred to it by the Parliamentary Bureau or by the Auditor General for Scotland, concerning financial control, accounting and auditing in relation to public expenditure.

2. No member of the Scottish Government or Junior Scottish Minister may be a member of the Committee and no member who represents a political party which is represented in the Scottish Government may be convener of the Committee.

3. Post-legislative scrutiny.

Culture, Tourism, European and External Relations Committee

1. The remit of the European and External Relations Committee is to consider and report on: (a) proposals for European Union legislation; (b) the implementation of European Communities and European Union legislation; (c) any European Communities or European Union issue; (d) the development and implementation of the Scottish Administration's links with countries and territories outside Scotland, the European Union (and its institutions) and other international organisations; (e) co-ordination of the international activities of the Scottish Administration.

3. The convener of the Committee shall not be the convener of any other committee whose remit is, in the opinion of the Parliamentary Bureau, relevant to that of the Committee.

4. The Parliamentary Bureau will normally propose a person to be a member of the Committee only if that person is a member of another committee whose remit is, in the opinion of the Parliamentary Bureau, relevant to that of the Committee.

5. Culture and tourism matters falling within the responsibility of the Cabinet Secretary for Culture, Tourism, and External Relations.

Equalities and Human Rights Committee

1. The remit of the Equal Opportunities Committee is to consider and report on matters relating to equal opportunities and upon the observance of equal opportunities within the Parliament.

2. In these Rules, 'equal opportunities' includes the prevention, elimination or regulation of discrimination between persons on grounds of sex or marital status, on racial grounds or on grounds of disability, age, sexual orientation, language or social origin or of other personal attributes, including beliefs or opinions such as religious beliefs or political opinions.

3. Human rights, including Convention rights (within the meaning of section 1 of the Human Rights Act 1998), and other human rights contained in any international convention, treaty, or other international instrument ratified by the United Kingdom.

Public Petitions Committee

1. The remit of the Public Petitions Committee is to consider public petitions addressed to the Parliament in accordance with these Rules and, in particular, to: (a) decide in a case of dispute whether a petition is admissible; (b) decide what action should be taken upon an admissible public petition; (c) keep under review the operation of the petitions system.

Delegated Powers and Law Reform Committee

1. The remit of the Delegated Powers and Law Reform Committee is to consider and report on: (a) (i) subordinate legislation laid before the Parliament or requiring the consent of the Parliament under section 9 of the Public Bodies Act 2011; (ii) has been deleted; (iii) motions to modify certain aspects of pensions; and, in particular, to determine whether the attention of the Parliament should be drawn to certain aspects of proposed statutory instruments; (b) proposed powers to make subordinate legislation in particular bills or other proposed legislation; (c) general questions relating to powers to make subordinate legislation; (d) whether any proposed delegated powers in particular bills or other legislation should be expressed as a power to make subordinate legislation; (e) any

failure to lay an instrument in accordance with section 28(2), 30(2) or 31 of the 2010 Act; (f) proposed changes to the procedure to which subordinate legislation laid before the Parliament is subject; (g) any Scottish Law Commission Bill; (h) any draft proposal for a Scottish Law Commission Bill; (i) any Consolidation Bill.

Most of the mandatory committees were originally concerned with organisational and procedural matters. The changes described above give some of them expanded remits which, in practice, allow them also to deal with certain wider policy areas, similar to those that are dealt with by subject committees.

A committee may consider any matter that is within its specific remit (referred to as a competent matter) or any other matter which is referred to it by the full Parliament or by any other committee. Where a matter is within its remit, or is otherwise referred to it, a committee can undertake a number of activities.[18] It can:

- consider the policy and administration of the Scottish Government on any competent matter;
- consider any proposals for legislation that relate to or affect any competent matter including both primary or secondary legislation, whether before the Scottish Parliament or the UK Parliament;
- consider any relevant EU legislation or international agreements or the like that may relate to or affect any competent matter;
- consider whether there is a need for law reform in its particular area;
- initiate bills on any competent matter for consideration by the Parliament;
- consider the financial proposals and financial administration of the Scottish Administration.

Ad Hoc Committees

The Parliament is able to set up ad hoc committees to allow consideration of issues on a broad basis in order to deal with matters that cut across the conventional boundaries of government (for example, public health, social inclusion and environmental sustainability). The Standing Orders do not make specific provisions for such ad hoc committees but they are sufficiently flexible to allow the establishment of such committees if the Parliament so wishes.

Composition of Committees

Each committee has between five and fifteen members. Members are appointed by the Parliament on a proposal from the Parliamentary Bureau and the Bureau has to have regard to the balance of the political balance in the Parliament.[19] Committees choose their own convener and deputy convener but the Parliamentary Bureau recommends to the full Parliament the party from which they are to be appointed and is required, in so doing, to have regard to the proportionate strength of the various parties in the Parliament. Committees normally meet in public unless the committee decides otherwise. When considering actual or potential proposals for legislation, a committee must meet in public unless it is taking evidence when it can decide to meet in private. Committees can, with the approval of the Parliamentary Bureau and the full Parliament, establish their own subcommittees.[20]

Ministers are not barred from becoming members of committees but, as a matter of practice, have not been appointed either to subject or to mandatory committees. However. a Minister does have the right to participate (but not vote) in proceedings of a committee concerning proposals for legislation in the relevant subject area (as does the individual member concerned in the case of a Member's Bill) and, in practice, Ministers do, on occasion, attend relevant committees.

A committee may decide, with the approval of the Parliamentary Bureau and the Conveners' Group,[21] to sit anywhere in Scotland, and a number of meetings have been held outside Edinburgh. However, the vast majority of committee meetings are held within the Parliament's own building in Edinburgh, notwithstanding the recommendation of the CSG that some committees should be permanently based outside Edinburgh 'to determine that the Parliament is a Parliament for the whole of Scotland'. Committees may appoint external advisers to assist them with their work[22] but the CSG recommendation that people who are not MSPs could be co-opted on to committees as non-voting members has not been incorporated into the Standing Orders. A committee may also appoint one of its members as a 'reporter' to report to it on any matter within its remit.[23] This allows the Scottish Parliament to make use of the rapporteur system, extensively used in the European Parliament and elsewhere, where such a person draws up a draft report for a committee. It was envisaged by the CSG that a rapporteur would act as a focal point for interest groups and individuals wishing to make representations to a committee. Parliamentary committees have begun to make use of the power to appoint a reporter although, as yet, such an appointment does not seem to have acquired the influence which can be wielded by a rapporteur in the European Union system. Among the problems which have emerged in the committee system is the perception that they were too large, had frequent changes in membership, and that some members sat on as many as three committees. Following the 2016 election, the new Presiding Officer proposed that committees should have a smaller number of members. This is being considered by the Commission on Parliamentary Reform (see below). It should be noted that the requirements to ensure that the political balance in the Parliament is reflected in the committees, along with parties' wishes to be represented, can lead to pressure for numbers to be larger.

Committee Substitutes

Any political party which has two or more members of the Parliament may nominate a member of the party to be a substitute for the members of the party on a particular committee.[24] The committee substitutes act in the place of any member of the same party who is unable to act because of illness, family circumstances, adverse weather conditions, a requirement to attend to other business in the Parliament or urgent constituency business. Committee substitutes are appointed for the duration of the relevant committee unless the membership of their political party group subsequently falls below two.

Conveners' Group

A Conveners' Group[25] has been set up which is not technically a committee. It consists of the Presiding Officer, who chairs the Group, and the conveners of the subject and the mandatory committees. Its functions include making recommendations as to the operation of the committees and to approve (along with the Parliamentary Bureau) the location of committee meetings and travel outside the UK of committee members in connection with their committees' remits. From 2011, this group began functioning as a 'liaison committee', holding evidence sessions with the First Minister several times a session. The Group normally meets in private. Matters which are to be decided by the Conveners' Group require the agreement of all members present.

In the early days of the Parliament, the committees were described as 'the Parliament's powerhouse'.[26] Their workload has turned out to be much heavier than was originally envisaged. They are intended to play a very active role in the Parliament's business, gathering information, scrutinising the policy of departments, holding inquiries and scrutinising primary and secondary legislative proposals. They can also initiate bills.[27] Committees can and have made important changes to bills as they progress through the various stages towards the statute book[28] and initially showed considerable independence from the government. Committee members develop expertise in the policy areas within their committee's remit and, in general, have acted in a less adversarial way than they do at meetings of the full Parliament. However, during the 2011–16 session, when the SNP had a majority of seats in the Scottish Parliament and therefore a majority of seats on committees, there was a tendency for the committees to function in a more partisan manner, that is, pro- or anti-government. In many cases, legislation was not scrutinised as carefully as it should have been and arguably resulted in poorly drafted Acts. This, combined with the lack of a revising chamber, such as the House of Lords, led the then Presiding Officer to call for an inquiry to be carried out.

By the time of the Scottish Parliament election in May 2016, the incoming Presiding Officer, Ken Macintosh MSP, acknowledged that progress with Parliamentary reform had, to some extent, stalled and a more fundamental look at reform was needed. In October 2016, he announced the establishment of an independent Commission on Parliamentary Reform. It is chaired by John McCormick, formerly the Electoral Commissioner for Scotland. It consists of five independent members and one member of each of the political parties with representation in the Scottish Parliament.

In announcing the Commission, the Presiding Officer commented:

In 1999 the Scottish Parliament was hailed as ground-breaking, bringing a new, inclusive style of politics to Scotland. However, over the last decade or more we have seen Scottish politics become increasingly tribal and divisive. This has, among other things, made it challenging for MSPs to find the space to develop their distinct role as parliamentarians.

Its remit is to consider ways in which the parliament can:

- be assured that it has the right checks and balances in place for the effective conduct of parliamentary business;
- increase its engagement with wider society and the public;
- clarify its identity as distinct from the Scottish Government.

The commission reported in June 2017 but reforms are yet to be made.

A further weakening of the scrutiny function of committee members was the appointment to various committees by the SNP Government of Parliamentary Liaison Officers whose role is to advise the relevant Minister of committee business and function as the Minister's 'eyes and ears'. This led to much criticism as the Parliamentary Liaison Officer committee members were seen to be unable to hold the government to account because they had a conflict of interest. However, in August 2016, the First Minister bowed to pressure and agreed to remove the Parliamentary Liaison Officers from the committees that scrutinise their Ministers.

POLITICAL PARTY GROUPS

There is little mention of the role that political parties play in the business of the Scottish Parliament in SA 1998 or in the Parliament's Standing Orders. In fact, however, the political parties have a significant influence in deciding what legislation is passed by the Parliament and how it operates. As we have seen in the previous chapter,[29] almost all MSPs are elected because they are nominated by their own political parties to stand for election, for either, or both, an individual constituency or for their own party's 'regional list'. A person who wants to become an MSP is extremely unlikely to be elected except as a party candidate.

It is normal for political parties to issue manifestos in advance of each election setting out the policies on which they seek voters' support. Those manifestos have no legally binding force but parties that breach their manifesto promises can face severe criticism from other parties and the electorate. Sometimes, failing to comply with a manifesto promise appears to attract little or no opprobrium from the public. In other cases, however, the consequence of breaking a manifesto promise can be severe, particularly if the promise is seen as a key feature of the party's programme. For example, it was widely considered that the Liberal Democrats' failure to keep their promise, in their manifesto for the 2010 UK general election, not to increase student tuition fees, was a significant factor in their sharp decline in support in the 2015 UK general election.

The manifestos of the parties that successfully form an administration in the Parliament can serve as a useful initial indicator to the civil servants of the policies that the administration will seek to pursue in office. Manifestos can also serve as a 'checklist' by which the parties can monitor their own performance in office in delivering their commitments to the electorate.

Within the Parliament, the members elected from each political party normally form a political group. The arrangements for the management and organisation of those groups are internal matters for the political parties themselves over which the Parliament has no say and which are not governed by any legislation. However,the role of the group is essentially the same in all parties. Party groups normally meet prior to all meetings of the Parliament and frequently its committees also. They will discuss the business of the meeting or, at least, its most important items and the line that the party leadership proposes to take on those items. All members of that group will normally be expected to vote in favour of that agreed line. Failure to do so is likely to lead to some form of disciplinary action by the party group, ranging from a letter to suspension or expulsion from the group. An MSP who is suspended or expelled (or resigns) from their political group does not cease to be a member of the Parliament. However, he or she may find themselves excluded from their party's list of candidates at a future election.[30] The party groups also have an important role in deciding the business of the Parliament. As described above,[31] the Parliamentary Bureau is made up by nominees of the leaders of political parties. In addition, the party groups, normally their business manager, will supply lists of their preferred speakers for debates and questions. The Presiding Officer will normally comply in broad terms with those requests although he or she may also call additional speakers whose names have not been put forward by their parties to speak.

CROSS-PARTY GROUPS

Cross-party groups are groups that consist of MSPs from each of the main political parties represented in the Parliament. They provide an opportunity for MSPs and members of the public and outside organisations to meet and discuss a shared interest in a particular subject or cause, and around fifty of them were formed during the life of the first Parliament. Examples of cross-party groups which have been established are the Animal Welfare Group, the Muscular Dystrophy Group, the Pakistan Group, and the Group on Industrial Communities. As these groups may be able to gain some influence within the Parliament, it was considered imperative that rules of good practice should be set down for their operation. Each group must apply to the Standards Committee for recognition, and only groups approved by the Committee are entitled to call themselves cross-party groups of the Scottish Parliament and to have access to Parliamentary facilities. Section 6 of the Code of Conduct sets out the framework of these rules for their operation.

HOLDING THE GOVERNMENT TO ACCOUNT

As well as making laws, most parliamentary assemblies have the important role of monitoring how governments implement the law once made, and how they carry out their functions in general. As with many other activities, the SA 1998 places no statutory requirements on the Parliament as to how it should go about the task of holding the executive arm of government to account. However, reflecting a widely held view that effective scrutiny of the Scottish Government should be incorporated into the practice of the Parliament, the CSG made detailed proposals on how such accountability could be put into effect.[32] The Standing Orders eventually adopted by the Parliament are broadly based upon the CSG proposals although they are not quite as comprehensive as was envisaged by the CSG. The following opportunities to ensure such accountability are available to the Parliament.

- MSPs may submit questions for either an oral or a written answer by a member of the Scottish Government.[33] Questions for oral answer are submitted in writing in advance but supplementary questions of which no notice has been given are permitted. General Question Time lasts for up to twenty minutes each week (normally on Thursdays) and First Minister's Question Time last for up to forty-five minutes (also on Thursdays). Portfolio Questions to Cabinet Secretaries are dealt with normally on Wednesdays, and Topical Questions on Tuesdays.
- The First Minister may, if he or she so wishes, make a statement to the Parliament outlining the proposed policy objectives and the legislative programme of the Scottish Government for the Parliamentary year ahead and, if such a statement is made, it will be debated by the Parliament.[34] This provision is optional, however, rather than mandatory, as the CSG seemed to suggest should be the case. (Neither was the CSG recommendation that, after each election, the Parliament should debate the four- or five-year legislative programme of a newly formed Scottish Government incorporated into the Standing Orders.
- Debates on general policy issues can be held from time to time, and a specified number of days are reserved for debates initiated by committees and opposition parties.

- At the end of each meeting of the Parliament there is a period of up to forty-five minutes for individual MSPs' business.[35]
- A motion of no confidence in either the entire Scottish Government or in an individual Minister or Junior Minister can be tabled by any MSP and, if it is supported by at least twenty-five members, it must be debated.[36] (It would appear, however, that, as the SA 1998 provides for only the resignation of the Scottish Government *en bloc* following a no confidence vote, only a vote of no confidence in the entire government would be binding. A vote of confidence in an individual Minister would seem to be advisory only (although no doubt such a vote would be most telling).
- A Minister can participate in the work of a committee when it is considering that Minister's legislative proposals, and such participation gives the committee members a further opportunity to scrutinise the activity of the Scottish Government.

SCOTTISH PARLIAMENTARY CORPORATE BODY (SPCB)

A brief mention should be made of the Scottish Parliamentary Corporate Body which was established by the SA 1998.[37] The principal function of this body, described in the Parliament's Standing Orders as the 'Parliamentary Corporation', is to provide the Parliament with the property, staff, and services it requires. This includes the staff who service committees, parliamentary researchers and librarians, and other ancillary staff. It makes decisions on a wide range of issues concerning the running of the Parliament, including the financing of the Parliament and the allocation of the budget, accommodation, and the use and security of parliamentary facilities. The SPCB is also responsible for the preparation of the Parliament's Official Report and its Journal (see below). It also arranges for the broadcasting of the Parliament's proceedings, subject to a code of conduct set down by the full Parliament.[38] The establishment of the SPCB ensures that these services are provided independently of the Scottish Government. The members of the SPCB, who direct its operation (subject to the Parliament's rights to give directions to it), are the Presiding Officer and five other MSPs. It was not envisaged by the CSG that these members would be appointed on a political basis but the Standing Orders say nothing on this point and, in fact, the four main parties in the Parliament agreed among themselves that they would each appoint one member of the SPCB when the first appointments of the body were made.

Any legal proceedings by or against the Parliament, its Presiding Officer or deputies, or any of its staff, are carried out by or against the SPCB on their behalf.[39] The SPCB is treated as a Crown body for the purposes of a number of important statutes, and given the privileges of such a body.[40]

PUBLIC ACCOUNTABILITY, OPENNESS AND ACCESSIBILITY

Investigating Complaints

As outlined above, the key principles adopted by the CSG include an emphasis on the Parliament being open and accountable to the wider Scottish public. The only provision of the SA 1998 giving any rights to the public over the system of government in Scotland is that of requiring the Parliament to set up a system to investigate complaints made by a member of the public to MSPs alleging maladministration which has caused injustice by members of the Scottish Government or any other office holder of the Scottish Administration (or any one acting on their behalf, including, of course, civil servants).[41] That provision was modelled on the existing UK Parliamentary Ombudsman system, and the obligation to set up such a system was restricted to complaints of the kind which that UK official is required to investigate (in essence, complaints of maladministration by government departments but excluding a number of matters such as the investigation of crime and commercial transactions).[42]

However, the SA 1998 allows the Parliament, if it wishes, to set up a wider investigatory system, including among others: the investigation of any action taken by, or on behalf of, the Scottish Parliamentary Corporate Body; any action taken by, or on behalf of, any Scottish public authority with mixed functions or no reserved functions; and any action concerning Scotland, and not relating to reserved matters, that is taken by, or on behalf of, a cross-border public authority.[43]

Initial arrangements for an ombudsman for the Scottish Parliament were put in place by the Secretary of State for Scotland under his powers to make transitional arrangements under the SA 1998.[44] These set up the office of Scottish Parliamentary Commissioner for Administration with powers and procedures modelled very much on the existing counterpart at UK Parliament level. The ombudsman appointed under these arrangements was the person who was the UK Parliamentary Commissioner for Administration at the time.

In 2002, the Scottish Parliament passed the Scottish Public Services Ombudsman Act which established the office of Ombudsman as a 'one-stop shop', assuming the statutory duties previously assigned to the Scottish Parliamentary Ombudsman, the Health Service Ombudsman and the Local Government Ombudsman. Over the years the SPSO has acquired jurisdiction over a number of other areas, such as housing associations, colleges, and prisons.

The Ombudsman may investigate complaints of maladministration and service failures. The number of complaints received number between five hundred and six hundred per annum, with about 50 per cent being fully upheld, about 55 percent of which are about the prison service.

Although the SA 1998 envisaged that all complaints of maladministration at Scottish Government level would be channelled through an MSP (the MSP filter), the Scottish Public Services Ombudsman Act 2002 does not contain such a restriction and complaints can be submitted directly by members of the public.

Public Petitions

Meaningful participation by the people of Scotland in the work of the Scottish Parliament was seen by the Scottish Constitutional Convention and the CSG as a key element of the operation of the Parliament. Both bodies recommended that the Standing Orders should enable members of the public to petition the Parliament. The Public Petitions Committee is one of the mandatory committees which the Parliament is required to establish under its Standing Orders.[45] Standing Orders also set out the procedures for bringing petitions to the attention of the Parliament.[46] A petition may be presented by an individual, a body corporate, or an unincorporated association of persons, either through an MSP or directly to the Parliament. Petitions should contain the name and address of the petitioner and those of anyone supporting the petition. There is, however, no requirement that a certain minimum number of signatures be obtained in support of the petition (as is the norm in many assemblies elsewhere in Europe).[47] Originally Standing Orders required the petition to be in English but that is now no longer the case. The petition may be lodged in writing with the Clerk of the Parliament or sent to the Clerk by email. There is also a facility for the electronic submission of petitions via an interactive form on the Parliament's website.[48] The clerk then sends it as soon as possible to the Public Petitions Committee. After arranging for the petition to be translated into English, if necessary, if the

Committee decides that the Scottish Parliament has the power to deal with the matter raised by the petition, it can deal with it in a number of ways. It can:

- refer the petition to the Scottish Ministers or any other appropriate body or person for information or consideration;
- refer it to the relevant subject committee;
- prepare a report for consideration by the Parliament Bureau or by the Parliament itself;
- or take any other action that the Committee considers to be appropriate.

The Committee may also meet outside Edinburgh to hear presentations of petitions. The petitioner must be notified, if necessary in a language other than English, of the action taken by the committee.[49]

In the first four-year session of the Parliament, the Public Petitions Committee considered 615 petitions, covering a wide range of subjects including housing, transport, the protection of heritage sites, genetically modified crops, and many others. The high number was partly due to the novelty of a petition system in government. In the 2010–16 period, the Committee considered 251 petitions, and 387 people started to hold various workshops in different parts of Scotland in advance of formal meetings. A new system for submitting and viewing petitions is currently being developed.

The subject matter of recent petitions includes making failure to recycle a criminal offence, the removal of unelected church representatives from local authority education committees, and sepsis awareness. The Committee is clearly fulfilling its role as a gateway for public involvement in the parliamentary process. In the first eight months of its operation, the Parliament considered more than ninety petitions, some emanating from particularly active petitioners who lodged petitions on various issues (in the case of at least one petitioner, causing the Public Petitions Committee some concern as to how it could deal with the volume of his petitions).

Consultation and Involving the Public

In 2012, Parliament Days were introduced which take the work of Parliament out of Edinburgh and into communities across Scotland. Each Parliament Day involves a range of activities, including formal meetings of committees, informal evidence-gathering, sessions in schools, and workshops.

The CSG also emphasised that, prior to legislation being submitted to the Parliament, there should be extensive consultation with organisations and individuals outside the Parliament. To achieve this, as described below,[50] it recommended that legislative proposals from the Scottish Government should be accompanied by a memorandum showing what public consultation has been undertaken, and the Standing Orders provide that such details must be included in a 'Policy Memorandum'.[51]

The CSG also suggested that there might be a role for forums bringing together particular interest groups: for example, a Civic Forum, a Business Forum, and a Youth Forum.[52] Proposals to establish the Civic Forum were announced by the Scottish Executive towards the end of 1999. The Civic Forum was made up of a diverse range of organisation in Scottish life – trade unions, churches, non-governmental organisations, national and local charities, business and professional organisations. The aim of the Forum was to build a new culture of active citizenship in which the people of Scotland have an opportunity to be involved in influencing government policies. It was mainly funded by the Scottish Government but funding was withdrawn in 2008.

A Scottish Youth Parliament was launched in 1999 and has a membership of around two hundred elected young people aged between fourteen and twenty-five. The Youth Parliament meets three times a year, discusses issues that affect young people across Scotland, and tries to propose solutions to these issues. It is supported financially by the Scottish Government.

The Scottish Parliament Business Exchange was set up in November 2001 with the aim of bringing the Parliament and the business community closer together in a non-partisan and non-lobbying way. It was registered as an educational charity and had a board that consists of parliamentarians, people with business and related interests, and a representative of the Scottish Trades Union Congress. The main funding for this organisation came from membership subscriptions but, because of deficits, it had to be rescued by the Scottish Government in December 2009 with a 'one-off' grant of £30,000 which later became an annual donation. The Scottish Government/ Scottish Parliamentary Corporate Body withdrew all support in 2015/16 and the Exchange wound up its activities in April 2016.

Public Access

The meetings of the Parliament and its committees and subcommittees are held in public, with very few exceptions. Members of the public are admitted to the large public gallery during any meeting of the Parliament, and visits by students and school parties are catered for. Access to the chamber itself is limited to MSPs, the Lord Advocate and Solicitor General for Scotland, to persons authorised by the Presiding Officer or Clerk and to persons invited by the Parliament to attend or to address the Parliament.[53] The Parliament has been addressed by, among others, Her Majesty the Queen, the Prime Minister, the president of Malawi, and the president of the European Parliament. The Parliament also frequently stages, normally in its public foyer, various displays and exhibitions on political and cultural themes. Its grounds are often used as a location for various rallies, demonstrations, and protests. The Parliament's authorities will, however, take steps to prevent such events becoming permanent fixtures.[54]

Use of Language

The wish to ensure that the Parliament is seen to represent the whole of Scotland is seen in the provision made in Standing Orders that, although the Parliament should normally conduct its business in English, members may also speak in Scots Gaelic or any other language with the agreement of the Presiding Officer as may persons addressing the Parliament on the invitation of the Parliament.[55] MSPs are required to make the oath, or affirmation, of allegiance in English but can then repeat it in any language they wish. In 2017, the oath or affirmation was also taken in Italian, Scots Gaelic, Urdu, Scots, and Doric (the vernacular form of Scots language as spoken in the north-east of Scotland).[56]

However, although interpretation facilities are provided within the building, the Parliament does not have its own interpreters available on a permanent basis, and those wishing to speak in a language other than English are required to give at least two weeks' notice in order to ensure that interpreters can be provided. Moreover, there is no automatic provision for MSPs' speeches to be interpreted into English or Gaelic or any other language. Accordingly, it is not possible for languages other than English to be used on a day-to-day basis, and it may be thought that the provision to allow the use of Gaelic is more of symbolic significance rather than practical utility for the normal business of the Parliament. However, a number of documents published by the Scottish Parliament are made available in Gaelic, including the Parliament's Annual Report; and both Gaelic and English and twelve other languages are used in the Parliament's website.

'Family-friendly' Hours of Business

The Parliament also adopted the suggestion of the CSG that it should avoid the long-standing Westminster practice of starting parliamentary sittings in the afternoons and continuing them until late at night. Instead, the Scottish Parliament has what are described as 'family-friendly' hours of business. The Standing Orders lay down that the Parliament will normally sit on Monday afternoons (to enable MSPs to travel from their constituencies on Monday mornings), from Tuesday to Thursday from 9.30 a.m. to 5.30 p.m. and on Friday mornings (to enable MSPs to travel back in the afternoon).[57] It was hoped that these hours would encourage people with family responsibilities to consider standing for election. In addition, when considering what weeks the Parliament should be in recess, the Parliament Bureau is obliged to take account of dates when schools in any part of Scotland are to be on holiday. This is in stark contrast to the UK Parliament which continues in session well into July despite the fact that Scottish school summer holidays start at the end of June.

Reporting of Proceedings and Other Publications

The Standing Orders also deal with the reporting of the proceedings of the Parliament and its committees,[58] recording all the items of business taken at any meeting, the results of any decisions taken and of any divisions or elections which took place. The minutes are printed and published as soon as possible. In addition, a substantially verbatim report of proceedings is made which contains all the contributions made in the Parliament and in committees both by MSPs and by any other speakers such as expert witnesses. It also contains all written questions together with the answers. This report is known as the Scottish Parliament Official Report and is the equivalent of Hansard in the UK Parliament. There are also arrangements for the broadcasting of the proceedings of the Parliament and its committees.

Standing Orders also provide for a Journal of the Scottish Parliament to be printed and published at intervals, containing minutes, notice of bills and Scottish Statutory Instruments and notice of reports by committees to the Parliament. The Journal is the authoritative record of what the Parliament has done in a parliamentary year and has been produced on an annual basis since 2000.

In addition to the publications of proceedings covered by the Standing Orders, the Parliament produces a large number of other documents which are available to the public. These include the Business Bulletin, published daily when the Parliament is in session, which details the business of the date, committee agendas, questions, motions and amendments and petitions lodged. From time to time briefing papers are published by SPICe (the Scottish Parliament Information Centre) covering topics such as the North Sea oil and gas industry, digital connectivity and the impact of Brexit on various sectors such as the Scottish economy and higher education. An Annual Report of the Scottish Parliament is published (in English and Gaelic) as well as an annual Statistical Report.

Proceedings may also be broadcast subject to conditions laid down by the Parliament.

Both the Scottish Government and the Scottish Parliament have comprehensive websites. The addresses are www.gov.scot and www.parliament.scot respectively.

NOTES

1. See, for example, Crick, Bernard and David Millar, *To Make the Parliament of Scotland a Model for Democracy* (1997).
2. SA 1998, S22.
3. SA 1998, Schedule 3.
4. These can be found in the Schedule to the Scotland Act 1998 (Transitory and Transitional Provisions) (Standing Orders and Parliamentary Publications) Order 1999, SI 1999/1095.
5. Rule 17.1 of the Standing Orders of Scottish Parliament. (Subsequent references to Rules are reference to the rules set out in these Standing Orders).
6. (1999) 'Shaping Scotland's Parliament' (referred to elsewhere in the book as the 'CSG Report').
7. See p. 129 on accountability etc.
8. See Chapter 5.
9. When elected, the Presiding Officer puts aside all political affiliation; the deputy officers do so only when called on to preside.
10. Rule 11.5.5.
11. Rule 11.9
12. Rule 3.5
13. Rule 3.1.3.
14. See Rules, Chapter 5.
15. Rule 9A.5.
16. Rule 6.1.

17. Rule 6.1.5.
18. See Rule 6.2.
19. Rules 6.3.1, 6.3.2.
20. See Chapter 12 of the Rules for the detailed provisions for Committee Procedures
21. For the Conveners' Group see p. 76.
22. Rule 12.7.A number of committees have made use of the power to appoint advisers.
23. Rule 12.6.
24. Rule 6.3A.
25. Rule 6A.1.
26. Winetrobe, Barry, *Realising the Vision: a Parliament with a Purpose* (The Constitution Unit, October 2001).
27. For committee bills see Chapter 5.
28. For example, committees made significant changes to the Public Appointments and Public Bodies etc. (Scotland) Act 2003.
29. See p. 39.
30. In some cases, a decision by the leadership of a party group to discipline one of its members can have the effect of increasing that member's popularity with the party's members outside Parliament, who may actually choose candidates. The classic example of a party 'rebel' gaining support from the party's rank and file in another legislature is Jeremy Corbyn. As a Labour MP, he had a record of disobeying his party's 'whip' on numerous occasions but was elected leader by a large majority of individual members of the Labour Party in both 2015 and 2016.
31. See p. 68.
32. CSG Report, 3.4.3.
33. See Chapter 13 of the Standing Orders: Rules on Statements and Parliamentary Questions.
34. Rule 5.7.
35. Rule 5.6.
36. See Rule 8.12 and the SA 1998, Sections 45, 47, 48, and 49.
37. SA 1998, Section 21.
38. See Rules 16.2–16.4.
39. SA 1998, Section 40.
40. Scottish Parliamentary Corporate Body (Crown Status) Order 1999, SI 1999/677.
41. SA 1998, Section 91.
42. See Parliamentary Commissioner Act 1967, Schedule 3.
43. SA 1998, Section 91(3).
44. Scotland Act 1998 (Transitory and Transitional Provisions) (Complaints of Maladministration) Order 1999, SI 1999/1351.
45. Rule 6.1.
46. Rule 15.4–8.

47. For example, Germany and Italy. See Chapter 4 of the report 'Parliamentary Practices in Devolved Parliaments' (Centre for Scottish Public Policy for the Scottish Office, 1998).
48. http://www.parliament.scot/gettinginvolved/petitions/CreateAPetition. aspx (last accessed 10 April 2017).
49. Rule 15.6.
50. See Chapter 5.
51. Rule 9.3.3.c (ii).
52. CSG Report, 2.38.
53. Rule 15.3.
54. In 2016, an eclectic group of supporters of independence, and other causes, established a camp in the Parliament's grounds. The Parliament eventually took legal action to remove the protesters, commonly described as the 'indy campers'. At the end of the case, the Court of Session made it clear there were limits to the Convention rights of assembly and freedom of expression: *Petition of Scottish Parliamentary Corporate Body*, [2016] CSOH 113.
55. Rule 7.1.
56. https://stv.tv/news/politics/248497-msps-to-take-oaths-in-six-languages/ (last accessed 10 April 2017).
57. Rule 2.2.
58. Rules 16.1–16.5

CHAPTER FIVE

Making Laws

INTRODUCTION

The Scottish Parliament has the power to make laws. As we have seen in Chapter 2, the areas in which it is able to exercise that law-making power are wide. This chapter looks at the way in which proposals for legislation proceed through the Parliament, taking into account the mechanisms put in place both by the Scotland Act 1998 (SA 1998) and by the Parliament's Standing Orders to ensure that the Parliament does not make legislation in areas outside its field of responsibility.

The way in which the Parliament deals with legislation is similar in many respects to the way in which legislation is dealt with by the Westminster Parliament at present. In the Scottish Parliament, just as at Westminster, a proposal for legislation – a 'bill' – is normally considered both by a committee and by the full Parliament. At the end of the process, a bill must receive Royal Assent before it can become law. When it has done so, it becomes an 'Act of the Scottish Parliament' or 'asp'.[1] In addition to Acts which are made by the Parliament in that way, a great deal of subordinate legislation is made by Scottish Ministers.[2]

There are also important differences, however, between the Scottish and the UK systems. First of all, there is no second chamber in the Scottish Parliament, unlike the UK Parliament where bills have to pass through the House of Lords as well as the House of Commons. Second, the Scottish Parliament and the Scottish Government have some limited power to take part in the law-making procedure in areas that do not otherwise fall within the Parliament's remit. And, perhaps most significantly, as the Parliament is restricted in its powers to making laws, the process whereby laws are made includes a number of features designed to ensure that the Parliament does not make laws in areas where it is not permitted to do so. With the passing of the Scotland Act 2016, a super-majority of two-thirds is required for legislation relating to certain matters called 'protected subject matters'.[3]

In this field, as in many others, the statutory requirements laid down in the SA 1998 were fleshed out in some detail by the CSG in its report, *Shaping Scotland's Parliament*, and subsequently embodied in the Parliament's Standing Orders.[4] In this chapter, the statutory provisions for bills to pass through the Parliament are examined, and the procedures set out in the Standing Orders are then looked at in some detail. Thereafter, the procedures for subordinate legislation are examined.

SCRUTINY OF BILLS TO ENSURE LEGISLATIVE COMPETENCE

Detailed provisions are built into the SA 1998 to ensure that each bill is subject to scrutiny to prevent the creeping in of any provision which is outside the powers of the Scottish Parliament. This process of scrutiny begins even before a bill is considered by the Parliament. On the introduction of a bill into Parliament, the Presiding Officer must provide a written statement which indicates whether or not, in his/her view, the provisions of the bill are within the legislative competence of the Parliament. If she/he thinks that any of the provisions are not within the competence of the Parliament, she/he must indicate what those provisions are and the reasons for his or her view. If the Presiding Officer takes the view, however, that the provisions of a bill are outwith legislative competence, this does not prevent the bill from being introduced.

If the bill is a government bill, the member of the Scottish Government in charge of it should also consider the matter and make a written statement to the Parliament that the bill is, in his or her view, within that legislative competence.[5] Both take legal advice before making such a statement.

At a later stage, before the bill is put before the Parliament for passing or rejection, the Presiding Officer must decide whether any provision of the Bill relates to a protected subject matter and state his/her decision.

After a bill has been passed by the Parliament, certain Law Officers – the Advocate General for Scotland, the Lord Advocate[6] and the UK Government's Attorney General – also have a role in the scrutiny of bills. If one of them has doubts as to whether any provision is within the legislative competence of the Parliament, including being related to a protected subject matter, he or she can refer the matter to the Supreme Court for a decision.[7] In contrast to the statement required at the time of the introduction of a bill, this power to make a reference can be exercised only after a bill has been passed by the Parliament. Such a reference has to be made within four weeks of each bill being passed by the Parliament and, during that period, the Presiding Officer must not submit the bill for Royal Assessment unless the Law Officers have waived their rights to make a reference.

If the Supreme Court decides that any provision of the bill is not within the legislative competence of the Parliament or that a provision relates to a protected subject matter, the Presiding Officer is not permitted to submit it in its unamended form for Royal Assent. Instead, the bill returns to the Parliament which may reconsider it and amend it so as to resolve the problem.[8] If the Law Officers waive their right to challenge the bill, the Presiding Officer can submit the bill for Royal Assent before four weeks have elapsed. Since the UK joined the European Community (now the European Union), it has been possible for UK courts to refer certain questions relating to the interpretation of EU law to its court, the Court of Justice of the European Union (CJEU), for a preliminary ruling. If a matter has been referred to the Supreme Court by one of the Law Officers, that court may make a further reference to the CJEU. Section 34 allows for the withdrawal of the reference if the Parliament decides that it wishes to reconsider the bill.

Secretaries of State in the UK Government also have the power to intervene.[9] Any one of them may make an order prohibiting the Presiding Officer from submitting a bill for Royal Assent in two sets of circumstances: first, where a Secretary of State believes that any provision would be incompatible with any international obligations (other than obligations under EU treaties, or arising from the European Convention on Human Rights) or the interests of defence or national security; and, second, where a Secretary of State believes that the bill contains provisions that would modify the law as it relates to reserved matters and there are reasonable grounds to believe that the modification would have an adverse effect on the operation of the law as it applies to reserved matters. As mentioned,[10] the Parliament does have limited powers to pass laws that affect matters reserved to the Westminster Parliament. The power given to a Secretary of State to prohibit legislation being submitted for Royal Assent allows the UK Government to prevent such legislation reaching the statute book. Like the Law Officers, a Secretary of State has only four weeks after the passing of a bill in which to decide whether to intervene and prohibit it from becoming law and, similarly, may waive that right. Again, where such an order is made by a Secretary of State, the Parliament can reconsider the bill and amend it to remove the offending provisions.

It should be noted that the power to make an order can be exercised by any UK Secretary of State. It can be envisaged that it might be the Secretary of State with the relevant departmental interest who actually exercises the power (for example, in the first case, the Foreign Secretary) but no doubt political factors will also have a part to play in the decision as to which Secretary of State exercises the power. For example, the UK Government might consider it politically preferable for this supervisory power over the Scottish Parliament to be exercised by the Secretary of State for Scotland or any successor office. In practice, it is the Secretary of State for Scotland who is informed on each occasion the Parliament passes a Bill.

As has been mentioned above, the Law Officers and Secretaries of State can inform the Presiding Officer, at any time, that they do not intend to intervene to prevent a bill from becoming law. If they do so, they cannot then change their minds and intervene later to prevent the bill receiving the Royal Assent but, if a bill is approved by the Parliament after reconsideration, the Law Officers and Secretaries of State have a further four-week opportunity to intervene again.

It should be noted that, while these powers of the Law Officers and the Secretaries of State are important 'backstop' powers, to date they have never been used in practice.

THE STAGES OF BILLS

In the UK Parliament, a bill has to go through a lengthy process in both the House of Commons and the House of Lords before it can receive Royal Assent and become an Act of Parliament. The stages in each House are:

- first reading – which is purely formal
- second reading – a general debate on the principle of the bill, at the end of which it can be rejected
- committee stage – the main amending stage
- report stage – a second amending stage, taken in the main chamber
- third reading – a final debate on whether to pass the bill; in the Lords, also involving a limited further opportunity for amendments.

The pressures of time in the House of Commons are enormous. It is quite common for important clauses in bills (including the Scotland Bills) to receive little or no scrutiny by MPs. The pace of business in the House of Lords is much more leisurely, and the Lords' principal role in the legislative process is to carry out more detached and detailed scrutiny and amendment so that any ambiguities and anomalies in a bill missed by the House of Commons may be removed. The arrangements made for the scrutiny of bills in the Scottish Parliament are designed to simplify the process considerably compared with Westminster. The arrangements in the Scottish Parliament also give the Parliament's committees a more prominent role and increase the opportunities for participation by the public.

The SA 1998 lays down that a bill should normally pass through the following minimum stages in the Parliament.[11]

- a general debate on a bill with an opportunity from MSPs to vote on its general principles;
- consideration by MSPs of the details of the bill (including an opportunity to vote on those details);
- a final stage at which a bill can be passed or rejected.

The Parliament's Standing Orders give effect to these requirements by specifying three stages for all Public Bills, namely Stage 1, Stage 2, and Stage 3. The Standing Orders also set out the minimum period of time which should elapse between Stages 1 and 2 and between Stages 2 and 3.

However, standing Orders also allow for an emergency measure to pass through all stages in the Parliament more quickly (though it is still subject to the scrutiny procedures described above).[12] In addition, in the case of Private Bills (see below) and certain bills of primarily a formal nature, the Parliament may use a different procedure from that set out above.[13]

The Parliament's Standing Orders are also required by the SA 1998 to cater for the situation that would arise if the Supreme Court has decided that a provision in a bill goes beyond the legislative competence of the Parliament, or a Secretary of State has intervened to prevent the bill being submitted for Royal Assent, as described above.[14] In either set of circumstances, the Parliament is required to reconsider the bill in question. This reconsideration stage enables the MSPs to remove the offending provisions and bring the bill within the legislative competence of the Parliament or, as appropriate, deal with the concerns relating to international obligations or defence and national security. At the end of this stage, the bill can again be approved or rejected.

The SA 1998, therefore, lays down only the basic framework for the passage of bills through the Parliament. The Parliament is given a great deal of freedom to regulate its own procedure in this respect but here, as in other areas, the CSG proposals offered a model on which the Parliament's Standing Orders were based.

CONSULTATION

As the Parliament has no second chamber to function as a revising chamber, care has to be taken before a bill begins its progress to ensure that ambiguities and anomalies are removed as far as possible. The CSG recognised this difficulty and, in its report, it recommended that legislative proposals go through an extensive consultation procedure both before their introduction into the Parliament and as they go through the legislative process. Such consultation would serve to provide an opportunity for such ambiguities and anomalies to be identified, and also to meet the political objectives of ensuring maximum public involvement in the Parliament's work, of securing agreement (so far as is possible) on policy and of airing substantive issues and objections.

The CSG emphasised that the consultation process should consist of more than an invitation to submit comments on specific legislative proposals. Accordingly, it recommended that legislative proposals from the Scottish Government should have completed a consultative process before they are presented to the Parliament. It suggested that the Scottish Minister responsible for an area of policy should inform the relevant committee regarding the Scottish Government's intentions in its area of interest and should discuss with it the relevant bodies to be involved in the consultation process. To ensure that the consultative procedure had been carried out, it recommended that the Parliament's Standing Orders should require a bill, when introduced to the Parliament by the Government, to be accompanied by a memorandum giving details of the consultative process undertaken in that case. That would allow the committee concerned to arrange for further consultation if it felt that the Government's consultation had been insufficient. In practice, however, quite a few bills have been introduced by the Scottish with virtually no prior consultation.

THE PASSAGE OF BILLS THROUGH THE PARLIAMENT

There are three main types of public bills, namely Executive Bills, now known as Government Bills, Committee Bills and Members' Bills. The Scottish Parliament may also pass Private Bills but these are relatively uncommon.

As described above, the SA 1998 requires bills normally to go through three stages. If a bill is rejected at Stage 1 or Stage 3 (it cannot be rejected at Stage 2), no further proceedings are to be taken on the bill and a bill in the same or similar terms may not be introduced within six months of the date on which it was rejected. A bill falls if it has not been passed by the end of the session in which it was introduced but a bill in the same or similar terms may be introduced in the following session.[15] A session of the Scottish Parliament is the four- or five-year period from one general election to the next.

A bill is introduced by being lodged with the Clerks by the member in charge of the bill. It must be in the proper form, be signed by the member introducing it, and it may also be signed by other MSPs who support it.[16] On introduction, a bill must be accompanied by a written statement from the Presiding Officer which indicates whether or not in his/her view the provisions of the bill are within the legislative competence of the Parliament. If there are provisions which would be outwith the Parliament's legislative competence, she or he must indicate what these provisions are and give reasons for this view.[17] A similar statement as to legislative competence must be made by the member introducing the bill. The bill must also be accompanied by a financial memorandum which sets out the best estimate of costs to which the provisions of the bill would give rise and the best estimate of the timescales over which these costs could be expected to arise. The financial memorandum must distinguish separately costs which could fall on the Scottish Administration, Scottish local authorities and other bodies, individuals and businesses.[18] Also required are explanatory notes which summarise objectively what each provision of the bill does and any other information necessary to explain the effects of the bill.

Government Bills

A Government Bill, which is a bill introduced by a member of the Scottish Government, must also have several other accompanying documents. These are:

- a statement signed by the member of the Scottish Government in charge of the bill which states that, in his or her view, the provisions of the bill would be within the legislative competence of the Parliament;[19]
- a policy memorandum which sets out
  - the policy objectives of the bill;

 - whether alternative ways of meeting those objectives were considered and, if so, why the approach in the bill was adopted;
 - the consultation, if any, which was undertaken on the bill's objectives and the ways of meeting them, and a summary of the outcomes of the consultation;
 - an assessment of the effects, if any, of the bill on equal opportunities, human rights, island communities, local government, sustainable development and any other matter that the Scottish Ministers consider relevant.[20]

If the bill contains any provision which charges expenditure on the Scottish Consolidated Fund there must also be an accompanying report signed by the Auditor General stating whether, in his/her view, the charge is appropriate.[21] So far, no such statement has been required.

If a Government Bill contains any provision conferring power to make subordinate legislation, the member in charge must lodge with the Clerk a memorandum setting out: the person or body on which the power is conferred and the form in which the power is to be exercised; why it is considered appropriate to delegate the power, and the Parliamentary procedures (if any) to which the power is to be subject.[22]

Once a bill has been introduced and printed, it is referred by the Parliamentary Bureau[23] to the committee of the Parliament within whose remit the subject matter of the bill falls. This committee is known as 'the lead committee' and it is the task of the lead committee to consider and report on the general principles of the bill. Where the subject matter of the bill falls within the remit of more than one committee, one of these is designated as the lead committee but the other committees may also consider the general principles of the bill and report their views to the lead committee. If the bill contains a provision which confers powers to make subordinate legislation, that provision must be referred to the Delegated Powers and Law Reform Committee which reports its views back to the lead committee.[24]

The introduction of a bill is roughly equivalent to the First Reading stage of a bill in the UK Parliament but much more is required of the member in charge of a bill in the Scottish Parliament by way of accompanying documents and in making a case for the bill to proceed than is required in the UK Parliament. The intention of these requirements is to give the members of the lead committee, and MSPs generally, more information and to improve the quality and the acceptability of Acts of the Scottish Parliament.

Stage 1

First, the lead committee considers the general principles of the bill, taking account of the views, if any, of other committees, and it also considers the Scottish Government's policy memorandum. It then prepares a report for the Parliament. The lead committee takes evidence, both oral and written, from a range of relevant witnesses, including individuals and interest groups. Other committees may also take evidence and report to the lead committee. Ministers, too, may give evidence to the lead committee (or to other committees). The evidence taken at the Stage 1 inquiry can lead to quite significant amendments to bills at Stage 2. For example, the Public Bodies and Public Appointments etc. (Scotland) Bill proposed the abolition of the Ancient Monuments Board for Scotland and the Historic Buildings Council for Scotland without making provision for their replacement by any statutory body that could advise Ministers on aspects of Scotland's historic environment. As a result of evidence given to the lead committee and incorporated into its Stage 1 report, the Scottish Government moved amendments to the bill at Stage 2 to provide for the establishments of an Historic Environment Advisory Committee for Scotland.

At least five days after the lead committee has published its report, the full Parliament considers the general principles of the bill in the light of the lead committee's report. (At this stage it is open to any MSP to move that the bill be referred back to the lead committee for a further report. If that motion is agreed to, the Parliament's consideration of the bill is postponed until the further report has been presented to it.) The Parliament then decides, on a vote if necessary, whether or not the bill's general principles are agreed to. If they are, the bill proceeds to Stage 2; if not, the bill falls.[25] The last part of this stage is equivalent to the Second Reading stage in the UK Parliament.

Financial Resolution

Where a bill contains provisions which introduce new expenditure or increase existing expenditure charged out of the Scottish Consolidated Fund or which impose or increase any tax or charge, there can be no proceedings after Stage 1 until the Parliament has, by resolution, agreed to this. Such a resolution can be moved only by a member of the Scottish Government or by a Junior Minister.[26]

Stage 2

The bill is now referred back to the lead committee for detailed consideration. There must be a period of at least five sitting days between the completion of Stage 1 and the beginning of Stage 2. The committee examines the bill section by section[27] and considers amendments. Each section, whether amended or not, must be agreed to. It is open to any MSP to move an amendment to the bill and participate in the debate on that amendment but an MSP who is not a member of the committee may not vote on the amendment. It is possible for Stage 2 to be taken by a Committee of the Whole Parliament or by a committee that is not the lead committee.[28] At the end of Stage 2, if the bill has been amended, the Clerk of Parliament arranges for the amended bill to be printed and published.

Stage 3

This stage is taken by the full Parliament and thus gives every MSP an opportunity to consider and to vote on the bill in its amended form. At Stage 3, the Parliament must decide whether to pass or reject the bill. It is open to any MSP to give notice of an amendment to be taken at this stage, and it is possible for the member in charge of the bill to move that no more than half the total number of sections should be referred back to the committee for further Stage 2 consideration but such a reference back may happen only once. If there is a vote on the question of whether the bill is passed, the result is valid only if the number of members voting is more than a quarter of the total number of seats in the Parliament, that is, at least thirty-three.[29] Stage 3 is the equivalent of the Report and Third Reading stages in the UK Parliament.

Subject to the four-week delay (referred to above[30]) and a possible reconsideration stage, the bill is now ready to be presented to the Queen by the Presiding Officer for Royal Assent.

The Commission on Scottish Devolution (the Calman Commission) which reported in 2009, recommended, inter alia, that the three-stage bill process should be changed to a four-stage process with Stage 3 becoming limited to a second main amending stage taken in the chamber, while the final debate on whether to pass the bill would become Stage 4. This would allow any substantial amendments made at Stage 3 to be referred back to the relevant committee for further Stage 2 consideration.[31] At the time of writing, this recommendation has not been taken up.

Reconsideration Stage[32]

On occasion, it may be necessary for the bill to be reconsidered by the Parliament. This will happen in the following circumstances:

- if one of the Law Officers has referred a question about legislative competence, including a protected subject matter, to the Supreme Court, and that court has made a reference to the European Court of Justice for preliminary ruling and neither of these references has been decided; or
- if the Supreme Court has decided that the bill or any provision of it is outwith the legislative competence of the Parliament; or
- if an order has been made by a Secretary of State prohibiting the Presiding Officer from presenting the bill for Royal Assent.

The reconsideration stage is taken by the full Parliament and the only amendments which may be moved at this stage are amendments to resolve the problem. Once the amendments have been disposed of, the Parliament decides the question of whether to approve the bill.

Figure 5.1, at the end of this chapter, shows how Government Bills make their passage through the Parliament.

Committee Bills

Committee Bills are an innovation in the UK law-making process and there is no equivalent procedure in the UK Parliament. The ability of committees of the Parliament to initiate legislation is in keeping with the spirit of giving them an opportunity to play a major part in the work of the Parliament. A proposal for a Committee Bill may be made either by a committee of the Parliament or by an individual MSP. If the proposal is made by an MSP, it is referred to the appropriate committee by the Parliamentary Bureau. (If a Committee Bill is introduced as a result of an MSP's proposal, it counts against the MSP's quota of two Member's Bills per session. See below.)

Prior to deciding whether to make a proposal, a committee may hold an inquiry into the need for the Bill. The proposal takes the form of a report to the Parliament setting out the committee's recommendations as to the provisions to be contained in the Bill, together with an explanation of the need for the Bill. If the Parliament agrees to the proposal, the convener of the committee may introduce the bill unless a member of the Scottish Government or a Junior Scottish Minister has indicated that Scottish Government legislation or UK Government legislation is to be introduced to give effect to the proposal. A Committee Bill must go through the same three stages as for a Government Bill, described above (with a reconsideration stage if necessary) except that, at Stage 1, it is referred immediately to the Parliament. A report by a lead committee on the Bill's general principles is not required on the grounds that the committee initiating the Bill has already carried out all the Parliamentary work necessary.[33]

Figure 5.1 at the end of this chapter shows how Committee Bills make their passage through Parliament. At the end of the first four-year session of the Parliament, three Committee Bills had been passed: the Protection from Abuse Act 2001; the Scottish Parliamentary Standards Commissioner Act 2002; and the Commissioner for Children and Young People (Scotland) Act 2003. A more recent example of an Act which started as a Committee Bill is the Scottish Parliamentary Commissions and Commissioners etc. Act 2010. In recent years, however, the committees seem to have lost their initial eagerness to propose bills.

Members' Bills

A Members' Bill is the equivalent of a Private Member's Bill in the UK Parliament. It is a bill that is introduced by an MSP who is not a member of the Scottish Government. Such members are sometimes (inaccurately) referred to as backbenchers. Each member is entitled to introduce two bills in any one session which gives a potential number of around two hundred in each session. The procedures for Members' Bills are much more satisfactory than the procedures at Westminster which can literally be a lottery where prospects of progress depend very much on how high a place the MP concerned draws in the ballot for private members' bills.[34]

There are two options open to an MSP who is not a member of the Scottish Government for the introduction of a bill.

Option 1
The MSP submits to the Parliamentary Bureau a draft proposal for a bill. The Parliamentary Bureau then refers the draft proposal to the relevant committee and the committee then decides whether to make the proposal as a Committee Bill (see Committee Bills above).[35] Such a bill is not technically a Member's Bill but it counts against the member's allocation of two per session.

Option 2[36]

An MSP wishing to introduce a Member's Bill must first lodge a draft proposal with the Clerk consisting of the proposed short title and a brief explanation of the purpose of the bill together with either: (a) a consultation document prepared as the basis for public consultation over a period of at least twelve weeks on the policy objectives of the draft proposal; or (b) a written statement of reasons why, in the MSP's opinion, a case for the bill has already been established by reference to specified published material, and that consultation is therefore unnecessary. The draft proposal is then published in the *Business Bulletin* and the Parliamentary Bureau refers it to a committee (or committees) within whose remit the subject matter of the draft proposal refers.

In the case of a proposal accompanied by a statement of reasons for not consulting, the committee may within one month decide either that it is satisfied with the reasons given for not consulting on the proposal or that it is not so satisfied. In the latter case, the proposal falls unless the member, within two months, lodges an appropriate consultation document with the Clerk. Once the proposal is finalised, it is printed in the *Business Bulletin*, for a period of one month, together with information as to whether a summary of consultation responses or the statement of reasons may be obtained and the names of any members who have supported the proposal.

To obtain the right to introduce the bill, the MSP must, within that month, gather the support of at least another eighteen MSPs, including members of at least half of the political parties represented in the Parliamentary Bureau. However, the right to introduce is subject to the right of the Scottish Government to intervene by making a statement to the effect that either it proposes to legislate to give effect to the member's proposal or that the UK Government is proposing to do so.

The right to introduce may be exercised only until the first sitting day in June or, exceptionally, with the consent of the Parliamentary Bureau, the last sitting day of September in the calendar year preceding the year in which the next ordinary Scottish Parliament election is to be held.

If the MSP does not obtain the right to introduce a bill, a proposal falls and a similar proposal may not be introduced by any MSP within six months. A Member's Bill must pass through the three stages of a bill described above, with a reconsideration stage and a financial resolution if necessary. It should be noted that at Stage 1, the lead committee may recommend to the Parliament that the general principles of the bill be not agreed to if in the opinion of the committee: (a) the consultation or the published material does not demonstrate a reasonable case for the policy objectives of the proposal or that legislation is required to achieve them; the Bill appears to be clearly outwith the legislative competence of the Parliament and it is unlikely to be possible to amend it satisfactorily at Stages 2 or 3; the Bill has deficiencies of drafting that make it unfit to be passed and are sufficiently serious as to make it difficult or impractical to resolve them at Stages 2 and 3. In such a case, if the Scottish Parliament agrees with the committee's recommendation, the bill falls[37]. Otherwise, the Bill proceeds to the next stage.

Figure 5.1 at the end of this chapter shows how a bill proposed by a member makes its way through the Parliament. At the end of the first session of the Parliament, eight members' bills had reached the statute book, including the Abolition of Poindings and Warrant Sales Act 2001, and the Protection of Wild Mammals (Scotland) Act 2002. More recent Members' Bills which have reached the statute book include the Control of Dogs (Scotland) Act 2010, the Scottish Register of Tartans Act 2008, the Health Boards (Membership and Elections) (Scotland) Act 2009, the High Hedges (Scotland) Act 2013, and the British Sign Language Act 2015.

Private Bills

A Private Bill is a bill that is introduced by an individual person, by a body corporate, or by an unincorporated association of persons. The person who introduces such a Bill is known as 'the promoter'. The promoter is seeking particular powers or benefits which go beyond, or are in conflict with, the general law. Thus, it is important that anyone who objects to the proposal has an opportunity to state his or her objections. A local authority, for example, may need additional powers to acquire land or building compulsorily and may acquire these powers by promoting a Private Bill.[38] An individual may promote a private bill in relation to his or her estate, property, status or style. Such bills, promoted by individuals (sometimes referred to as 'personal bills'), are likely to be fairly rare. The procedures for Private Bills are fairly complicated and only a brief outline is given here. Readers who wish more detail are referred to Chapter 9A of the Parliament's Standing Orders.

A Private Bill can be introduced into the Parliament on any sitting day by being lodged with the Clerks and it must be signed by or on behalf of the promoter. Depending on the nature of the Bill, a wide range of accompanying documents may be required. The accompanying documents should include details of the advertisement of the promoter's intention and a statement as to where various relevant documents may be inspected. 'Works Bills' for the acquisition of land in order to construct harbours, airports, ring roads, previously dealt with by way of Private Bills, no longer exist. Anything meeting that description is now processed outwith the Parliament by a separate approval process under the Transport and Works (Scotland) Act 2007.

After the Bill has been introduced, the Parliament establishes a Private Bill Committee to consider it. A Private Bill Committee must have no more than five members, none of whom should reside in or represent an area to be affected by the Bill. The members are expected to attend all the meetings of the committee. There is a sixty-day 'objection period' during which objections may be lodged with the clerks either in writing or by email (later confirmed in writing).

A Private Bill goes through three stages:

- a Preliminary Stage at which the Private Bill Committee considers the general principles of the bill and whether it should proceed as a Private Bill. At the end of this stage, the Parliament takes a decision as to whether to agree those general principles and whether the Bill should proceed or not;
- a Consideration Stage at which the details of the Bill are considered by the Private Bill Committee. At this stage the promoter and objectors are invited to give evidence to the members, and the Bill may be amended by the committee in much the same way as at Stage 2 of a Public Bill;
- a final stage at which the Parliament may further amend the Bill and then decide whether to pass or reject it.

As with Public Bills, a Private Bill may have to go through a Reconsideration Stage.

At the end of the first session of the Scottish Parliament only one private bill had reached the statute book – the National Galleries of Scotland Act 2003. More recent examples include the Edinburgh Tram Lines Act 2006, the Glasgow Airport Rail Link Act 2007, the William Simpson's Home (Transfer of Property etc.) (Scotland) Act 2010, Burrell Collection (Lending and Borrowing) (Scotland) Act 2014, and the City of Edinburgh (Portobello Park) Act 2014.

Private Bills which have not reached the statute book by the end of a Parliamentary session are carried over into the new Parliamentary session. Figure 5.2 at the end of this chapter shows how a Private Bill makes its way through the Parliament.

Emergency Bills

The process described above for Government Bills has inbuilt delays of at least two weeks between Stages 1 and 2 and between Stages 2 and 3.[39] But there must be a procedure which allows the Scottish Government to deal with emergencies. The SA 1998 allows for this and the Parliament's Standing Orders thus make special fast-track provisions for such situations.[40]

Any member of the Scottish Government or a Junior Scottish Minister may move that a bill introduced as a Government Bill shall be treated as an Emergency Bill. If the Parliament agrees, the Bill is referred immediately to the Parliament for Stage 1 consideration without the necessity of a report on the Bill's general principles from a committee. Stage 2 is taken by a Committee of the Whole Parliament. The requirement of minimum intervals between Stages 1 and 2 and between Stages 2 and 3 is dispensed with and all stages of the Bill are normally taken in a single day. The first bill passed by the Scottish Parliament – the Mental Health (Public Safety and Appeals) (Scotland) Bill 1999 – was treated as an Emergency Bill and passed through all stages and received Royal Assent within a fortnight.

The controversial Offensive Behaviour at Football and Threatening Communications (Scotland) Act 2012 was introduced into the Parliament as an Emergency Bill but the Parliament later decided that it should no longer be treated as an Emergency Bill, thus allowing more time for consideration, debate and amendment.

Budget Bills

A Budget Bill is a Government Bill, the purpose of which is to authorise sums to be paid out of the Scottish Consolidated Fund or to authorise sums received to be applied without being paid into the fund.[41] A Budget Bill can be introduced only by a member of the Scottish Government and does not need to be accompanied by a Financial Memorandum, Explanatory Notes or a Policy Memorandum.[42]

At Stage 1 a Budget Bill is referred immediately to the full Parliament for consideration of its principles and a decision as to whether these are agreed to. A report from a committee on general principles is not required and Stage 2 of the Bill is taken by the Finance Committee. The normal minimum intervals between stages do not apply but Stage 3 is not to begin earlier than twenty days after introduction of the Bill. If Stage 3 is not completed before the expiry of thirty days after introduction, the

Bill falls. Amendments to a Budget Bill may be moved only by a member of the Scottish Government or by a Junior Scottish Minister.[43]

If a Budget Bill is dependent on the Parliament passing a tax-varying resolution[44] which would result in an increase of the basic rate of income tax for Scottish taxpayers and the Parliament rejects such a resolution, the Bill falls. However, if a Budget Bill falls or is rejected at any stage a bill in the same or similar terms can be introduced at any time thereafter.[45]

Miscellaneous Other Bills

The Scottish Parliament may also pass:

- Hybrid Bills.[46] These are Public Bills, introduced by Scottish Ministers, which adversely affect the private interests of individuals or bodies in a manner different from the private interests of others in the same category or class. For example, a bill to construct some major building may involve the compulsory purchase of privately owned land. In such a case, consultation with all who would be affected (the mandatory consultees) is very important and an advertisement of the proposal must be one of the accompanying documents if the bill affects heritable property. Hybrid Bills go to a Hybrid Bill Committee consisting of three to five members. There is also an objection period during which objections may be lodged by persons or bodies likely to be affected. Hybrid Bills are fairly rare. An example is the Forth Crossing Act 2011;
- Consolidation Bills, the purpose of which is to restate existing law with or without amendments, to give effect to recommendations of the Scottish Law Commission or of the Scottish Law Commission and (English) Law Commission jointly.[47] The first Consolidation Bill – the Salmon and Freshwater Fisheries (Consolidation) (Scotland) Act 2003 – was passed at the end of the Parliament's first four-year session;
- Statute Law Repeals Bills, the purpose of which is to repeal, in accordance with the Scottish Law Commission's recommendation, statute law which is out of date and no longer relevant;[48]
- Statute Law Revision Bills, the purpose of which is to revise statute law by repealing Acts that are no longer in force or have become unnecessary and re-enacting provisions of Acts of the Scottish Parliament or the UK Parliament which are otherwise spent.[49]

CHALLENGES TO THE LEGISLATION

As mentioned earlier in this chapter, bills are subject to pre-legislative consideration and to further scrutiny after they have been passed to ensure that they do not stray beyond the Parliament's legislative competence. The courts, however, have power even after legislation has been enacted to decide that an Act (or part of it) deals with matters outside the Parliament's legislative competence, and by so doing in effect strike down its legislation. This is because section 29(1) of the SA 1998 states that an Act of the Scottish Parliament is not law so far as any provision of it is outside the legislative competence of the Parliament.

There are also provisions in section 40(3) of the SA 1998 stating that a court cannot make an order for suspension or reduction against the Parliament. At first sight, this might suggest that a court cannot 'cancel' an item of legislation made by the Parliament but only grant a declarator that it is beyond the Parliament's legislative competence. In practice, however, challenges to legislation normally arise in the course of legal proceedings between other parties rather than involving the Parliament itself. The purpose of section 40(3) would appear to be to prevent interference in the way that the Parliament goes about its business rather than to protect the Parliament's legislation from challenge.

Challenges to the Parliament's legislation are considered in more detail in Chapters 8 and 9 below.

SUBORDINATE LEGISLATION MADE BY SCOTTISH MINISTERS

Much UK legislation is enacted not as primary legislation which must pass through the full Parliamentary procedure but as subordinate legislation usually in the form of a statutory instrument. Such legislation consists of either an order (or regulations, rules, etc.) made by a Minister or an Order in Council made by the Queen on the advice of her Ministers. Some existing powers to make subordinate legislation under Acts of the UK Parliament were transferred to the Scottish Ministers when the Scottish Parliament and Executive were first established in 1999. In addition, Acts of the Scottish Parliament may confer powers on Scottish Ministers to make subordinate legislation in any area in which the Scottish Parliament has legislative competence.[50] The SA 1998 places some restrictions on the power to make subordinate legislation under an

Act of the Scottish Parliament. For example, serious criminal offences cannot be created by such legislation.[51]

A piece of subordinate legislation made in the form of a statutory instrument under an Act of the Scottish Parliament is called a Scottish Statutory Instrument (SSI).

Procedures for Making Subordinate Legislation

The SA 1998 does not lay down procedures for the making of subordinate legislation within devolved areas. Instead, the procedures were initially set out in a statutory instrument made under the SA 1998.[52] Provisions for scrutiny of Scottish Statutory Instruments are set out in the Parliament's Standing Orders.[53] The procedures are largely based on the Westminster model.

As at Westminster, most instruments are subject to either a negative procedure (subject to annulment) or an affirmative procedure (requiring approval by resolution). Under the negative procedure, the instrument becomes law unless the Parliament resolves that nothing further is to be done under the instrument, that is, to annul the instrument. Under the affirmative procedure, the Parliament must resolve to approve the instrument for it to become law. The affirmative procedure is thus the stronger form of scrutiny. The parent Act[54] lays down which procedure is to be used and, in some cases, the parent Act may provide that the instrument is to be made without being subject to either affirmative or negative procedure, or even without requiring it to be laid before Parliament.

Scrutiny by Committees

The Scottish Parliament has a committee called the Delegated Powers and Law Reform Committee,[55] similar to the Joint Committee on Statutory Instruments at Westminster, which scrutinises the technical aspects of every piece of subordinate legislation that is laid before the Parliament. The Delegated Powers and Law Reform Committee also has the power to scrutinise provisions in bills that confer powers on Scottish Ministers to make subordinate legislation. Subordinate legislation is also scrutinised by at least one subject committee of the Scottish Parliament or by the Parliament as a whole, a procedure that has no direct Westminster parallel.

An instrument or draft instrument (that is, an actual or a proposed piece of subordinate legislation) is said to be laid before the Parliament if a copy of it is lodged with the clerks during office hours. Once laid, the clerks refer the instruments to the Delegated Powers and Law Reform Committee and to the lead committee, that is, the subject committee within whose remit the subject matter of the instrument falls, unless the Parliament has decided that the instrument should be considered by the full Parliament. If the subject matter falls within the remit of more than one subject committee, one of the committees is designated as the lead committee and the instrument is sent to the other committee(s) as well which may make recommendations to the lead committee.[56]

The remit of the Delegated Powers and Law Reform Committee is to decide whether the attention of the Parliament should be drawn to the instrument on the following grounds:[57]

- it imposes a charge on the Scottish Consolidated Fund[58] or contains provisions requiring payments to be made to various bodies;
- it is made under an Act (the parent Act) which specifically excludes challenge in the courts;
- it appears to have retrospective effect although the parent Act does not confer the authority to do so;
- there appears to be unjustifiable delay in publishing the instrument or in laying it before the Parliament;
- there appears to be a doubt as to whether it is *intra vires*;
- it raises a devolution issue;
- it has been made by what appears to be an unusual or unexpected use of the powers conferred by the parent Act;
- for any special reason its form or meaning could be clearer;
- its drafting appears to be defective;

or on any other ground which does not impinge on its substance or the policy behind it. The committee must report its decision with its reasons to the Parliament and to the lead committee normally within twenty days and, in any event, no later than twenty-two days of the laying of the instrument.[59]

Motion for Annulment (Negative Procedure)

The negative procedure is a weaker form of control of subordinate legislation because the instrument becomes (or remains) law after a certain period if no MSP successfully moves its annulment. No later than forty days after the instrument has been laid, any MSP (whether or not a member of the lead committee) can propose to the lead committee that nothing further be done under the instrument. The lead committee is allowed to have a debate of no more than ninety minutes on this proposal, and the MSP who has made that proposal (if not a member of the committee) along with the Minister in charge of the instrument, may participate in the debate but not vote on the proposal.

The lead committee then reports to the Parliament, within forty days of the instrument being laid, with its recommendations. If the lead committee recommends that no further action should be taken, that is, that the instrument should not be made, a very limited debate takes place, a vote is taken if necessary and, if the motion to annul is agreed, the Minister is then required to annul the instrument.[60]

Motion for Approval (Affirmative Procedure)

The affirmative procedure is a stronger form of control of subordinate legislation because the instrument cannot become (or remain) law unless it has been approved by the Parliament. The lead committee must decide whether to recommend to the Parliament that an affirmative instrument should be approved. Any member of the Scottish Government or a Junior Minister, even if not a member of the lead committee, may propose to the lead committee that it should recommend approval. As with the negative procedure, that member and the Minister in charge of the instrument (if not members of the committee) may participate in the ninety-minute debate but may not vote. The lead committee must make its recommendation to the Parliament within forty days of its being laid. If approval is recommended, only very limited debate is allowed and, if the motion to approve is agreed to, after a vote if necessary, the instrument becomes (or remains) law.[61]

Instruments Which Do Not Require the Parliament's Approval

Some Acts of the Scottish Parliament may provide that an instrument laid before the Parliament may be made without the Parliament's approval. Such instruments should not be contentious but the Parliament's Standing Orders do allow MSPs to have some control over them. The procedure is very similar to the negative procedure described above. No later than forty days after the instrument has been laid, any MSP may propose to the lead committee that the committee should recommend to the Parliament that the instrument be not made. The MSP and the Minister in charge of the instrument are entitled to participate in the ninety-minute debate but may not vote if they are not members of the lead committee. If the lead committee recommends to the Parliament that the instrument should not be made, the procedure is as described above.[62]

Although the Scottish Ministers normally make subordinate legislation only in areas in which the Parliament has legislative competence, some possibilities exist for Scottish Ministers to make subordinate legislation in areas where the Parliament itself has not been given powers to legislate. The SA 1998 contains a power allowing for functions exercisable by a UK Minister to be transferred, by Order in Council, to Scottish Ministers (or to be exercised concurrently by UK and by Scottish Ministers), in so far as the functions concerned relate to Scotland.[63] This allows Scottish Ministers to make subordinate legislation in relation to matters concerning Scotland but in which legislative power has not been devolved to the Parliament. (Such a transfer, however, can take place only with the approval of the Scottish Parliament, and also both Houses of the UK Parliament.)

THE LEGISLATIVE LOAD

As the beginning of the first session of the Parliament, the First Minister announced a legislative programme of eight Executive Bills for the first year of the Parliament. At the end of December 1999, when the Parliament had been in existence for six months, only one Act of the Scottish Parliament had reached the statute book – the Mental Health (Public Safety and Appeals) (Scotland) Act 1999 – and that arose from an Emergency Bill. Three other Executive Bills and one Member's Bill were at the proposal stage. No committee bills had been introduced by that date. In contrast, the Parliament had made around two hundred Scottish Statutory Instruments (SSIs) within the same period.

By the close of the Parliament's first session on 31 March 2003, the Parliament had passed sixty-two Acts. Of these, fifty had been introduced as Executive Bills, three as Committee Bills, eight as Members' Bills and one as a Private Bill. Very few of these would have reached the statute books if there had not been a Scottish Parliament because the UK Parliament did not make much time available for Scottish bills. In addition to the sixty-two Acts of the Scottish Parliament, nearly two thousand Scottish Statutory Instruments had been made.

The figures for the second session of the Parliament, 2003–07 are rather similar because there was still a coalition government in place.

The election in May 2007, however, resulted in a minority government formed by the SNP and it had to rely on winning support for its proposals from two or three of the opposition parties. This was not always easy and thus the number of Executive (renamed Government in 2012) Bills to reach the statute book fell. Only seven Acts were passed in 2008 and twelve in 2009. The number of statutory instruments remained about the same each year.

In the election of 2011 the SNP won a majority and the number of Acts passed rose again. With the loss of a majority in 2016, it is expected that the number of Acts passed may decline. The average per year has been around fifteen.

As the 2011 and 2016 terms are for five years rather than four, to avoid clashes with UK elections, the number of Acts passed in these sessions is likely to rise. However, only four Acts were passed between the Scottish Parliament election in May 2016 and August 2017. This will probably have an impact on the number passed in the session 2016–21. It has been suggested by some commentators and by opposition parties that this is because of the SNP Government's concentration on holding a second referendum on independence following the UK-wide referendum on leaving the EU which took place in June 2016, a month or so after the Scottish election in which the SNP formed a minority administration.

UK SUBORDINATE LEGISLATION AND THE SCOTTISH PARLIAMENT AND MINISTERS

The SA 1998 also gives the Parliament and Scottish Ministers a degree of involvement in respect of other matters in which legislative competence has not been devolved to the Parliament.[64] The powers include those listed below and can be grouped into three types.

First, certain provisions which enable subordinate legislation to be made by Order in Council can be exercised only with the approval of the Parliament, as follows (in all but the first two cases the approval of both Houses of the UK Parliament is also required):

- the power to disqualify specified public office-holders from becoming an MSP;[65]
- the power to make payment to opposition political parties to assist MSPs in carrying out their duties;[66]
- the power to modify the list of reserved matters on which the Parliament cannot legislate;[67]
- the power to transfer additional functions from UK Ministers to Scottish Ministers;[68]

- the redistribution of functions exercisable by Scottish Ministers in whole or in part to UK Ministers;[69]
- the power to add new devolved taxes[70]
- the power to regulate the Tweed and Esk fisheries;[71]
- certain powers regarding the qualified transfer of functions to a Scottish tribunal.[72]

Second, there are certain matters in respect of which the Scottish Parliament can annul proposals for UK subordinate legislation, as follows:

- the transfer of property and liabilities from UK Ministers to Scottish Ministers or the Lord Advocate (and vice versa);[73]
- specifying functions which a UK Minister can arrange by agreement to be carried out by a Scottish Minister or the Lord Advocate (and vice versa);[74]
- an order made by the Scottish Minister setting the level of the deposit (caution) which has to be lodged by a person seeking the disqualification of an MSP;[75]
- the adaptation of the functions of a 'cross-border public authority'[76] and the transfer of the property and liabilities of such bodies (unless, in these cases, the Parliament (and the UK Parliament) has previously approved the subordinate legislation in question).[77]

(If the UK subordinate legislation in the above cases, except in the case of setting the level of caution, changes the text of an Act of Parliament, the Scottish Parliament and both Houses of the UK Parliament have to approve the proposal by a positive vote in support of it.)

Third, there are certain cases in which the Scottish Ministers either have to give their agreement or be consulted before subordinate legislation is made by the relevant UK authority, including the following:

- an order made by the UK Treasury designating those government receipts which are to be payable into the Scottish Consolidated Fund – the Treasury is required to consult the Scottish Ministers before making such designation;[78]
- the exercise of certain powers by UK Ministers over cross-border public authorities – in some circumstances the UK Minister must consult the Scottish Ministers before exercising functions in relation to a cross-border public authority;[79]
- subordinate legislation transferring certain functions to Scottish Ministers where that modifies certain obligations under international or EU law – the Scottish Ministers must be consulted before any such legislation is made;[80]

- the exercise of certain reserved powers concerning fuel poverty-support schemes, the promotion of reductions in carbon emissions, and the promotion of reductions in home-heating costs;[81]
- the exercise of certain powers by the Secretary of State to make provision about the combination of polls for elections.[82]

The Scottish Parliament
Pàrlamaid na h-Alba

Stages in the passage of a Public Bill

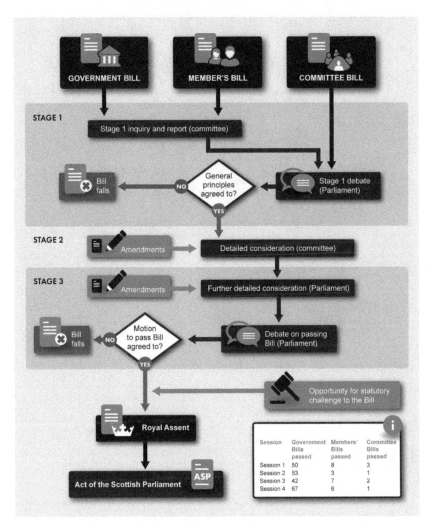

Figure 5.1 Passage of a Government Bill through Parliament.

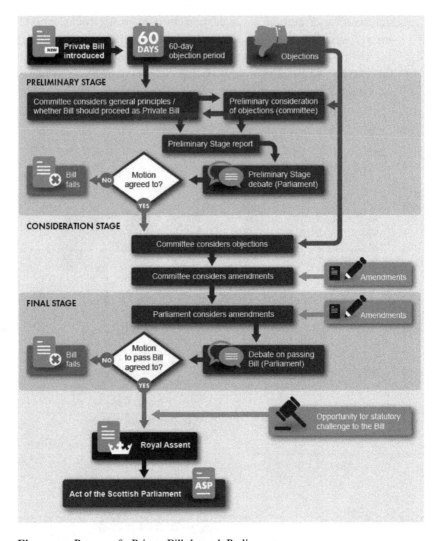

Figure 5.2 Passage of a Private Bill through Parliament

NOTES

1. SA 1998, section 28.
2. SA 2016, section 11.
3. SA 2016, section 11.
4. The first Standing Orders for the Scottish Parliament were made by a statutory instrument of the UK Parliament (SI 1999/ 1095). In December 1999, the Parliament resolved to adopt its own Standing Orders. These are

largely based on the Standing Orders made by SI 1999/1095. The rules relating to the procedures for bills are set out in Chapter 9 of the Standing Orders. (Subsequent references to Rules are references to the rules set out in the Standing Orders.)

5. SA 1998, section 31.
6. See p. 136.
7. SA 1998, section 33.
8. SA 1998, section 36.
9. SA 1998, section 35.
10. See Chapter 2.
11. SA 1998, section 36.
12. Rule 9.21.
13. Rule 9.17–9.20.
14. Rule 9.9.
15. Rule 9.5.5.
16. Rule 9.2.
17. Rule 9.3.1. This is part of the pre-legislative scrutiny of a bill. See p. 92.
18. Rule 9.3.2.
19. This is also part of the pre-legislative scrutiny of the bill. See p. 68.
20. Rule 9.3.3.
21. Rule 9.3.4. For the Scottish Consolidated Fund and the Auditor General, see Chapter 10.
22. Rule 9.4A.
23. For the Parliamentary Bureau, see Chapter 4.
24. Rules 9.6.1, 9.6.2.
25. Rule 9.6.7.
26. Rule 9.12.7.
27. Note that a Scottish Parliament bill is divided into sections. A UK Parliament bill is divided into clauses that become sections when the bill becomes an Act of Parliament.
28. Rule 9.7.1.
29. Rule 9.8.9.
30. See p. 93
31. Commission on Scottish Devolution, 2009, Recommendation 6.2 6.4. For the Calman Commission generally, see Chapter 2.
32. Rule 9.9.
33. Rule 9.15.
34. There is a number of separate routes for introducing Private Members' Bills in the Commons, of which the annual ballot is only the best known and most likely to be successful. Occasionally bills brought in by back-bench MPs through the 'Ten Minute Rule' bill process have also successfully made it on to the statute book. There is no ballot process for Lords' Private Members' Bills which also have quite a good record of success.
35. Rule 9.15.4.

36. The revised rules for Members' Bills are set out in Rule 9.14 of the Standing Orders to which the reader is referred.
37. Rule 9.14.18.
38. It should be noted that all bills which are not Private Bills are Public Bills.
39. See p. 95.
40. SA 1998, section 36 (2) and Rule 9.21.
41. For the Scottish Consolidated Fund, see Chapter 10.
42. Rule 9.16.2.
43. Rules 9.16.3–9.16.6.
44. That is, in accordance with SA 1998, section 73.
45. Rules 9.16.7–9.16.8.
46. Rule 9.17 and Chapter 9A of the Rules.
47. Rule 9.18A.
48. Rule 9.19. Such laws are known as 'spent enactments'.
49. Rule 9.20.
50. SA 1998, section 112.
51. SA 1998, section 113(10).
52. Scotland Act 1998 (Transitory Provisions) (Statutory Instruments) Order 1999, SI 1999/1096.
53. The rules for making subordinate legislation are contained in Chapter 10 of the Parliament's Standing Orders.
54. The parent Act is the Act which empowers ministers to make subordinate legislation relating to that Act.
55. The Delegated Powers and Law Reform Committee is one of the mandatory committees of the Scottish Parliament, that is, the Parliament must establish such a committee. See Chapter 4.
56. Rules 10.1, 10.2.
57. Rule 10.3.
58. For the Scottish Consolidated Fund, see Chapter 10.
59. Rule 10.3.
60. Rule 10.4.
61. Rule 10.6.
62. Rule 10.5.
63. SA 1998, section 63. There is a parallel provision allowing for the transfer of functions from Scottish Minister to UK Ministers in section 108.
64. SA 1998, Schedule 7.
65. SA 1998, section 15.
66. 6. SA 1998, section 97.
67. SA 1998, section 30.
68. SA 1998, section 63.
69. SA 1998, section 108.
70. SA 1998, section 80B.
71. SA 1998, section 111.
72. Schedule 5, Part III, paragraph 2A.

73. SA 1998, section 109.
74. SA 1998, section 93.
75. SA 1998, section 18.
76. SA 1998, section 89.
77. SA 1998, section 90.
78. SA 1998, section 64.
79. SA 1998, section 88; and see Chapter 9.
80. SA 1998, section 106.
81. SA 2016, sections 58–60.
82. SA 2016, section 4(1).

CHAPTER SIX

The Scottish Government

INTRODUCTION

The establishment of a Scottish Parliament gave Scotland not only a legislature but also a government which may take executive action over the whole range of devolved functions. The Scotland Act 1998 (SA 1998) describes it as the Scottish Administration but for the first eight years of its existence, under the Labour–Liberal Democrat coalitions from 1999 to 2007, the term Scottish Executive was generally used to describe not just the Scottish Ministers as the SA 1998 provides but also the government as a whole, including its departments and civil servants. The SNP minority administration, which took power in 2007, decided very soon after its inception that the term Scottish Government would be adopted. The Scotland Act 2012, section 12, formally changed the name to the Scottish Government (though the term Scottish Executive is still occasionally used, particularly for formal legal or Parliamentary purposes and the term Scottish Administration is used for the whole of devolved central government in Scotland).

The structure of the Scottish Government is based on the Westminster model of Parliamentary government. The Ministers are drawn from the ranks of the MSPs and are accountable to them. In the UK Government the rules relating to the appointment of the Prime Minister and the other Ministers of the UK Parliament are largely unwritten and are based on convention. The equivalent rules for the appointment of the First Minister and the other Ministers of the Scottish Parliament are statutory and are to be found in Part II of the SA 1998.

The Scottish Government consists of the First Minister, Scottish Ministers, and the Scottish Law Officers, that is, the Lord Advocate and the Solicitor General for Scotland.[1] No person who holds ministerial office in the UK Government is allowed to be appointed as a Minister in the Scottish Government. Thus, anyone who is elected to the Scottish

Parliament and who already holds ministerial office in Her Majesty's Government in any of the UK departments of state has to give that office up if he or she is to become a Scottish Minister. This rule applies also to the First Minister. Thus, Donald Dewar, who was Secretary of State for Scotland prior to the first general election to the Scottish Parliament in 1999, resigned from that office in order to be appointed as a member of the Scottish Executive, as it was then called, and First Minister. (There is no bar, however, on Scottish Ministers serving as members of either the House of Commons or House of Lords in the UK Parliament.)

THE FIRST MINISTER

The First Minister is the equivalent of the Prime Minister. He or she is nominated by the Parliament and appointed by the Queen from among the members of the Scottish Parliament within twenty-eight days of a general election and holds office 'at Her Majesty's pleasure'.[2] Theoretically, this means that the First Minister could be dismissed by the Queen for good reason or for none. In practice, the First Minister holds office as long as he or she can command the support of the majority of the MSPs or, at the very least, as long there is not a majority of MSPs prepared to vote against him or her.

Because the electoral system to the Scottish Parliament has an element of proportional representation in it, it is difficult for any one single party to win a clear majority of the seats. In the first elections the Labour Party won fifty-six of the 129 seats and thus did not have a clear majority. A coalition agreement was reached with the Liberal Democrats[3] and, as part of the agreement, the leader of the Labour Party, Donald Dewar, emerged as the favoured candidate for the post of First Minister with the leader of the Liberal Democrats, Jim Wallace, as his deputy. In the elections of 2003, the Labour Party won fifty seats and was still the largest party. Again, they formed a coalition with the Liberal Democrats (who had won seventeen seats) and Jack McConnell, the leader of the Labour Party became First Minister with Jim Wallace again as his deputy.[4]

It was generally assumed, until the elections in 2007, that the First Minister would need to lead a party, or coalition of parties, which commanded support from a majority of MSPs. After the close result of the 2007 election, however, (where the SNP won most seats, forty-seven, but only one ahead of Labour on forty-six, in both cases representing a little over a third of the seats in the Parliament) neither the SNP nor Labour was able to form a majority coalition, and the SNP formed a minority administration.[5] That administration could have been over-thrown at any time by the combination of sufficient MSPs of the opposition parties but, in spite of some threats and murmurs from time to time that this might happen, the SNP minority administration survived for a full five-year term.[6]

In the Scottish general election of 2011, the SNP won an outright majority and formed the Government. It lost its majority in the 2016 election, however, and formed a minority government again.

The Parliament's Standing Orders set out the procedure for the nomination of an MSP for appointment as First Minister.[7] Any member may nominate a candidate by submitting a nomination to the Clerk of the Parliament in writing. To be valid, the nomination must be seconded by another MSP. The candidates must have taken the oath of allegiance before voting takes place. An electronic voting system is normally used but, if the Presiding Officer thinks that that system cannot be used for any reason or that it has produced an unreliable result, the vote may be taken by ballot or by roll call or any other method. The names of the candidates are read out by the Presiding Officer and then there is a vote or a series of votes until one single candidate emerges who has the support of the majority of MSPs voting.[8] The quorum for this vote is 25 per cent plus one which seems very low for such an important decision. Following the selection of the candidate by the Parliament, the Presiding Officer recommends that candidate to the Queen for appointment and the Queen appoints the candidate.

If the office of First Minister is vacant, or he or she is for any reason, such as prolonged illness, unable to act, his or her functions are exercisable by another MSP designated by the Presiding Officer.[9] No doubt the Presiding Officer would, in such a situation, consult the party leaders privately to try to identify a member who would be generally acceptable. When the First Minister Donald Dewar became ill in 2000, the Deputy First Minister, Jim Wallace, deputised as he did in the immediate period after Donald Dewar's death.

The First Minister may resign at any time and must do so if the Scottish Government loses the confidence of the Scottish Parliament.[10] A new First Minister must be nominated for appointment within twenty-eight days of the post becoming vacant, otherwise an extraordinary general election must be held.[11]

THE FUNCTIONS OF THE FIRST MINISTER

The First Minister is, in many ways, the Scottish Prime Minister. He or she is normally the leader of the party with the largest number of seats in the party or in the coalition forming the majority in the Scottish Parliament (or, in the event of no party or coalition having a majority, the party that forms a minority administration) and the leader of the Scottish Government. During the first eight years of the Scottish Parliament when the First Minister was from the same party as that which formed the UK Government, the First Minister was also the chief channel of communication with the UK Prime Minister. Since the formation of the SNP Governments, that last role has continued to a certain extent although the form of communication has often taken the form of public argument rather than private discussion!

As head of the Scottish Government, the First Minister is responsible for the overall development, implementation and presentation of the administration's policies and for promoting and representing Scotland at home and overseas.

Certain powers of appointment are specifically conferred on the First Minister by the SA 1998 which, in the case of the UK Prime Minister, are largely conventional. The First Minister, with the agreement of the Parliament, recommends names to the Queen for appointment as Ministers, junior Ministers, and the Law Officers.[12] Ministers and junior Ministers may be removed from office by the First Minister. In the case of the Law Officers, the First Minister may, with the agreement of the Parliament, recommend to the Queen their removal.[13] The Act allows for executive functions to be conferred on the First Minister alone, and the doctrine of collective responsibility does not apply to his or her acts or omissions.[14]

The crucial difference between the Scottish First Minister and the UK Prime Minister is that the former's party will normally not have a majority in the Scottish Parliament. He or she is likely to be either be the head of a coalition government or lead a minority administration. By contrast, the UK Prime Minister will normally have a working majority – at least as long as the first-past-the-post system of voting is retained for elections to Westminster.

Coalition with another political grouping, or the lack of a majority, inevitably constrains the freedom of action of the First Minister. If there is a coalition, the First Minister has to negotiate with the leader of the smaller party or parties in the coalition as to how many ministerial posts each party will have when portfolios are allocated to Ministers.

The Labour–Liberal Democrat coalition, which emerged after the first elections in May 1999, allocated two ministerial posts and two junior ministerial posts to the Liberal Democrats. In 2003 the coalition agreement gave the Liberal Democrats three ministerial posts and three junior ministerial posts. The UK Prime Minister does not normally have this constraint in the allocation of portfolios, though there was a UK coalition government between the Conservatives and the Liberal Democrats from 2010 to 2015, and, of course, a First Minister who leads a minority administration is similarly free from having to negotiate with a coalition party, though his or her appointment of Ministers will have to be approved by the Scottish Parliament. If there is a coalition administration, there will also be interparty negotiation about the policies to be adopted, the prioritisation of bills, the allocation of convenerships of committees, and many other aspects of the business of government.[15] If the coalition parties can agree on such matters, they should of course normally be able to ensure majority support for them in any votes in the Scottish Parliament. With a minority administration, however, its support cannot be guaranteed, and the minority SNP Governments of 2007 and 2016 have lost a number of important votes on matters of policy, none of which so far has provoked its leader and First Minister, to resign.

Whether as head of a majority coalition or a minority administration, however, the office of First Minister is a very powerful one. By presiding at Cabinet meetings, and setting its agenda to a large extent, the First Minister can control discussion and the process of decision-making. He or she is expected to make major policy statements and intervene in the pressing issues of the day, such as Scottish industrial closures. The press and other media see the First Minister as Scotland's Prime Minister and give him or her enormous public exposure.

SCOTTISH MINISTERS

The First Minister appoints a team of Scottish Ministers. Each Minister must be a member of the Scottish Parliament. Ministers are appointed with the Queen's approval but the First Minister must first seek the agreement of the Parliament to the nominations before submitting names to the Queen.[16] This is different from the procedure at Westminster where the Prime Minister can recommend to the Queen the appointment to ministerial office of whomsoever he or she wishes, subject, of course, to political considerations, without having to secure the agreement of Parliament. Standing Orders allow the First Minister to seek the Scottish

Parliament's approval for the appointment of Scottish Ministers either individually or en bloc. The Parliament is able to reject, but not to substitute, the names of particular individuals in the First Minister's list. A simple majority of those voting is sufficient to secure Parliament's agreement, and again, the quorum is 25 per cent plus one.[17] The allocation of portfolios to Ministers is a decision for the First Minister alone, subject to negotiation with the coalition partner(s), if any, and is not included in the motion seeking the Parliament's approval to appointment.

Scottish Ministers, like the First Minister, hold office at Her Majesty's pleasure. They may be removed from office by the First Minister and must resign if the Scottish Government loses the confidence of the Parliament.[18]

The Presiding Officer notifies the Parliament of any resignation made by a member of the Scottish Government. Ministers cease to hold office if they become disqualified to be MSPs for any reason (other than the calling of an election), such as bankruptcy or insanity.

In the UK Parliament, whose members are elected under the first-past-the-post system, it is usual for one party to have an outright majority. Thus, UK Ministers are normally MPs from one single political party, the party of government. In the Scottish Parliament, some of whose members are elected under the regional list system discussed above,[19] coalition government or minority government is the norm, and Scottish Ministers are appointed from the MSPs of the parties forming the coalition. The number of Ministers in the UK Cabinet is normally around twenty-two, although it has become common for a few Ministers, other than those with Cabinet responsibilities, also to attend Cabinet meetings. The number of Scottish Ministers appointed to the first Scottish Executive was ten and, after the election in 2003, the First Minister again appointed ten Ministers to his Cabinet (though two of these were appointed at the rank and salary of junior Ministers). The SNP administration which came to power in 2007, however, decided upon a radical restructure of the ministerial and departmental structure. Five 'Cabinet secretaries' were appointed, bringing together in most cases responsibilities which were previously held by different ministers, forming the Scottish Cabinet along with the First Minister. After the 2016 general election, eight Cabinet Secretaries were appointed in addition to a Deputy First Minister.

In addition to the oath of allegiance to the Queen, which all members of the Scottish Parliament must take on election, members of the Scottish Government must take the official oath as laid down in the Promissory Oaths Act 1868, in the following terms: 'I do swear that I will well and truly serve Her Majesty Queen Elizabeth in the office of Scottish Minister'.

THE SCOTTISH LAW OFFICERS

There are two Scottish Law Officers, namely the Lord Advocate and his or her deputy, the Solicitor General, who act as the senior legal advisers to the Scottish Government and are themselves members of the Scottish Executive. They are not usually members of the Scottish Parliament but are appointed by the Queen on the recommendation of the First Minister. In other words, they are political appointments. The Lord Advocate is also the head of the systems of criminal prosecution and investigation of deaths in Scotland and must act independently in those capacities.

Unlike the rest of the Scottish Ministers, they do not have to be Members of the Scottish Parliament and none of the Lords Advocate or the Solicitors General appointed so far has been an elected member of the Scottish Parliament. They do not have to be members of a political party and, though under the Labour–Liberal Democrat administration, the Scottish Law Officers were normally, though not always, members of the Labour Party, the SNP administration decided that it would make the Scottish Law Officers 'non-political' appointments. As part of this change in political, though not legal, status, the new SNP administration decided in May 2007 that the Scottish Law Officers would no longer attend meetings of the Scottish Cabinet, except in special circumstances. (The participation by the Scottish Law Officers in the party political decision-making process had already attracted some criticism[20] and, as a result, from 2000 the Lord Advocate ceased to vote in the Scottish Cabinet although he or she continued to attend its meetings until 2007.)

Like Scottish Ministers, the Scottish Law Officers have to have the approval of Parliament before they can be appointed,[21] and the same procedure as that used for the appointment of Scottish Ministers is used for securing the agreement of Parliament.[22] If they are not members of the Parliament, they can still participate in Parliamentary proceedings but they may not vote.[23] They are able to participate in debates and answer questions, attend sessions of committees, and steer through Parliament any bills or secondary legislation for which they have responsibility. If asked any question in Parliament, however, or asked to produce any document by the Parliament which relates to the operation of the system of criminal prosecution in a particular case, they may decline to do so on the grounds that it might prejudice criminal proceedings in that case or would otherwise be contrary to the public interest.

The First Minister, having obtained the agreement of the Parliament to their nominations, recommends the appointments to the Queen. They may resign at any time and must do so if the Scottish Government loses the confidence of the Parliament. If, however, the Lord Advocate has to resign as a result of a vote of no confidence in the Scottish Government, she or he is deemed to remain in office as head of the systems of criminal prosecution and investigation of deaths in Scotland until a successor is appointed.[24]

This is one of a number of provisions in the SA 1998 designed to safeguard the independence of the Scottish Law Officers. In addition, it is outwith the legislative competence of the Scottish Parliament to attempt to pass an Act which contains a provision that would remove the Lord Advocate from his/her position as head of the systems of criminal prosecution and investigation of deaths in Scotland.[25] Any decisions taken by the Lord Advocate in either of those capacities must be taken by him/her independently. The independence of the Scottish judicial system is further enhanced by section 1 of the Judiciary and Courts (Scotland) Act 2008 which places a specific duty to uphold the continued independence of the judiciary on a number of persons, including the First Minister and other Scottish Ministers, the Lord Advocate, and members of the Scottish Parliament (MSPs).

JUNIOR SCOTTISH MINISTERS

The First Minister may also appoint junior Scottish Ministers.[26] They are not technically members of the Scottish Government as defined in the SA 1998, Section 44 although they are considered as such. Section 49 of the SA 1998, which deals with their appointment, does not set any limit to their number. In the UK Government there is a statutory limit. Not more than ninety-five members of the House of Commons may hold ministerial office. The purpose of this (in theory, at least) is to prevent the executive from dominating the legislature in Parliament. Political considerations and public opinion no doubt work together to ensure that a reasonable limit is set in the Scottish Parliament and, in the first Parliament, the number of junior Ministers appointed was ten. In the Parliament elected in 2003, seven junior Ministers were appointed. Ten junior Ministers were appointed by the SNP administration after 2007 (although this was accompanied by a substantial reduction in the number of 'senior' Ministers). Junior Scottish Ministers are appointed in the same way as Scottish Ministers are. Twelve Junior Ministers were appointed after the 2016 general election.

With the agreement of the Parliament, the First Minister recommends their appointment to the Queen. They, too, hold office at Her Majesty's pleasure, may be removed from office by the First Minister, may resign at any time, and must do so if the Scottish Executive loses the confidence of the Scottish Parliament.

PARLIAMENTARY LIAISON OFFICERS

A small number of MSPs may be appointed as Parliamentary Liaison Officers (often referred to as 'PLOs'), previously known as Ministerial Parliamentary Aides. As the earlier title suggests, they assist Cabinet Ministers in the discharge of their parliamentary duties. These are very junior posts and attract no additional financial allowance. They are roughly equivalent to Parliamentary Private Secretaries in the UK Government. The role became controversial when Parliamentary Liaison Officers were appointed to the committees that scrutinise the policies and work of the Ministers to whom they are aides. Following the 2016 general election, the First Minister attempted to continue this practice but, following severe criticism from other political parties and from the media, change was made and the Parliamentary Liaison Officers are no longer to be appointed to the principal scrutiny committee that scrutinises the ministerial portfolio to which the Parliamentary Liaison Officers are attached. This change has been added to the Ministerial Code.

The Ministerial Code

The Scottish Ministerial Code provides a code of conduct and guidance on procedures for the First Minister, Cabinet Secretaries. Junior ScottishMinisters, the Law Officers and Parliamentary Liaison Officers. All Scottish Ministers are expected to behave in a way that upholds the highest standards of propriety. They are expected to observe the Seven Principles of Public Life which were defined in 1995 by the Committee on Standards in Public Life (the Nolan Committee). These are:

- selflessness
- integrity
- objectivity

- accountability
- openness
- honesty
- leadership

The Code is to be read against the overarching duty on Ministers to comply with the law, to uphold the administration of justice, and to protect the integrity of public life.

The Code is in eleven sections. It was last updated in 2016. The general principles are set out in section 1(2). They include: the principle of collective responsibility; the duty to account for, and be held to account for, their policies, decisions, and actions as Ministers; the duty to give accurate and truthful information to the Parliament; to be as open as possible with the Parliament and the public; the duty to ensure no conflict arises between public duties and private interests; to uphold the political neutrality of the Civil Service.

In addition, the Code provides that, in all their dealings with the Parliament, Ministers should seek to uphold and promote the key principles which guided the work of the Consultative Steering Group in 1998. These are: sharing power; accountability; openness; accessibility; and equal opportunities.

SCRUTINY OF THE SCOTTISH GOVERNMENT BY THE SCOTTISH PARLIAMENT

Questions[27]

There are arrangements for the answering of Written Questions and various categories of questions for oral answer.

Written Questions

Written questions may be answered by the First Minister, the Lord Advocate, or by a Minister or junior Minister as appropriate. Questions must be admissible (comply with various requirements) and must be lodged with the Clerk of the Parliament. Normally an answer is provided within ten working days. The answer, along with the original question, is published in the Official Report. There is no limit to the number of questions that a member may ask but members are asked not to abuse this by lodging too many.

Oral Questions

As is the case of MPs in the UK Parliament, any member of the Scottish Parliament may ask a question of the Scottish Government to be answered in the Parliament. Under the Standing Orders (Rule 13) of the Parliament, a question must relate to a matter for which the First Minister, the Scottish Ministers or the Law Officers have a general responsibility, that is, devolved matters. This rule has been stretched on occasion, however, to cover matters, such as defence, which are reserved.

The Scottish Ministers also use 'planted' questions to enable them to make a statement to the Parliament. This is done by arranging for an MSP who is a member of the same political party to lodge a friendly question. This type of question undermines the scrutiny element of questions in Parliament.

First Minister's Questions

Donald Dewar, the first First Minister of the Scottish Parliament, had been a member of the UK Parliament for many years and was steeped in the Westminster traditions. He was keen that the First Minister's Question Time in the Scottish Parliament should be based on the Westminster model. Prime Minister's Question Time in the House of Commons, however, is seen as a bit of a bear pit with many noisy interruptions. Transferring the Westminster model to Scotland has done little to increase public respect for the Scottish Parliament.

The First Minister's Question Time normally takes place on a Thursday and lasts for forty-five minutes. Questioners are limited to one question but are allowed one brief supplementary question.

In addition to First Minister's Question Time, there are arrangements for Portfolio Questions (to Cabinet Secretaries) and General Questions on Wednesdays and Thursdays and for Topical Questions on Tuesdays. There are also arrangements for Emergency, Local, and Urgent questions.

Motions of No Confidence

It is a convention of the UK constitution that the Prime Minister and his/her Ministers resign if they lose a motion of no confidence. The SA 1998 puts this into statutory form. sections 45(2), 47(3)(c), 48(2) and 49(4)(c) require the resignation of the First Minister, the

Scottish Ministers, the Law Officers and Junior Ministers respectively if Parliament resolves that the Scottish Executive no longer enjoys the confidence of the Parliament. If the Parliament subsequently fails to nominate a successor as First Minister, an extraordinary general election has to be called.[28]

Any MSP is able to move a motion of no confidence in the Scottish Executive. The motion must be supported by at least twenty-five other MSPs in order to be included in the business programme of the Parliament. Normally, at least two days' notice of a motion of no confidence should be given but the Parliamentary Bureau may decide that a shorter period is appropriate.[29] Such a motion requires a simple majority of those voting (subject to a quorum) for approval. The Parliament is also able to consider a motion of no confidence in a named Minister. This would not automatically lead to the resignation of the Minister as the SA 1998 does not require this. The position of that Minister might become untenable, however, after losing the confidence of the Parliament, and the First Minister might ask the Minister to resign.

MINISTERIAL FUNCTIONS

Ministers of the UK Government exercise various powers, most of which are conferred on them by an Act of Parliament. A few derive from the common law and are called prerogative powers. As the Scottish Parliament began to pass its own Acts, powers were conferred by these Acts on Scottish Ministers. The SA 1998, however, contains a section that transferred existing prerogative and executive functions relating to devolved matters virtually in their entirety from UK Ministers to Scottish Ministers.[30] This was a sensible provision for the early days of the Scottish Parliament. Many of the early decisions taken by the Scottish Government derived from powers conferred by an Act of the UK Parliament on a Secretary of State, usually the Secretary of State for Scotland. This section enabled the Scottish Ministers to take over immediately without requiring any other piece of empowering legislation.

As the Scottish Parliament started to enact its own legislation, section 52 of the SA 1998 enabled functions to be conferred directly on the First Minister, the Lord Advocate and the Scottish Ministers by Acts of the Scottish Parliament or by subordinate legislation. In the UK Parliament, the duties of Secretaries of State are, in theory, interchangeable and this theory is continued into the Scottish Parliament with the provision that statutory functions may be exercised by any member of the Scottish Government. The acts and omissions of any of them (other than the specific functions conferred on the First Minister or the Lord Advocate) are to be treated as the acts and omissions of each of them. This puts into statutory form the doctrine of collective responsibility.

There are some exceptions to the general rule about the transfer of powers from the UK Ministers to the Scottish Ministers where it makes sense for a UK Minister to share powers with Scottish Ministers – for example, the provision of grants or loans for transport infrastructure, the promotion of exports and the funding of scientific research. UK Ministers also retain the power to make regulations for Scotland in order to implement European Community obligations, and Scottish Ministers have no power to make subordinate legislation or to do any act which is incompatible with EC law or with rights under the European Convention on Human Rights.[31]

COLLECTIVE RESPONSIBILITY

The acceptance of the constitutional doctrine of collective responsibility formed part of the coalition agreement between the Labour Party and the Liberal Democrats,[32] when they agreed that both partners in the coalition would accept that all the business of the Scottish Executive, including decisions, announcements, expenditure plans, proposed legislation and appointments, should be supported collectively by all members of the Executive and that there should be an appropriate level of consultation and discussion to ensure the support of all Ministers. Under the doctrine of collective responsibility, Ministers have the opportunity to express their views frankly as decisions are reached, and opinions expressed and advice given within the Executive remain private. Once a decision is reached, however, it is to be binding on all Ministers. Any Minister who cannot accept a decision of the Executive is expected to resign. In practice, however, the doctrine has occasionally been undermined by the actions of some Ministers who have been unable to support decisions but who, nevertheless, remained in post.[33] The SNP Administrations after 2007 had no political requirement to make any formal declaration of collective responsibility of this type, not being a coalition, but, in practice, it has also applied the same doctrine to its Ministers.

EXECUTIVE DEVOLUTION IN RELATION TO RESERVED MATTERS

The White Paper made it clear that the Scottish Executive was to be responsible for the exercise of certain administrative functions in areas where the law-making powers are reserved to the UK Government. This is termed executive devolution. Prior to devolution, most of these functions were performed by the Secretary of State for Scotland. These included:

- the administration in Scotland of European Structural Funds;
- civil nuclear emergency planning;
- powers and duties in relation to electricity supply;
- administration of firearms licensing;
- establishment and operation of certain public sector pension schemes;
- enforcing medicine legislation;
- designation of casino areas;
- various powers and duties relating to transport.

In most cases these are now transferred to Scottish Ministers for them to exercise instead of UK Ministers. Some are exercisable concurrently by Scottish Ministers and by UK Ministers while others are exercised by a UK Minister but only after consultation with, or with the consent of, the Scottish Ministers.

The original Scotland Act 1998 made provision for additional executive functions to be transferred from the UK Government to the Scottish Administration[34] and, since 1999, there has been a steady stream of statutory instruments passed by the UK Parliament transferring functions in this way. Most of the transfers have been relatively minor[35] but there have also been some major transfers of authority to Scottish Ministers, such as regarding the renewable electricity obligation and the franchising of rail services.[36]

A further substantial extension of executive devolution was introduced by SA 2016 as a result of the recommendations of the Smith Commission. Scottish Ministers were given powers in a number of areas where the legislative power was still retained by the UK Parliament, including the following:

- information sharing regarding social security functions[37]
- the Scottish functions of the Crown Estate Commissioners (subject to the Treasury using the powers given to it in SA 2016 section 36 to transfer them);[38]

- certain powers regarding traffic signs, speed limits and parking;[39]
- various powers concerning the Gaelic Media Service,[40] the Commissioners of Northern Lighthouses,[41] and the Maritime and Coastguard Agency;[42]
- the ability to award a franchise for rail services in Scotland to a public service operator;[43]
- extensive powers to make fuel-poverty support schemes,[44] to place obligations on energy companies to reduce carbon emissions and to reduce home-heating costs,[45] and regarding offshore renewable energy installations;[46]
- powers to make references to the Competition and Markets Authority.[47]

THE APPOINTMENT AND REMOVAL OF JUDGES

The SA 1998 gave the First Minister significant powers over the appointment and removal of judges.[48] The two most senior judges in Scotland are the Lord President of the Court of Session and the Lord Justice-Clerk. The Prime Minister recommends the names of appropriate persons to the Queen but he or she cannot recommend anyone for appointment who has not first been nominated by the First Minister. The First Minister also recommends to the Queen the names of persons for appointment as the other judges of the Court of Session, sheriffs principal and sheriffs but only after consultation with the Lord President.

In practice, until fairly recently, it was the Lord Advocate[49] who selected candidates for appointment as judges and sheriffs and recommended them to the First Minister (or prior to devolution, the Prime Minister). From the earliest days of devolution, however, there was a considerable and growing body of opinion that the appointment of judges should be removed from the political process.

Reflecting these concerns, in the spring of 2000, the Scottish Executive issued a consultation paper on the possibility of a judicial appointments commission.[50] The responses to the consultation paper indicated substantial support for such a body and, in 2001, the Justice Minister announced the establishment of the Judicial Appointments Board for Scotland. The Board was initially set up on an administrative basis in 2002 but was given a statutory foundation by the Judiciary and Courts (Scotland) Act 2008. This provides that the relevant Scottish Minister (including the First Minister) may only appoint, recommend, or nominate an indi-

vidual to a judicial office within the Board's remit[51] if the Board has recommended that individual for appointment to that office.[52] The Minister
concerned may reject that recommendation but he or she has no power
to make an alternative appointment which has not been recommended
by the Board. As far as the two most senior judicial offices are concerned
(the Lord President and the Lord Justice Clerk), the Act provides that
the First Minister must establish a panel[53] to recommend individuals
who are suitable for appointment to fill the vacancy. The First Minister
cannot make a nomination for someone to fill the vacancy until the panel
has made a recommendation. The First Minister is obliged only to 'have
regard' to the panel's recommendation;[54] in practice, it would seem very
difficult for the First Minister not to nominate someone who was not
recommended by the panel although, if the panel recommends more than
one person as suitable, the First Minister would have the power to decide
which name to put forward to the Prime Minister.

The Judicial Appointments Board for Scotland is required to have
lay members whose number must equal the total number of judicial
and legal members.[55] The board's recommendations are to be made on
merit[56] but, subject to this overriding requirement, the board also has to
have regard to the need to encourage diversity in the range of individuals
available for selection to be recommended for appointment to judicial
office.[57] All vacancies are publicly advertised and no candidate is recommended for appointment without being interviewed.

The power to remove a judge of the Court of Session is even more
controversial and provoked a great deal of debate during the passage of
the SA 1998 through the House of Lords. Prior to the establishment of
the Scottish Parliament, there was no power to remove such a judge from
office in Scotland. The position in England is different: a judge may be
removed from office following an address from the House of Commons
and the House of Lords to the Queen. The Scotland Bill as originally
drafted would have allowed the First Minister to recommend to the
Queen the removal of a Court of Session judge and the Chairman of the
Scottish Land Court following a resolution of the Parliament which was
supported by at least two-thirds of the total number of MSPs. These
provisions were amended by the House of Lords to build in a further
stage to protect the independence of the judges.

The position now is that, if there is any question of a judge of the
Court of Session or the Chairman of the Scottish Land Court being
unfit for office through inability, neglect of duty, or misbehaviour, the
First Minister may set up a tribunal of at least three persons, chaired by
a member of the Judicial Committee of the Privy Council, to investigate

and report on the matter.[58] The First Minister must set up such a tribunal if requested to do so by the Lord President of the Court of Session and may do so in other circumstances if it is considered to be necessary. If the tribunal reports, in writing and with reasons, that the judge is unfit for office for one of the reasons given above, the First Minister is to move a resolution before the Parliament that a recommendation should be made to the Queen that the judge be removed from office. The First Minister must obtain the approval of the Parliament but there is now no requirement of a special majority. If the judge to be removed from office is either the Lord President or the Lord Justice Clerk, the First Minister must consult the Prime Minister. The lesser penalty of suspension may be imposed. The detailed procedure which must be followed is now set out in the Judiciary and Courts (Scotland) Act 2008.[59]A tribunal must similarly be established in the case of temporary judges and sheriffs though, here, the decision to remove, if the tribunal reports appropriately, can be made by the First Minister (subject to annulment by the Scottish Parliament in the case of sheriffs).[60]

THE CIVIL SERVICE

Scottish Ministers may appoint such staff as they consider appropriate. These staff are in the Home Civil Service, as are staff serving in other departments of the Scottish Government.[61]The holders of various offices such as the Registrar General of Births, Deaths and Marriages for Scotland and the Keepers of the Records and Registers of Scotland are also in the Home Civil Service as are their staff. The UK Government considers that maintaining a unified Home Civil Service is essential for the preservation of the Union. It also preserves a career structure in the UK for civil servants and ensures that their terms and conditions of service are appropriately protected. Responsibility for the management of that staff ultimately remains with the Minister for the Civil Service (that is, the Prime Minister) but, in practice, responsibility for the day-to-day management of staff is delegated to the Scottish Ministers as happens for UK Government departments.

The departments of the Scottish Government are known as directorates. These are grouped under six Directors-General:

Education, Communities and Justice
Exchequer
Economy

Health and Social Care
Organisational Development and Operations
Constitution and External Affairs

As well as the directorates which have responsibility for service delivery for different areas of Scottish Government, there is also a number of directorates that provide central services for the rest of the Scottish Administration: for example, communications, human resources and corporate services, procurement, and the Scottish Government legal directorate.

THE SCOTTISH PARLIAMENT AND OTHER PUBLIC BODIES

Despite the wide range of services delivered by local and central government, in Scotland, there is a huge range of public services which are delivered by unelected public bodies. Most of these are officially called Non-departmental Public Bodies (NDPBs) but they are popularly known as quangos.

They take a number of different forms. The latest national Public Bodies Directory for Scotland lists them as follow:

- Executive NDPBs (36), including the Scottish Law Commission, Children's Hearings Scotland, and Creative Scotland;
- advisory (6), including the Judicial Appointments Board for Scotland, the Scottish Law Commission and the Local Government Boundary Commission for Scotland;
- tribunals (8), including the Lands Tribunal, the Mental health Tribunal for Scotland and the Parole Board;
- public corporations (4), including Scottish Water, Scottish Canals and Glasgow Prestwick Airport;
- various NHS Bodies (23);
- executive agencies (7) including Disclosure Scotland, Education Scotland and the Scottish Prison Service;
- non-ministerial departments (8) including the Office of the Scottish Charity Regulator, the Scottish Housing Regulator, Food Standards Scotland and Revenue Scotland (created in 2105 to administer and collect Scottish devolved taxes);
- Commissioners and Ombudsmen (6), including the Scottish Public Services Ombudsman, the Scottish Human Rights Commission, and the Standards Commission for Scotland[62]

- Other Significant National Bodies, of which there are twenty-nine, ranging from the Accounts Commission to the Court of Lord Lyon.

The total of national bodies is currently 111 and there are well over 100,000 people employed in them. Many of their chief executives earn more per annum than the First Minister.

There have been many criticisms of public bodies, not the least of which are the lack of direct accountability to the public and the lack of transparency in the appointment of their members and, in the case of some, their large budgets.

Prior to the establishment of the Scottish Parliament, the Labour Party in Scotland had called for 'a bonfire of quangos'. In the White Paper, *Scotland's Parliament*, the UK Government expressed concern at the extent to which vital public services are run by unelected bodies.[63]

Responsibility for all Scottish public bodies whose remits run wholly within devolved areas passed to the Scottish Parliament and Government under the rules governing the Parliament's legislative competence (which have been dealt with above).[64] The Parliament is able to wind them up, alter their remits or merge some of them together. Scottish Ministers have the powers to make appointments to their boards, to fund them and generally direct their activities.

The McIntosh Commission, which was appointed in 1998 by the Secretary of State for Scotland to consider the relationship between the Scottish Parliament and local government, recommended that, in any review of other bodies delivering public services, the option of transfer to local government should always be considered. Likewise, where new services are being developed prior consideration should always be given to whether local government should be the vehicle of delivery, subject to efficiency and cost-effectiveness.[65]

The initial response of the Scottish Government to McIntosh's recommendations was to confirm that, whenever a periodic review of a quango is carried out, the option of the transfer of its functions to local government would be considered as one of the options. In February 2000, the Finance Minister announced a major consultation exercise on the appointment of members to quangos. The key objectives of the procedures for making public appointments system were:[66]

- to ensure public confidence in the appointment process by making it fair, open and transparent with appointments being made on merit;
- to be proportionate, that is, appropriate to the nature of the posts and the weight of their responsibilities;

- to provide clarity and structure;
- to secure quality outcomes;
- to encourage a wider range of people to apply for public appointments;
- to be accessible and informative.

The Scottish Government also wished to increase the number of women and people from an ethnic minority background on public bodies. In June 2001, the Scottish Government issued a White Paper, *Public Bodies: Proposals for Change*. In this, the Scottish Government announced its intention to abolish fifty-two public bodies. Closer inspection of the list, however, revealed that only eleven were to be completely abolished. Of the others, some were to be declassified as public bodies, others (such as the three Water Authorities and NHS Health Boards and Trusts) were to be merged or reorganised, while others were to have their status reviewed. Most of the bodies proposed for abolition were advisory NDPBs rather than the more controversial Executive NDPBs which have big budgets and significant executive functions. There were no proposals to transfer quangos' functions to local government.

Some of the reorganisations and abolitions could be achieved by the Scottish Government without the need for primary legislation while others (bodies which had been set up by statute) could be abolished only by primary legislation. For example, the water authorities were merged under the Water Industry Act 2002. A miscellany of other bodies appeared as candidates for abolition in the Public Appointments and Public Bodies etc. (Scotland) Act 2003. These were:

- Ancient Monuments Board for Scotland
- Historic Buildings Council for Scotland
- Scottish Hospital Trust
- Scottish Medical Practices Committee
- Scottish Conveyancing and Executry Services Board
- Royal Commission on the Ancient and Historical Monuments of Scotland (RCAHMS).

As a result of successful lobbying, the Royal Commission on the Ancient and Historical Monuments of Scotland[67] was removed from the list and survived the cull while the Ancient Monuments Board and Historic Buildings Council, though technically dissolved, re-emerged as the Historic Environment Advisory Council.

The Public Appointments and Public Bodies etc (Scotland) Act 2003 also provides for the appointment of a Scottish Commissioner for Public

Appointments in Scotland whose functions are the regulation and monitoring of appointments to quangos by Scottish Ministers and the investigation of complaints arising from appointments.

The general election of 2007 brought about a change of political control with the formation by the SNP of a minority administration, rebranded as the Scottish Government. Like its predecessor, the Labour–Liberal Democrat coalition Scottish Executive, the new Scottish Government soon set about reorganising Scottish public bodies.

In October 2007, it published a list of 199 national public sector organisations for which it is responsible and committed itself to reducing this number by 25 per cent by 2011 through what is called a Simplification Programme. By March 2009, the number of organisations had been reduced to 165. This included the abolition of twenty-six Justice of the Peace Advisory Committees announced by the previous administration. Some executive agencies, such as the Scottish Agricultural Science Agency, the Scottish Building Standards Agency and the Mental Health Tribunal Agency for Scotland, were abolished as stand-alone agencies and transferred into the Scottish Government. Some new executive NDPS were established, such as the Scottish Legal Complaints Commission and Skills Development Scotland and the Scottish Futures Trust.

The Public Services Reform (Scotland) Act 2010 took the Simplification Programme further. The Deer Commission and the Advisory Committee on Sites of Special Scientific Interest were transferred to Scottish National Heritage, and several other advisory bodies were dissolved. On the other hand, the Act created a new national body for arts, culture and the creative industries, called Creative Scotland, with the consequent dissolution of the Scottish Arts Council and Scottish Screen. Two new scrutiny bodies were established, Social Care and Social Work Improvement Scotland, now known as the Care Inspectorate, and Healthcare Improvement Scotland to replace existing scrutiny bodies in these areas.

Ministers were given additional order-making powers which enable them to modify, confer, abolish, transfer or provide for the delegation of any function of bodies or persons in a long list of existing public bodies.

The bonfire of quangos in Scotland has thus far not amounted to very much. The total number has certainly been reduced but some of that by what might be described as sleight of hand. Most of the executive quangos remain untouched and a few quite useful advisory committees have gone. The Scottish Government has clearly realised, as have other executives before them, that public bodies have a role to play both in advising government and in delivering services.

It should be noted that the Ethical Standards in Public Life etc (Scotland) Act 2000 provides for a model code of conduct for members of the various devolved public bodies. The Standards Commission has powers to censure, suspend or remove from office a member who breaches the code.

CROSS-BORDER PUBLIC AUTHORITIES

Certain public bodies have remits that cover matters some of which are within the legislative competence of the Parliament and others outwith it. Such bodies include the British Wool Marketing Board, UK Sport, the Hazardous Substances Advisory Committee, Visit Britain and many others. These are known as cross-border authorities.[68] The SA 1998 designated sixty-five public bodies as cross-border public authorities. Scottish Ministers have the right to be consulted by their UK counterparts on the appointment of members and officers and on any specific function whose exercise might affect Scotland. The SA 1998 also makes it possible for the exercise of certain functions of cross-border public bodies to be transferred from UK Ministers to Scottish Ministers.[69] It is also possible for the Scottish Parliament to set up separate Scottish bodies to handle the specifically Scottish and devolved aspects of the cross-border authorities' work.

Some public bodies deal solely with matters which are reserved to the UK Parliament. These include the Commission for Equality and Human Rights, the BBC and the Post Office. Though they deal with matters which are reserved, their activities continue to be of great interest to Scots. The Scottish Parliament's Standing Orders enable committees to invite the submission of reports and the presentation of oral evidence[70] to its committees. In certain cases, the Scottish Government may be consulted prior to the appointment of chairpersons or governors. In the case of the BBC Trust member for Scotland, the Scottish Government has to give its agreement to the person selected by the UK Minister for that appointment.[71]

NOTES

1. SA 1998, section 44.
2. SA 1998, section 45(1)

3. The terms of the coalition agreement are to be found in *A Partnership for Scotland: An Agreement for the First Scottish Parliament* (May 1999).
4. The terms of the second coalition agreement are to be found in a *Partnership for a Better Scotland* (May 2003).
5. The number of MSPs elected for each party was as follows: SNP forty-seven, Labour forty-six, Conservative seventeen, Liberal Democrat sixteen, Green two, Independent one. As a result, unless the two principal rivals, SNP and Labour formed a coalition, any coalition would have had to have had the support of at least three parties to form a majority. The SNP's Alex Salmond was eventually elected first minister by forty-nine votes to the forty-six received by the outgoing first minister, Jack McConnell, with the Green MSPs supporting Alex Salmond and the Conservatives, Liberal Democrats, and Independent MSPs abstaining.
6. The nearest that the Parliament came to giving serious consideration to such a motion was probably in January 2009 when, following the SNP's initial failure to have its budget passed, the Labour Party indicated it might put forward a vote of no confidence in the Scottish government but, ultimately, it decided to accept an amended budget.
7. The rules relating to the nomination of the first minister and the appointment of members of the Scottish government are contained in Chapter 4 of the Parliament's Standing Orders.
8. The procedures relating to the selection of the first minister are to be found in rule 11.10 of the Parliament's Standing Orders.
9. SA 1998, section 45(4).
10. SA 1998, section 45(2).
11. See Chapter 3, p. 46.
12. SA 1998, sections 47–9.
13. SA 1998, section 48.
14. SA 1998, section 52(5)(a).
15. See *Partnership for a Better Scotland* (May 2003).
16. SA 1998, section 47(2).
17. The procedures relating to the appointment of Scottish ministers are found in Rule 4.6 of the Parliament's Standing Orders.
18. SA 1998, section 47(3).
19. See Chapter 3.
20. For example, the comments by one of Scotland's most senior judges, Lord McCluskey (a former Labour Solicitor General) in The Herald, 27 December 1999.
21. SA 1998, section 48.
22. The procedures relating to the appointment, removal and parliamentary participation of the Law Officers are contained in Rules 4.3–4.5 of the Parliament's Standing Orders.
23. SA 1998, section 27.
24. SA 1998, section 48(3).

25. SA 1998, section 29(2)(e).
26. SA 1998, section 49.
27. The rules about questions are to be found in Chapter 13 of the Standing Orders.
28. SA 1998, section 3(b)
29. The procedures relating to motions of no confidence are found in Rule 8.12 of the Parliament's Standing Orders.
30. SA 1998, section 53.
31. SA 1998, section 57.
32. Partnership for a Better Scotland (May 2003), section 5.
33. Mike Watson, the MSP for Glasgow Cathcart who was a Minister in 2002/03, found himself unable to accept a Cabinet decision to close a hospital in Glasgow. He did not resign but, following the election in 2003, he was not reappointed as a minister.
34. SA 1998, section 63.
35. For example, SI 1999/1750, SI 1999/3321, SI 2000/1563, SI 2002/1630, SI 2003/415, SI 2004/2030, SI 2005/849, SI 2006/304, SI 2006/1040, SI 2006/3258, SI 2007/2915, SI 2008/1776.
36. SI 2001/3504, SI 2001/954
37. SA 2016, sec 34
38. Transferred by section 36 of SA 2016. One effect of this transfer is that, as the functions concerned will no longer be exercised by the Crown Estate Commissioners, these functions will no longer be reserved by virtue of the general reservation concerning the Crown. See Schedule 5, Part I, paragraph 1(a) of SA 1998 and section 36(4) of SA 2016.
39. SA 2016, sections 41–3.
40. SA 2016, section 54.
41. SA 2016, section 55.
42. SA 2016, section 56.
43. Unlike in England and Wales, where a passenger rail franchise cannot be awarded to a public service operator. See section 57, SA 2016.
44. SA 2016, section 58.
45. SA 2016, section 59. See also Section 60 regarding the apportionment of targets.
46. SA 2016, section 62.
47. SA 2016, section 63.
48. SA 1998, section 95.
49. For more information on the Lord Advocate, see p. 126.
50. Judicial Appointments: An Inclusive Approach (2000).
51. Effectively, all judicial offices other than the Lord President or Lord Justice Clerk [see Section 10(1)].
52. Ibid. section 11(1).
53. Ibid. section 18(1).
54. Ibid. section 18(5).

55. Ibid. Schedule 1, paragraph 4(1).
56. Ibid. section 12(2).
57. Ibid. section 14(1).
58. SA 1998, section 95.
59. Judiciary and Courts (Scotland) Act 2008 sections 33–5.
60. Judiciary and Courts (Scotland) Act 2008 sections 37–8.
61. SA 1998, section 51.
62. See Chapters 4 and 8.
63. *Scotland's Parliament* Paragraph 6.7.
64. See Chapter 2.
65. The McIntosh Report, paragraph 62.
66. Scottish Executive, *Appointments to Public Bodies in Scotland: Modernising the System, Consultation Paper* Chapter 2.
67. RCAHMS did not survive as a separate body for much longer, however. In 2015 it was merged with Historic Scotland to become Historic Environment Scotland.
68. SA 1998, section 88.
69. SA 1998, section 89.
70. Standing Orders of the Scottish Parliament, Rule 12.4.
71. SA 1998, section 90A.

CHAPTER SEVEN

Relations between Scotland and Westminster

INTRODUCTION

As we have seen in Chapter 2, the Scottish Parliament has its powers devolved to it by the UK Parliament, and the UK Parliament has not relinquished its sovereignty. The Scottish Parliament is, therefore, a body subordinate to the UK Parliament. The SA 2016 introduced provisions designed to 'entrench' the existence of the Scottish Parliament in the UK constitutional order, stating that 'The Scottish Parliament and the Scottish Government are a permanent part of the United Kingdom's constitutional arrangements', and that they should not be abolished 'except on the basis of a decision of the people of Scotland voting in a referendum'.[1] Moreover, these provisions are described as signifying 'the commitment of the Parliament and Government of the United Kingdom to the Scottish Parliament and the Scottish Government', and it was made clear by Ministers at the time of their introduction that this was a 'political declaration of permanence'.[2] It remains the case, however, that the UK Parliament has retained its supremacy and sovereignty over the Scottish Parliament and could abolish the Scottish Parliament if it so wished. It can nevertheless be expected that, as long as the Scottish Parliament remains popular as an institution with the Scottish people, the UK Parliament is unlikely to take such drastic action. Nevertheless, the UK Parliament retains some important controls over the Scottish Parliament.

LEGISLATIVE AND EXECUTIVE CONTROLS

As has been explained in Chapter 2,[3] two areas reserved to the UK Parliament by Schedule 5 to the Scotland Act 1998 (SA 1998) are the Union of the Kingdoms of Scotland and England and the Parliament of the UK, and most of the provisions of the SA 1998 are protected from modification by Schedule 4. A Scottish Government dominated by parties in favour of independence, therefore, would not be able to pass a valid Act of the Scottish Parliament declaring Scottish independence. Indeed, as a decision on independence would clearly affect a reserved matter, it is debatable whether it would even be in the competence of the Scottish Parliament to agree to hold a referendum on independence.

The SA 1998 sets out a complex pattern of provisions designed to prevent the Scottish Parliament from passing a bill, and Scottish Ministers from taking action which would either be beyond the powers given by the Act or which the UK Government would consider to be against the interests of UK defence or national security. As has already been discussed in Chapter 5, the Advocate General for Scotland, who is a Law Officer of the UK Parliament, has the power, under section 33(1) of the Act, to refer the question as to whether a bill or any provision of a bill is within the legislative competence of the Scottish Parliament to the UK Supreme Court for decision. This approach dictates that the final decision is made by judges.

In some circumstances, a political, rather than a judicial, approach is considered appropriate. A Secretary of State of the UK Parliament has the power under the SA 1998, section 35 to make an order prohibiting the Presiding Officer from submitting a bill for Royal Assent if he or she believes it would be incompatible with the UK's international obligations or its defence or national security interests. This power is also available to a Secretary of State if a bill makes modifications to the law concerning reserved matters, as it can do in certain limited circumstances,[4] and he or she is concerned such modifications may adversely affect the operation of that law.[5] A similar power is given to a Secretary of State under section 58(4).

Similarly, under sections 58(1)–(3), a Secretary of State may prevent a member of the Scottish Executive from taking a proposed action or may require such a member to take action under certain circumstances. The circumstances cover situations where a UK Minister has reasonable grounds for believing that a member of the Scottish Government is about to act in a way which is incompatible with any international obligation. On the other hand, if he or she believes that some action is required for giving effect to an international obligation, a Secretary of State can direct by order that the action be taken by a member of the Scottish Government. Such an action might even include introducing a bill in the Scottish Parliament though it is difficult to see how MSPs, particularly those from political parties different from that of the UK Government, could be forced to vote for such a bill. In that case, the UK Government would probably fall back on the power of the UK Parliament, described in the following paragraphs, to make laws for Scotland and pass the bill itself. Such a situation would lead to a serious political confrontation between the two governments and, no doubt, strenuous endeavours would be made behind the scenes to avoid such a crisis. An order made under any of the provisions of section 58 must contain reasons.[6]

In addition, there are powers shared between UK Ministers of the Crown and Scottish Ministers[7] which need to be handled by liaison arrangements. Functions in relation to the observation and implementation of European Union rights and rights under the European Convention on Human Rights continue in the main to be dealt with by UK Ministers.[8]

As well as this set of provisions giving the UK Government the ability to intervene in would-be legislation of the Parliament or actions of Scottish Ministers, the UK Government also has the much more direct ability to take action in Scottish matters as a result of section 28(7) of the SA 1998 which states in unequivocal terms that the power given to the Parliament does not affect the power of the UK Parliament to make laws for Scotland. Such a power allows the UK Parliament, if it were to wish to do so, not only to pass laws in relation to devolved matters but also to change the SA 1998 itself and so change the powers of the Scottish Parliament or Scottish Ministers.

In fact, notwithstanding the wide range of powers available to the UK Government to prevent legislation or actions by the Scottish Parliament or Government of which it disapproved, they have never been used. As we shall see later in this book,[9] the few successful challenges that there have been so far have been initiated by private individuals or corporate bodies rather than by other governmental bodies.

THE 'SEWEL CONVENTION' AND UK LEGISLATION ON DEVOLVED MATTERS

When the Scottish Parliament was set up, it was widely expected that these provisions allowing the UK Parliament to legislate on issues devolved to the Scottish Parliament would be used rarely[10] and that the SA 1998, section 28(7) was more likely to come into play in the event of some constitutional crisis setting the Scottish Parliament and Executive at odds.

It was always envisaged, however, that there could be instances where it would be more convenient for legislation on devolved matters to be passed by the UK Parliament.[11] The UK Government made it clear during the passage of the Scotland Bill through the UK Parliament that it was its expectation that this power would be used only with the agreement of the Scottish Parliament. This position was spelt out in the debate in the House of Lords on the Scotland Bill when the then Government Minister, Lord Sewel, stated that [the government] 'would expect a convention to be established that Westminster would not normally legislate with regard to devolved matters in Scotland without the consent of the Scottish parliament'.[12]

This convention, very soon to become known as the 'Sewel Convention', has, in fact, come into play much more regularly than one imagines its author expected. Westminster's power to legislate on devolved matters has been used extensively but on every occasion with the consent of the Scottish Parliament expressed through a motion agreeing that the measure in question should be considered by the UK Parliament. These motions have come to be known as 'Sewel motions' or, more formally, 'Legislative Consent Motions', in that they signify the consent of the Scottish Parliament to the UK Parliament legislating on the matter in question. In the first term of the Scottish Parliament (1999–2001), the Sewel motion procedure was used on forty occasions, and the rate of use scarcely dropped in the second term when it was used on thirty-nine occasions. Even after the election of the SNP Administration in 2007, the rate of use of the Sewel motion did not drop significantly. In the period of SNP minority government from 2007 to 2011, Sewel motions were used on thirty-two occasions. That small drop may simply have reflected the smaller amount of legislation the SNP was able to take through the Parliament, compared with its 'majority coalition' predecessors. In the period of SNP majority government from 2011 to 2016, the rate of use of Sewel motions increased slightly, being used on thirty-eight occasions.[13] The status of Sewel motions was further enhanced following the report by the Smith Commission established after the 2014 Scottish independence referendum. That body recommended that 'The Sewel Convention will be put on a statutory footing.'[14] This recommendation was put into legislation in the SA 2016 which amended Section 28 of the SA 1998 by qualifying the terms of subsection 28(7) (restating the UK Parliament's overriding power to legislate for Scotland) with a new subsection 28(8) in the following terms: 'But it is recognised that the Parliament of the United Kingdom will not normally legislate with regard to devolved matters without the consent of the Scottish Parliament'.

As soon as an amendment of this nature to the SA 1998 was first proposed, however, there was considerable debate as to whether subsection 28(8) could have any practical legal effect. The position was made clear beyond any doubt in the 2017 Supreme Court decision on the process that the UK Government would have to follow to trigger the Article 50 process to commence formally the UK's withdrawal from the European Union following the Brexit referendum.[15] In that case (the *Miller* case), (which was substantially about whether the government required Parliamentary approval to trigger Article 50), the Lord Advocate (acting, of course, as the Scottish Government's Law Officer) argued that the UK Government, as well as obtaining approval from the UK Parliament, would also engage the Legislative Consent Motion convention. It therefore also required the consent of the Scottish Parliament to the triggering of Article 50 (though he also accepted, somewhat confusingly, that the courts would have to accept the validity of such an Act if it were passed by the UK Parliament *without* the consent of the Scottish Parliament). The Supreme Court's answer was robust. The consent of the devolved legislatures was not required for the passage of such an Act. The court stated that 'we do not underestimate the importance of constitutional conventions' and recognised that 'The Sewel Convention has an important role in facilitating harmonious relationships between the UK Parliament and the devolved legislatures". However, 'the policing of its scope and the manner of its operation does [*sic*] not lie within the constitutional remit of the judiciary, which is to protect the rule of law.[16]

THE USE OF THE SEWEL CONVENTION IN PRACTICE

Notwithstanding its status as a convention rather than as a rule of law on which the courts can rule, there is a number of reasons why the use of Sewel motions has proved attractive to government in both Edinburgh and Westminster. First, there are many occasions in which UK bills deal with matters that are undoubtedly reserved in general but have a bearing on, and require, changes in devolved legislation to make them fully effective in Scotland. Good examples of such legislation are UK Acts of Parliament dealing with immigration and asylum matters, which are reserved, but which legislation also required changes in certain provisions devolved to the Scottish Parliament, for example. in housing, education and social work.[17]

Second, there are areas of policy where both the UK and the Scottish Governments have felt that a UK-wide approach to the issue concerned would be more effective than if separate approaches were to

be pursued in Scotland and England. An early example of such legislation was the Food Standards Act 1999 which established a Food
Standards Agency. The legislation passed through the UK Parliament
after the Scottish Parliament had acquired its full powers, and food
safety is a matter that is devolved to the Scottish Parliament. The UK
and Scottish Governments decided, however, that it would be appropriate for the legislation to be introduced on a UK-wide basis, if the
Scottish Parliament consented, as it duly did. It should be noted that
the Food Standards Agency was established with a separate Scottish
executive machinery and advisory committee, and had to report to both
the Scottish and UK Parliaments. The example of the Food Standards
Agency also illustrates how the use of a Sewel motion is not irreversible
and does not detract from the underlying division of powers between the
UK and Scottish Parliaments. It was made clear in the Food Standards
Act 1999 that it did not detract from the Scottish Parliament's right to
legislate in the area of food safety if it so wished, and that is precisely
what the Scottish Government did some sixteen years after the passage
of the 1999 Act. Following organisational changes in the delivery of the
food-safety regime in England and Wales, and also some high-profile
examples of failures in the food-safety regime, the Scottish Government
decided after consultation that the functions of the Food Standards
Agency would be transferred, in Scotland, to a new independent Scottish
agency, Food Standards Scotland. This policy decision was brought into
effect by the passage of the Food (Scotland) Act 2015. It should be noted
that, because this legislation was entirely within devolved competence, a
Sewel motion did not have to be passed by the Scottish Parliament (even
though one had been required to allow the UK Parliament to give the
original Food Standards Agency functions in Scotland), nor did the UK
Parliament need to pass legislation to amend the UK Food Standards
Act 1999 to allow Food Standards Scotland to take over those functions
of the Food Standards Agency.[18]

It should be noted, also, that it has become accepted that a Sewel
motion is appropriate not just when the UK Parliament is considering
legislation on devolved matters but also where it is proposed to alter the
legislative competence of the Parliament or the executive competence
of Scottish Ministers.[19] In many cases, the legislative proposal before
the UK Parliament may well do all of those things. Of the 111 Sewel
motions passed in the Scottish Parliament sessions from 1999 to 2016,
ninety included some measure legislating on devolved matters (in some
cases of a very minor nature but in others of much more significance).
Though only three proposed to alter the legislative competence of the

Parliament (two of which related to what eventually became the SA 2012 and the SA 2016), eighty-one concerned proposals to alter the executive competence of Scottish Ministers and, in the vast majority of those cases, they were made alongside proposals for the UK Parliament to legislate on devolved matters.[20] (It should be noted that in all but a handful of cases, the alteration of the legislative or executive competence concerned had the effect of extending devolved powers.) The wish to ensure a UK-wide approach by government has also been evident in measures seeking to tackle serious crime and international crime where, on a number of occasions since 1999, the UK Parliament has passed measures that include sometimes extensive provisions affecting matters which fall within the powers of the Scottish Parliament, for example, the Anti-Terrorism, Crime and Security Act 2001, and the Terrorism, Prevention and Investigatory Measures Act 2011. A striking example of such a measure was the Proceeds of Crime Act 2002 which was notable for the considerable extent to which it included separate Scottish provisions, in a UK bill, to take account of the different Scottish legal system. Other areas in which legislation on devolved matters has been passed by Westminster include those dealing with the UK's international obligations that have consequences for both reserved and devolved matters, for example, the International Criminal Court Act 2001.

Another reason why the use of Sewel motions can be attractive is that, if the Scottish Government wishes to introduce legislation in Scotland to parallel legislative initiatives which are taking place elsewhere, in England, it does not need to put aside time in the Scottish Parliament's programme to allow for the passage of essentially the same legislation. That avoids a situation where such parallel legislation could not be introduced as quickly in Scotland because of lack of Parliamentary time, or at the expense of other elements within the Scottish Government's programme. Passing Scottish legislation through Westminster also has the advantage for the Scottish Government that such legislation cannot be challenged as being ultra vires, whereas Scottish Parliament legislation can be challenged on the grounds that it goes beyond the powers of the Scottish Parliament. It could therefore be an attractive route to follow in the case of legislation that the Scottish Government fears might be challenged in the courts as being beyond its powers.[21]

From time to time, regular use of these motions has been disputed, particularly though not exclusively, by Scottish nationalists who have objected that the procedure has the effect of taking decision away making from the Scottish Parliament.[22] As we have seen, however, since the SNP formed its first Administration in 2007, the Scottish Government and Parliament have continued to make regular use of the Sewel motion procedure, the official position of the SNP Government being that, as long as the current constitutional arrangements are maintained, the procedure is an important part of the framework of relationships between Westminster and Holyrood.[23]

There has also been objection, and this time not just from nationalists, to the fact that the terms of the Sewel motion which gives initial agreement to the UK Parliament legislating on a devolved matter are normally very broad. Even though such a motion is normally accompanied by a memorandum setting out the purpose and effect of the proposed Westminster bill in more detail, which memorandum can be the subject of debate in the Scottish Parliament in committee, it does not appear that there is always extensive debate in committee on the terms of such memorandums. Moreover, the eventual legislation which emerges from Westminster may eventually be amended to a substantial degree so that it varies considerably from the legislation that the Scottish Parliament originally thought it was consenting to being dealt with at UK level. Though it has been accepted by government at both Westminster and Scottish levels that, if there are substantial changes made at Westminster subsequent to the agreement to a Sewel motion by the Scottish Parliament, the Scottish Parliament might have the opportunity to look at the issue again, this has in practice happened rarely.[24] On the other hand, the fact that the use of Sewel motions is now well established means that any attempt by Westminster to use its powers to legislate on devolved Scottish matters without the consent of the Scottish Parliament expressed through a 'Sewel motion' would stand out much more clearly as a measure that was being imposed on Scotland without Scottish consent. To take such a course of action would therefore be liable to cause political difficulties for any UK Government that did take such a drastic step. Following the decision of the Supreme Court in the *Miller* case referred to above, however, it is clear that the provisions regarding Sewel motions apply strictly to devolved matters only. They cannot be relied upon to give the Scottish Parliament even a non-binding consultative role, let alone a constitutional right, requiring its consent to any other matters which affecting Scotland might concern the Scottish Parliament.

The fact that Sewel motions have been regularly used since 1999, by both Labour/Liberal Democrat and SNP Governments, majority and minority alike, suggests that they are now an established feature in the post-devolution landscape of Scottish Government, particularly now that they have been given a statutory foundation by section 28 (8).

In contrast to the regular use of the Sewel motion procedure, the UK Government has not found it necessary to make any use of the various provisions described above[25] allowing it to stop the passage of proposed legislation through the Scottish Parliament, or to intervene in the activity of Scottish Ministers. During the earlier years of the Scottish Parliament's existence, it was suggested by some that this was due, at least in part, to the fact that the leading political force at both UK and Scottish Government levels was identical, viz. the Labour Party. The fact that the use of Sewel motions has continued unabated under SNP Government in Scotland since 1999, however, suggests that as much of the activity of government and the political establishment, still takes place at a UK, or at least a British, level, the Scottish electorate may at times be attracted by policies being promoted in England. That appears to be the case notwithstanding the growth of devolved political institutions in many parts of the UK. That may, in turn, influence Scottish Governments, of all political colours, to introduce policy initiatives broadly similar to those being promoted elsewhere in the UK. There is, it has been suggested, an inevitable pressure for uniformity which will tend to limit deviation from the UK norm in the case of legislation and government activity alike.[26]

LIAISON ARRANGEMENTS

If the various executive and legislative controls described above were ever to become used on a frequent basis, that would be an indication that the devolution settlement was under strain. The clear hope of the government when it launched its proposals for a Scottish Parliament was that a good working relationship between the UK Government and the Scottish Executive would allow areas of difficulty to be dealt with at an early stage, through joint working, consultation, and other more informal mechanisms, and thereby avoid the need for what would almost inevitably be a controversial use by central government of its ultimate executive and legislative supremacy. To put such arrangements on a firm footing, the UK Government entered into a number of agreements with the Scottish Ministers (and the other devolved administrations in the UK) which seek to set out the terms on which the different administrations will work together, at both political and official levels.[27]

Though the texts establishing these arrangements described them as 'agreements', it should be noted that it is clearly stated that the agreements should not be legally binding. It is also clear that the agreements are not intended to give either the various administrations which are signatories to them, nor indeed any other individual or corporate person, any rights that they can enforce through legal proceedings. They are, instead, statements of principle, intended to be 'binding in honour only'. Notwithstanding their non-binding nature, however, the various agreements are of great practical significance in setting down the basis on which the devolved administrations will work with the UK Government. Moreover, the very terminology of the agreements is clearly designed to give them a special status, marking them out as having a constitutional significance beyond the ordinary government document. Indeed, although the agreements make it clear that they do not create new legal rights and obligations, one might expect that, in due course, attempts could be made in court proceedings to suggest that they can at least be used to provide a background against which a particular action of a Minister can be judged though, so far, there does not seem to have been any attempt to do so.

The main elements of these arrangements are described below.

The Memorandum of Understanding

The principal agreement is the Memorandum of Understanding which sets out the principles that are to underlie relations between the UK Government and the devolved administrations, and contains a number of important provisions.

- It commits the various administrations to seek to alert each other to relevant developments within their areas of responsibility; to give appropriate consideration to the views of each other's administration; and, where appropriate where there is shared responsibility, to establish arrangements that allow for policies to be drawn up jointly between the administrations.
- It makes provisions for the exchange of information, statistics and research, and commits each administration to provide any information that may reasonably be required by another administration.
- It places on each of the administrations a responsibility to respect any confidentiality restrictions imposed by the provider of any information.
- It restates the convention that the UK Parliament would not normally legislate on devolved matters without the agreement of the devolved legislature. It states that the UK Parliament retains the right to discuss any devolved matter, and similarly the Scottish Parliament, and the other devolved assemblies, will be entitled

to debate non-devolved matters. The UK Government commits itself, however, to encourage the UK Parliament to bear in mind the primary responsibility of devolved legislatures and administrations in these fields; and the devolved executives will encourage each devolved legislature to bear in mind the responsibility of the UK Parliament in these matters.[28]

- It affirms that the legal controls over the Scottish Parliament and the other devolved assemblies are to be used by the UK Government as a last resort only. It sets out a detailed dispute avoidance and resolution procedure, in the hope that matters can be resolved amicably between the administrations concerned.
- It restates, as a matter of law, that international relations and relations with the European Union remain the responsibility of the UK Government and Parliament. It recognises, however, that the devolved administrations will have an interest in international and European policy-making in relation to devolved matters, notably where implementing action by the devolved administrations may be required.

The Joint Ministerial Committee

The Memorandum also established a Joint Ministerial Committee. This comprises the UK Prime Minister, the Scottish, Welsh and Northern Ireland First Ministers, (together in all cases with a deputy or other colleague) and the Secretaries of State for Northern Ireland, Scotland, and Wales, together with other members of the various administrations as appropriate. It was originally envisaged that the Joint Ministerial Committee would meet in this structure on a plenary basis at least once a year but, in practice, it has met much less frequently.[29] Indeed, after its meeting in 2002, it did not meet again until June 2008. In addition, the Joint Ministerial Committee may meet in other 'functional' formats: for example, if dealing with environment issues, it will be made up of the relevant environment Ministers, and, if agriculture, the relevant agriculture Ministers, and meetings of this type have been more frequent. Indeed, the plenary Joint Ministerial Committee which met in June 2008 established an additional format for meetings, the JMC (Domestic), which met in March 2009 to discuss welfare issues, and, in May 2009, dealt with migration.[30]

The Joint Ministerial Committee, in whatever format, is to meet for two purposes: first, to take stock of the way that devolution is working, either generally or in a particular area; and, second, to deal with particular problems between two or more administrations (if other attempts to resolve them have been unsuccessful). Meetings of the Joint Ministerial Committee, in the appropriate functional format, are held at the request of the UK Government or any of the devolved administrations. The committee is staffed by a Joint Secretariat, and is shadowed by a committee of officials from the various administrations. The secretariat and committee prepare matters for meetings, and also allow for contact and discussion at official level on the manner in which the devolution arrangements are working, again both in general terms and in the context of any particular difficulty that might arise. In practice, potential differences between the various administrations have been resolved at official level in the secretariat, or the committee of officials, rather than in the Joint Ministerial Committee itself.

The Concordats

Accompanying the Memorandum and the Joint Ministerial Committee are the concordats which seek to set out detailed working arrangements between the different administrations. Concordats were drawn up shortly after the first elections to the Scottish Parliament and the National Assembly for Wales to deal with matters affecting all the devolved administrations with the aim of providing a broadly similar framework applicable to them all. These cover the following areas of government activity:[31]

- Co-ordination of European Union Policy Issues
- Financial Assistance to Industry
- International Relations

The concordats on the Co-ordination of European Policy issues, and on International Relations, are discussed in Chapter 11 below. The concordat on Financial Assistance to Industry was produced to fulfil commitments made in the White Papers 'Scotland's Parliament' and a 'Voice for Wales' that the devolved powers to give financial assistance to industry would be subject to common UK guidelines, and consultation arrangements to be set out in a published concordat. It includes a number of provisions requiring the different administrations to consult on proposals for new legislation, and on particular cases where an administration plans to offer financial assistance to large investments which breach EU financial limits and involve relocation from one part of the UK to another; and, more generally, where two or more parts of the UK are in competition with each other for inward investment.

In addition to these broad-ranging concordats, it was also agreed that bilateral concordats be set up between individual UK Government departments and their Scottish and Welsh counterparts to deal with working relationships on a more detailed basis, and a large number of such agreements have been drawn up.[32] Such agreements can be entered into by two or more administrations as and when they are required.

Devolution Guidance Notes

These various arrangements are backed up by a number of Devolution Guidance Notes produced by the UK Cabinet Office in consultation with the devolved administrations in Scotland, Wales and Northern Ireland.[33] These deal with matters such as the way in which bilateral relations between different administrations should be conducted, correspondence, ministerial accountability, how to conduct parliamentary business when it concerns an item which is the responsibility of a different Parliament or Assembly, and the notification of legislative proposals. It is pointed out in Devolution Guidance Note 1 that, although concordats are intended to regulate many working relationships between different administrations, other, less formal, arrangements (or simply ad hoc arrangements) will be appropriate in many cases and, in practice, such less formal arrangements have been of much more significance in ensuring good working relations between Westminster and the devolved administrations than the more formal liaison machinery set out in the Memorandum of Understanding.[34]

That this is the case is underlined by the infrequency of use of the Joint Ministerial Committee arrangements, as referred to above, and by the fact that no use appears to have been made of the provision in the Memorandum that concordats could be regularly reviewed (even though, in many cases, the functions of the relevant government departments have changed since the concordats were established). As with the overarching Memorandum of Understanding, it is made clear that these notes do not constitute binding agreements or contracts, and do not give rise to legal obligations. Rather, they are intended to 'guide the work of the UK Government', in accordance with the principles set down in the Memorandum of Understanding.

Among other matters, Devolution Guidance Note 1 emphasises that good communications between administrations are essential and, if one administration is planning action that impinges on the responsibilities of another, it should give adequate forewarning. The principal channel of communication between administrations should be through bilateral links between the relevant departments of each administration, at official or ministerial level. Where disagreements or disputes do arise between administrations, they can be referred to the machinery of the Joint Ministerial Committee (JMC) established by the Memorandum of Understanding with a view to settling the matter in line with the agreed procedures.

Devolution Guidance Note 1 has a number of specific provisions dealing with how Parliamentary business should be dealt with when there is a potential overlap between reserved and devolved matters. It states that the UK Government and devolved administrations have agreed to co-operate to enable each party to meet its obligations to its respective Parliament or Assembly, having regard to the principles set out in the Memorandum of Understanding in doing so. It makes clear, however, that it is for the authorities of each legislature to decide whether or not the subject of a question or a proposed debate falls within the remit of that legislature, and how to treat questions and proposed subjects for debate which concern both devolved and non-devolved matters, such as EU business on a devolved matter. It is stated that, as a general principle, the UK Government will normally answer UK Parliamentary questions purely on devolved matters of fact by making it clear that such questions should be addressed to the relevant devolved administration. Similarly, the devolved administrations should make it clear in answer to Parliamentary or Assembly questions in relation to non-devolved matters of fact that such questions should be addressed to the UK Government unless the administration concerned has executive responsibility in the relevant area.

The note restates the UK Government's commitment to the Sewel Convention, and commits itself to alerting the relevant devolved administration(s) to proposals for UK legislation on non-devolved matters in policy fields which may impinge on devolved matters. Each devolved administration is also expected to alert the UK Government to all its legislative proposals. Each administration is also expected to alert the other administrations to legislative proposals in policy fields that fall within the competence of those other administrations.

Devolution Guidance Note 10 sets out in some detail how UK Government departments should seek to give effect to the Sewel Convention in practice. It points out that, although the convention refers to the Scottish Parliament, UK departments will, in practice, deal with the Scottish Executive (now Government). It will be for the Scottish Executive to indicate the view of the Scottish Parliament and to take whatever steps are appropriate to ascertain that view. It reminds UK

Government departments that although a Legislative Consent Motion is only needed for legislative provisions which are specifically for devolved purposes, or which alter the legislative competence of the Parliament or the executive competence of the Scottish Ministers, departments are expected to consult the Scottish Executive on changes in devolved areas of law even though they are only incidental to, or consequential on, provisions made for reserved purposes.

The series of Devolution Guidance Notes also sets out arrangements on a wide range of other matters affecting relations between the UK Parliament and Government, and their devolved counterparts, including on handling correspondence, attendance of UK Ministers and officials at the committees of devolved legislatures, and requests for meetings between Ministers (UK and devolved) and Ministers and members of another legislature, and arrangements for orders to transfer further legislative competence to the Scottish Parliament ('section 30' orders which are discussed above).[35]

In addition to these arrangements, it should also be noted that the Secretary of State for Scotland (as with the other territorial Secretaries of State) was originally envisaged as continuing to play an important role as a channel of communication between the UK Government and the Scottish Executive at the highest level. Indeed, the Memorandum of Understanding gives these Secretaries of State a specific role in trying to resolve differences between the UK Government and a devolved administration before it needs to be considered by the Joint Ministerial Committee. The role of the Secretary of State is also the subject of a specific Devolution Guidance Note (Note 3), and that is considered further in the relevant section later in this chapter.

FINANCIAL CONTROLS

The financing of the Scottish Parliament is dealt with in detail in Chapter 10. Suffice it to say at this point that the UK Government and Parliament retain considerable financial controls over the Scottish Parliament although these have been reduced somewhat by the provisions in the SA 2012 and SA 2016. The biggest single element of finance for the Scottish Government's expenditure is a block grant determined annually by the Treasury. The Treasury also has the power to require the Scottish Ministers to provide any information it may reasonably request.

When originally established, the Scottish Parliament had only very limited tax-raising powers but these were substantially extended, first by the SA 2012 and then by the SA 2016. As yet, however, the Scottish Government has made very limited use of its wider powers over taxation as can be seen from the account given in Chapter 10.

The SA 1998 requires the Scottish Parliament to make provision by legislation for financial control, accounts and audit,[36] and one of the first measures introduced into the Parliament was a bill to deal with such matters[37].

THE OFFICE OF THE SECRETARY OF STATE FOR SCOTLAND

The office of the Secretary of State for Scotland has a long history, dating back to the days before the union of the Scottish and English Parliaments in 1707. After the Jacobite rebellion of 1745, the office lapsed in the following year, and the Lord Advocate became the chief Scottish Minister. This arrangement lasted until 1885 when the office of Secretary for Scotland and a Scottish Office were re-established. In 1892 the Secretary for Scotland was given a seat in the Cabinet and has retained that seat ever since except in time of war. In 1926, the title was changed to that of Secretary of State for Scotland. In 1939, St Andrew's House in Edinburgh was opened as the headquarters of the Scottish Office, and the powers of the Scottish Office were directly vested in the Secretary of State.

There are many references to the Secretary of State in the SA 1998. As has been explained above,[38] the offices of Secretary of State are interchangeable and, in some cases, the powers conferred by the SA 1998 will be exercisable by other Ministers of the Crown. The Secretary of State for Scotland was given many important powers to be exercised in the seven months between the passing of the SA 1998 and the formal opening of the Scottish Parliament by the Queen on 1 July 1999. When, however, the Parliament received its full legislative powers and most of the powers of the Secretary of State were transferred to the Scottish Executive in 1999, the role of the Secretary of State was undoubtedly diminished. The size of the ministerial team was cut to reflect the reduced legislative and executive powers over Scottish matters remaining with the UK Government and Parliament. During the Scottish Parliament's first term, from 1999 to 2003, the two Scottish Secretaries (first John Reid, and then Helen Liddell) emphasised the continuing importance of the post in Scotland's public life, and the post continued to be of some importance in Scotland's political life. Its important role was certainly recognised in Devolution Guidance Note 3 which describes the holder of the post as being 'the custodian of the Scotland Act 1998' who is expected to 'represent the interests of Scotland in Cabinet', particularly in those matters reserved to the government by the Scotland Act. He or she is responsible for the smooth running of the Scotland's devolution settlement and functions as guardian of the Scotland Act. The Secretary of State and any other Scotland Office Minister are normally members of any Cabinet committees and subcommittees which have a bearing on their role.

The continued existence of the post has from time to time, however, been criticised by many commentators and politicians as anomalous after devolution. It was therefore no great surprise when the then Prime Minister, Tony Blair, took the opportunity during a government reshuffle in June 2003 to alter significantly the role of the Secretary of State for Scotland. Though the post remained, it was added to the existing responsibilities of another member of the Cabinet who also represented a Scottish constituency (Alistair Darling, the Secretary of State for Transport). (The post of Secretary of State for Wales was similarly combined with another Cabinet post although the post of Secretary of State for Northern Ireland was retained because of the continuing suspension of devolved government within Northern Ireland at that time.) The Scotland Office (successor to the Scottish Office) was abolished as a separate department and taken under the umbrella of a new Department for Constitutional Affairs now headed by its own Secretary of State. A full-time Junior Minister for Scottish Affairs was retained, normally with the status of Parliamentary undersecretary although this post was similarly located in the new department (and thereafter in the Ministry of Justice).

At the end of 2008, however, the UK Government decided to reappoint a Secretary of State for Scotland who had no other departmental responsibilities, with the appointment of Jim Murphy MP to the post (assisted by a Junior Minister). The reason for this return to the previous arrangement appears to have been the difficulty of a Secretary of State holding two offices avoiding criticism (whether justified or not) that his or her focus on one office detracted from his attention to the other office held. This was a criticism which was made particularly frequently by opposition parties during the period when the Scottish Secretary held as his other post one which inevitably led to a heavy focus on international issues (for example, Douglas Alexander and Des Browne, who combined the post of Secretary of State for Scotland with that of International Development and Defence, respectively). A Secretary of State for

Scotland whose ministerial duties were focused on Scotland only would also to give the UK Government a better opportunity to play a more active part in Scottish politics. The practice of the Secretary of State being a full-time post continued under the subsequent Conservative–Liberal Democrat coalition between 2010 and 2105, and, thereafter, under the majority Conservative administration after 2015. The fact that there was a renewed focus on the future constitutional status of Scotland in relation to the rest of the UK was no doubt a significant factor in the continuation of that practice.

Because only one Conservative MP had been elected from Scotland, it was not surprising that the post was held by a Liberal Democrat MP between 2010 and 2015 (firstly Danny Alexander, for only eighteen days, and thereafter Michael Moore and then Alistair Carmichael). Since 2015, the post has been held by David Mundell who until 2017 was the only Conservative MP from Scotland.[39] Though the Scotland Office is small by comparison with other UK Government departments, it has a high profile, particularly in Scotland. Its output of publicity material, putting the case for Scotland to remain in the UK has been substantial.

ADVOCATE GENERAL FOR SCOTLAND

The devolution arrangements introduced by the SA 1998 transformed the offices which had previously provided legal advice and litigation services in Scotland for the UK Government, the Lord Advocate and the Solicitor General for Scotland, into Scottish Ministers and members of the Scottish Administration. As a consequence, the office of Advocate General for Scotland was created as part of the devolution arrangements. The Advocate General for Scotland has a small number of staff, based in Edinburgh and London. The Advocate General is the UK Government's Law Officer in relation to Scotland. That includes providing legal advice to UK Government departments on policy and legislation affecting Scotland and the Scottish devolution settlement. The Advocate General also has important statutory functions under the SA 1998 which allows the post-holder to intervene to require Scottish Parliament legislation and acts of its Ministers (and those responsible to them) to be scrutinised by the courts if a question of possible unlawfulness arises. Those functions are considered elsewhere in this book.[40]

The Advocates General appointed to date have all been, or become, Queen's Counsel, although there is no statutory requirement that they should have any particular legal qualification. Unlike the Law Officers to the Scottish Government, the post continues to be appointed on a political basis, and all holders so far have been members of one of the political parties in the government of the day. The first office-holder, Lynda Clark QC, was a Labour MP at the time she was appointed, and she continued as such until 2005. She was then appointed to the House of Lords, and continued to hold the office of Advocate General until 2006. All the Advocates General since then have been members of the House of Lords, or have been made life peers on their appointment.

CONCLUSION

The first two terms of the Scottish Parliament showed, therefore, that it was possible for devolution to operate without any major conflict between governments and legislatures at Westminster and in Scotland and, indeed, with hardly any need to make use of the mechanisms set up after 1999 to ensure liaison and co-operation between the two tiers. The use of 'Sewel motions', however, and the changes to the role of the Scottish Secretary, emphasise how in this area, as in many others, Scotland's new constitutional relationship with the rest of the United Kingdom continued to evolve, even without changing any of the parameters of the underlying devolution legislation itself. The substantial changes to the devolution settlement brought about by the SA 2012 and the SA 2016 have changed that context significantly. Their provisions, particularly those in the SA 2016, have introduced substantial complexity into the devolution settlement which, it can be envisaged, may lead to greater potential for conflict and dispute between the UK and Scottish administrations, which will test both the formal and informal mechanisms designed to resolve such disagreements.

There have, of course, been significant differences between the UK and Scottish Governments since the SNP first formed the Scottish Administration in 2007, particularly arising from the 2014 independence referendum and the 2016 referendum on UK membership of the European Union. Such differences, however, have not challenged the structures set up after 1999, modified to a limited extent since then, with the objective of managing disagreements and disputes. Those challenges to the devolution settlement have, for the most part, taken place outside the devolution arrangements themselves, which have proved remarkably resilient in the face of such challenges. In fact, to date, in only four cases has legislation passed by the Parliament been successfully challenged in court proceedings, and none of those challenges was made by either the

Scottish or UK Governments. These challenges are discussed further in Chapter 9 below.

NOTES

1. SA 2016 section 1, inserting new section 63A in SA 1998.
2. See ministerial comments in Committee of the Whole House on the Bill in the House of Lords (Hansard, 8 December 2015).
3. See p. 19.
4. SA 1998, Schedule 4, paragraph 3.
5. SA 1998, section 35.
6. SA 1998, section 58(5).
7. Conferred by section 56, SA 1998. See Chapter 5.
8. SA 1998, section 57.
9. See Chapter 9.
10. Donald Dewar, the first first minister in the Scottish Parliament, said in the House of Commons, when still Secretary of State for Scotland, that there was 'a possibility, in theory, of the UK Parliament legislating across those [devolved] areas, but it is not one which we anticipate or expect'. (Hansard HC Debs, vol. 305, cols 402–3, 28 January 1998).
11. See White Paper *Scotland's Parliament*, paragraph 4.4.
12. HL Debs, 21 July 1998, vol. 592, c. 791.
13. Annex 1 to Written Case of Lord Advocate in the *Miller* case, *R.* (on the application of Miller and another) v. *Secretary of State for Exiting the European Union*, [2017] UKSC 5.
14. Report of the Smith Commission, www.smith-commission.scot, paragraph 21.
15. *R.* (on the application of Miller and another) v. *Secretary of State for Exiting the European Union*, [2017] UKSC 5.
16. Ibid. paragraph 151.
17. See the Immigration and Asylum Act 1999 and the Nationality, Immigration and Asylum Act 2002.
18. Food Standards Act 1999, section 35(3).
19. See Devolution Guidance Note 10, Department for Constitutional Affairs (November 2005), paragraph 4.
20. Annex 1 to Written Case of Lord Advocate in the *Miller* case.
21. See memorandum by Scotland Office to Scottish Parliament Procedures Committee inquiry into the Sewel Convention, Office of the Deputy Prime Minister, October 2002. See also Written Memorandum given in evidence by Professor Alan Page to the House of Lords Select Committee on the Constitution's Inquiry into *Devolution: Inter-Institutional Relations in the United Kingdom*, HL Paper 147, July 2002, p 185, paragraph 12.

22. See, for example, the comments by SNP MSP Mike Russell in Scottish Parliament Official Report, 30 January 2002, c5881–2.

23. See, for example, the evidence given by the SNP Minister for Parliamentary Business, Bruce Crawford, to the House of Commons Justice Committee enquiry into 'Devolution: 10 Years on': 'I think it is because of the attitude we take to Legislative Consent Motions. We are not predisposed to being against Legislative Consent Motions because we have got the settlement we have got. We might like to see Scotland as an independent country but we have got a system that has got to work within the confines of the current constitutional settlement and, therefore, inevitably people who have got the best will of the Scottish people or, indeed, the UK at heart will do their best to make the system work and that is what goes on a general basis.' (5th report of the Justice Committee, 2008–9 session, Evidence paragraph 234.)

24. On these workings of the Sewel Convention, see Page, Alan and Andrea Batey, *Scotland's other Parliament: Westminster legislation about devolved matters in Scotland since devolution*, Public Law, autumn 2002, pp. 501–23; Cabinet Office Devolution Guidance Note 10, https://www.gov.uk/government/uploads/system/uploads/attachment_data/file/60985/post-devolution-primary-scotland.pdf (last accessed 10 April 2017); and Oral Evidence given by George Foulkes MP, Minister of State at the Scotland Office, to House of Commons Scottish Affairs Committee, 7 November 2001, qs 17–18.

25. See p. 146.

26. Page, Alan and Andrea Batey, *Scotland's other Parliament: Westminster legislation about devolved matters in Scotland since devolution*, Public Law, autumn 2002 pp. 521–3.

27. Devolution: memorandum of understanding and supplementary agreements between the United Kingdom Government, Scottish Ministers and the Cabinet of the National Assembly of Wales. Originally published as Cm 5240 in December 2001. Updated in October 2013. The memorandum contains the underlying agreement together with the first 'concordats'.

28. Practical experience suggests these commitments to refrain from such discussion are frequently ignored.

29. See evidence by Deputy Prime Minister John Prescott MP to the House of Lords Select Committee on the Constitution's Inquiry into Devolution: Inter-Institutional Relations in the United Kingdom, HL Paper 147, July 2002, p. 27, q 55.

30. See 'Serving Scotland Better: Scotland and the United Kingdom in the 21st century', Commission on Scottish Devolution, Final Report June 2009, paragraph 4.30

31. The original concordats included one on statistics but this was not included in the October 2013 version of the Memorandum of Understanding and Supplementary Agreements as it was considered that it was no longer necessary because of new legislation which had established

new arrangements for statistical work across the UK (see paragraph 3 of the Memorandum).

32. By early 2002 more than forty such concordats had been drawn up between Westminster and the various devolved administrations, of which eighteen affected Scotland.

33. Published at https://www.gov.uk/guidance/guidance-on-devolution# devolution-guidance-notes

34. See, for example, the Oral Evidence given by Minister for Parliamentary Business, Patricia Ferguson MSP, to the House of Lords Select Committee on the Constitution's Inquiry into Devolution: Inter-Institutional Relations in the United Kingdom, HL Paper 147, July 2002, pp 113–14.

35. See p. 18.

36. SA 1998, section 70.

37. Public Finance and Accountability (Scotland) Act 2000, introduced in the Parliament on 7 September 1999, and enacted 17 January 2000.

38. See earlier in this chapter.

39. He had held the post of junior minister in the Scotland Office during the entirety of the 2010–15 coalition government.

40. See p. 92.

CHAPTER EIGHT

Challenging the Legislation of the Parliament and the Actions of Ministers

INTRODUCTION

As we have seen in the previous chapter, the SA 1998 contains detailed provisions designed to ensure that the Scottish Parliament does not seek to pass legislation outwith its competence. These provisions were not affected by the subsequent revisions to the devolved arrangements made by the 2012 and 2016 Scotland Acts. These provisions are reinforced by numerous mechanisms allowing the UK Government to intervene if it considers that the Scottish Parliament or Government has strayed beyond the boundaries of the powers conferred on them by statute, before the proposed legislation becomes law, although none of these has ever been used so far. There is always the possibility, however, that an individual or corporate body may also wish to challenge a provision as being beyond the Parliament's powers, even though the UK Government does not wish to do so. It is also conceivable that the UK Government might wish to challenge a provision after it has passed through all its stages in the Parliament (including the receipt of Royal Assent) if it appeared subsequently that the provision did, in fact, stray beyond the limits of devolved competence. Similarly, there will be occasions when a particular action taken on behalf of the Scottish Government might be claimed to be invalid as being outside the authority given to it by the SA 1998. Such legal challenges to the validity of provisions could potentially arise in a wide range of circumstances. They could involve disputes between the Scottish Government and the UK Government, between an individual and the Scottish Government or between individual or corporate bodies. To date, however, all the challenges to the validity of Acts of the Scottish Parliament or actions of the Scottish Government have arisen from individuals or from private organisations.

THE LEGISLATIVE BASIS FOR CHALLENGES

Such questions as to whether Acts of the Scottish Parliament or actions of the Scottish Government have strayed beyond their powers are described in the SA 1998 as 'devolution issues' and Schedule 6 to the Act sets out in considerable detail both what constitutes a 'devolution issue' and how such issues are to be handled. A 'devolution issue' can arise before virtually any court or tribunal, in civil or in criminal cases.

Part I of Schedule 6 first defines a devolution issue as 'a question whether an Act of the Scottish Parliament or any provision of an Act of the Scottish Parliament is within the legislative competence of the Parliament'. As mentioned above, however, a devolution issue may arise in areas other than Acts of the Scottish Parliament. For example, questions of legislative competence may arise over the executive actions of Scottish Ministers. Schedule 6 further defines devolution issues as including the following:

- a question whether any function is a function of the Scottish Ministers, the First Minister or the Lord Advocate;
- a question whether the purported or proposed exercise of a function by a member of the Scottish Executive is, or would be, within devolved competence;
- a question whether a purported or proposed exercise of a function by a member of the Scottish Government is, or would be, incompatible with any rights under the European Convention on Human Rights or with European Union (EU) law;
- a question whether a failure to act by a member of the Scottish Government is incompatible with any of the rights under the European Convention on Human Rights or with EU law;
- any other question about whether a function is exercisable within devolved competence in or as regards Scotland and any other question arising by virtue of the SA 1998 about reserved matters.

A devolution issue, however, is not to be taken to arise in any legal proceedings simply because one of the parties argues that it does if the court considers that contention to be 'frivolous or vexatious'.

An important qualification to this list of 'devolution issues' was introduced by SA 2012 which provided[1] that in criminal proceedings in Scotland a question which would otherwise be considered a devolution issue would not be considered as such if it related to the compatibility with any of the Convention rights or with EU law of:

(a) an Act of the Scottish Parliament or any provision of an Act of the Scottish Parliament;
(b) a function;
(c) the purported or proposed exercise of a function;
(d) a failure to act.

The effect of this change is that, if a person wishes to raise such an issue, for example, whether some particular provision of Scottish legislation making an action criminal breached Convention rights by doing so, it cannot be done by raising it as a 'devolution issue'. Instead, such issues arising in the course of criminal proceedings have to be pursued through a different 'compatibility issues' procedure which is described later in this chapter.

A further change was made in the same section[2] of the SA 2012 which extended the exemption that, in the original form of the Scotland Act, had allowed certain acts of the Lord Advocate to be challenged as being beyond devolved competence. Such challenges could therefore be raised as 'devolution issues'. In its amended form, the SA 1998, which prevents members of the Scottish Government from doing any act which is incompatible with any of the Convention rights or with EU law, does not apply to any act of the Lord Advocate in prosecuting any offence or in the capacity as head of the systems of criminal prosecution and investigation of deaths in Scotland.[3]

The reason for the latter change arose from the fact that, after the SA 1998 came into force, and the Scottish Parliament and Government were established, 'devolution issues' were raised in a large number of cases. In the vast majority of those, the challenge was made to actions of the Lord Advocate in his capacity as head of the criminal prosecution system in Scotland, alleging that he, or someone acting on his behalf (for example, a procurator fiscal), had brought or was conducting a prosecution that was in some way incompatible with the European Convention on Human Rights. As a result, it was argued that such prosecution was invalid (because the Lord Advocate, as a member of the Scottish Government, had no power under SA 1998 as originally enacted to act in a way which was incompatible with Convention rights). This large number of cases led to complaints from the judiciary that the ability to raise 'devolution issues' in this way had led to challenges to acts of prosecutors and a plethora of disputed issues which resulted, in turn, to delays in the handling of criminal business. As a result of the change made by SA 2012, the matters coming within the terms of the amended provisions cannot now be raised as 'devolution issues'.

It should be noted, however, that this exception applies only to the Lord Advocate in his or her role as prosecutor and as head of the criminal prosecution service and in his or her capacity as head of the systems of criminal prosecution and investigation of deaths. Accordingly, any of his or her other actions can still be challenged by use of the 'devolution issues' procedure in court proceedings.

In addition, the Lord Advocate continues to be subject to the provisions of section 6(1) of HRA 1998 which requires him or her to act in a manner which is compatible with Convention rights.

Almost all the other challenges to actions of the Scottish Government have also been made on grounds that such actions breach 'Convention rights' in some way. There have been few challenges to an Act of the Scottish Parliament itself, as distinct from some action taken under the authority of a member of the Scottish Government. These are described later[4] but it can be noted that only four such challenges have been successful so far. Interestingly, it was not until thirteen years after the Scottish Parliament came into existence that the first challenge was successful, in the case of *Cameron* v. *Cottam*, [2012] HCJAC 19, 2013 J.C. 12, 2012 S.L.T. 173.

THE RELATIONSHIP BETWEEN THE SCOTLAND ACTS AND HUMAN RIGHTS LEGISLATION

The fact that virtually all the challenges described above have been based on a claim that the Scottish Parliament or Executive has breached a 'Convention right' illustrates the close interrelationship between the SA 1998 and the Human Rights Act 1998 (HRA 1998). Indeed, for the first year-and-a-half of the new devolved arrangements, Scotland was the only part of the UK where the European Convention on Human Rights had been partially incorporated into domestic law. This was because the provisions of the SA 1998 requiring legislation, and actions of the Scottish Government (including, of course, actions of those acting on behalf of its members), to be compatible with the European Convention on Human Rights came into effect when the Scottish Parliament and the members of the Scottish Executive acquired their respective powers in stages in mid 1999. By contrast, the HRA 1998, which incorporated 'Convention rights' into UK law, did not come into force until October 2000, and, as a result, transitional provisions were put in place so that the Convention rights provided for in the HRA 1998 would apply to the relevant sections of the SA 1998 as if the HRA were already in force.[5] It was therefore hardly surprising that the opportunity to raise alleged breaches of Convention rights as devolution issues was taken up so extensively, given the fact that it was not initially possible to make use of the HRA 1998.

After the HRA 1998 came into force, there was some uncertainty as to whether a claim that an action of the Scottish Executive was incompatible with the European Convention on Human Rights could be raised under the HRA 1998 as well as, or instead of, being raised as a 'devolution issue'. The issue was conclusively resolved in 2007 by the House of Lords in *Somerville* v. *Scottish Ministers*, [2007] 1 W.L.R. 2734, 2008 S.C. (H.L.) 45, 2007 S.L.T. 1113, which held that such a claim could be brought under either Act. The court also found that the time bar (of one year), which was expressly contained within HRA 1998, did not apply to claims brought under SA 1998 but the SA 1998 was amended in 2009 to include a one-year time limit in relation to such incompatibility claims. Alhough the amendment was brought as a response to litigation by prisoners, it has amended the protection afforded to all under the Scotland Act. Challenges to Acts of the Scottish Parliament have been few but, of the four that have so far been successful, three have been raised as 'devolution issues' under the SA 1998, and one as a 'compatibility issue'. One was raised by way of judicial review, two by accused persons in criminal trials, and one in a dispute over tenancy rights in a case in the Scottish Land Court. The next chapter examines in detail those challenges, along with some unsuccessful challenges, which have been made to Scottish Parliament legislation since it was established.

LEGAL PROCEEDINGS IN SCOTLAND

Part II of Schedule 6 to the SA 1998 deals with legal proceedings in Scotland (those in England and Wales are dealt with in Part III, and in Northern Ireland in Part IV). Proceedings may be instituted by the Advocate General (that is, the UK Government's Law Officer for Scotland) or the Lord Advocate. The Lord Advocate may defend proceedings instituted by the Advocate General. A court or tribunal must order intimation of any devolution issue arising before it to the Lord Advocate and the Advocate General and they may take part as a party in the proceedings so far as they relate to a devolution issue, even if they are not parties to the substantive dispute.

In practice, however, devolution issues have arisen before the courts in the course of proceedings raised by parties other than the Advocate

General or the Lord Advocate. Such proceedings might be raised for the specific purpose of challenging the legitimacy of legislation by the Scottish Parliament or Government (in which case they will need to be raised by judicial review). Judicial review is the method by which an aggrieved party can ask the court to quash any action or decision of a public body, or body carrying out public duties, on the ground that it has acted or decided unlawfully. That unlawful behaviour can consist of taking action or making decisions without any statutory basis for that action or decision. Legislation of the Parliament, or actions of Scottish Ministers, which go beyond the powers it or they have been given by the SA 1998 and other statutes is therefore unlawful and can be struck down by the courts. Such questions do not arise only in actions raised against Scottish Ministers. If a person believes that action by another body carrying out public functions has acted on the basis of legislation by the Parliament that it ought not to have made (because it was beyond the legislative competence of the Parliament, or some other reason), then that action will be raised against the public body concerned. The Scottish Government will normally be able to join in that action, however, if it wishes to argue that its legislation on the question in dispute was lawful. Judicial review proceedings can be raised only in the Court of Session and are now normally subject to a time bar of three months from the date of the action or decision complained of, or 'such longer period as the Court considers equitable having regard to all the circumstances'.[6] The rules of procedure for judicial review proceedings are found in Chapter 58 of the Rules of the Court of Session.

Devolution issues, however, which raise questions of the validity of legislation of the Scottish Parliament or Government (or actions taken by Scottish Ministers) are not restricted to challenges made by way of judicial review. They can arise in any legal proceedings. For example, if a person were to defend an action raised by a local authority, on the ground that the authority was relying on Scottish Parliament legislation that she/he considered the Parliament could not have lawfully passed, then that would raise devolution issues. Similarly, a person, accused of an action which had been defined as a crime by an Act of the Scottish Parliament, who claimed that the legislation in question had been outside devolved competence, would be raising a devolution issue in his or her defence.

APPEALS AND REFERENCES

Whether a challenge arises from judicial review proceedings, aimed specifically at questioning Scottish Parliament legislation, or in the course of wider proceedings, Schedule 6 of SA 1998 sets out a detailed set of rules for how the devolution issues arising from such challenges shall be dealt with.

In civil proceedings before a lower court (that is, the sheriff court or the Outer House of the Court of Session) or a tribunal, a devolution issue which arises may be referred to the Inner House of the Court of Session. A tribunal from which there is no right of appeal must make such a reference. In criminal proceedings before JP (Justice of the Peace) courts, the sheriff court or before a single judge in the High Court of Justiciary, a devolution issue, if it arises, may be referred to a larger bench of judges in the High Court of Justiciary.

Any court consisting of three or more judges of the Court of Session (normally a civil appeal court) or two or more judges of the High Court of Justiciary (a court of criminal appeal) may refer a devolution issue to the UK Supreme Court (unless the issue had been referred to either of them by a lower court, in which case the issue has to be decided by the superior Scottish court). Where the Court of Session has decided a devolution issue referred to it by a lower court, an appeal lies to the Supreme Court.

There are two courts in Scotland from which there was, prior to devolution, normally no further appeal to the House of Lords. These are the High Court of Justiciary, sitting as a court of criminal appeal, and the Lands Valuation Appeal Court. SA 1998 introduced a right of appeal from their decisions on devolution issues. If a decision on a devolution issue has been made by one of these courts, an appeal can be made to the Supreme Court with the permission of the court concerned or with the permission of the Supreme Court if permission is refused by the court concerned.

Originally, such references were made to the Judicial Committee of the Privy Council but, with the establishment of the UK Supreme Court by the Constitutional Reform Act 2005, that court took over, from 2009, both the function of the Appellate Committee of the House of Lords, including its role as the final court of appeal for Scottish civil cases, and the functions of the Judicial Committee of the Privy Council in respect of devolution issues.

The Law Officers of Scotland, England, and Northern Ireland may require a court or tribunal before which a devolution issue has arisen to refer it to the Supreme Court. A direct reference to the Supreme Court may also be made by the Law Officers of Scotland, England and Northern Ireland of a devolution issue which is not the subject of legal proceedings. This will involve the judges in ruling on hypothetical issues rather than on concrete facts – an extremely unusual procedure for British judges. This procedure has never been used so far in Scotland although it was used in Wales in the case of *Attorney General* v. *National Assembly for Wales* [2013] 1 AC 792.

A comprehensive set of rules has been brought into effect specifying how devolution issues are to be raised in both the lower courts and in the Scottish appeal courts, and how appeals and references from the lower courts should be dealt with.[7]

COMPATIBILITY ISSUES

As described above, as a result of changes introduced by the SA 2012, in criminal cases, challenges to certain Scottish Parliament legislation, or actions of Scottish Ministers can no longer be raised as 'devolution issues'. Instead, they must be raised as 'compatibility issues'.[8] A 'compatibility issue' is defined as a question, arising in criminal proceedings, as to:

(a) whether a public authority has acted (or proposes to act);
  (i) in a way that is made unlawful by section 6(1) of the Human Rights Act 1998; or
  (ii) in a way that is incompatible with EU law; or
(b) whether an Act of the Scottish Parliament or any provision of an Act of the Scottish Parliament is incompatible with any of the Convention rights or with EU law.

The procedure whereby courts deal with compatibility issues is broadly similar to that which applies in devolution issues. Where a compatibility issue arises in criminal proceedings before a JP court, sheriff court, or single judge of the High Court of Justiciary, the court may, instead of determining it, refer the issue to the High Court of Justiciary. The Lord Advocate or the Advocate General for Scotland, if a party to those criminal proceedings, may require the court to refer to the High Court of Justiciary any compatibility issue which has arisen in the proceedings. In turn, the High Court of Justiciary may refer a compatibility issue to the Supreme Court rather than determining it itself, whether that has come to it by way of reference or in the course of an appeal. The Lord

Advocate or the Advocate General for Scotland, if a party to criminal proceedings before a court consisting of two or more judges of the High Court, may also require the court to refer to the Supreme Court any compatibility issue that has arisen in the proceedings otherwise than on a reference.

In dealing with a reference which has been submitted to it in this manner, the Supreme Court cannot make a final determination of a compatibility issue as it can with a devolution issue. The Supreme Court's powers are restricted to the determination of the compatibility issue which has been referred to it only. Once it has done that, the Supreme Court must remit the proceedings back to the High Court of Justiciary to determine the case applying, of course, the decision of the Supreme Court on the compatibility issues.

The Advocate General is also given a right of appeal in a case where a person is acquitted or convicted, in proceedings in which the Advocate General was a party to the proceedings. The Advocate General may refer the case to the High Court of Justiciary for its opinion on any devolution issue, or any compatibility issue, which has arisen in the proceedings.

As well as a reference, an appeal may also be made to the Supreme Court against a determination of the High Court of Justiciary in criminal proceedings sitting as an appeal court. Once again, the Supreme Court's powers are restricted to the determination of the compatibility issue. When it has done that, it must remit the case back to the High Court of Justiciary as with a reference. Such an appeal can be made only with the permission of the High Court or, failing that, with the permission of the Supreme Court (unless it is an appeal by the Lord Advocate or the Advocate General on a compatibility issue).

The key distinction between the powers of the Supreme Court in proceedings dealing with compatibility issues is that it does not have the power to decide the case as a whole but only the compatibility issue. That means that for these cases, which in practice will be most Scottish criminal cases that come before it, the final determination in the case will be made by the High Court of Justiciary, preserving thereby its position as the highest court of appeal in Scotland on criminal matters. The position was explained by the Supreme Court in the case of *Macklin* v. *Her Majesty's Advocate (Scotland)* [2015] UKSC 77, 2016 S.C. (U.K.S.C.) 47, in the following terms:

> It is important to understand the nature of the jurisdiction exercised by this court under section 288AA of the 1995 Act. The court

does not sit as a criminal appeal court exercising a general power of review . . . In terms of section 288AA(2) of the 1995 Act, the powers of the Supreme Court are exercisable only for the purpose of determining the compatibility issue . . . When it has determined the compatibility issue, the Supreme Court must remit the proceedings to the High Court.

To date, there has been only one case in which the compatibility issues procedure introduced by the SA 2012 has been utilised for a successful challenge to legislation of the Scottish Parliament. That was the case of *AB* v. *HM Advocate*, [2017] UKSC 25, which is considered in more detail in the next chapter.

The SA 1998 also includes a provision for subordinate legislation to be made by a UK Minister to remedy ultra vires provisions in Acts of the Scottish Parliament. Subordinate legislation may also be made to remedy any improper exercise of functions by Scottish Ministers. Such subordinate legislation may be retrospective in effect. This can remedy any problems which have arisen and put third parties into the position they thought they were in before the flaw in the Act or subordinate legislation was discovered.

There is a further provision in the SA 1998, section 102, which allows any court or tribunal to remove, limit or suspend any retrospective effect of its decision that a provision of an Act of the Scottish Parliament or subordinate legislation is ultra vires. In *Salvesen* v. *Riddell*, 2013 S.C. (U.K.S.C.) 236, 2013 S.L.T. 863, the effect of their judgment that the Scottish Parliament legislation found to be beyond legislative competence was suspended by the Supreme Court for twelve months to allow the Scottish Government to make the necessary amendments to legislation. In the case of *Christian Institute & Ors* v. *Lord Advocate*, [2016] UKSC 51, 2016 S.L.T. 805, the Supreme Court, having decided that the legislation and guidance were defective, decided to continue the case for forty-two days to decide whether or not to make an order under section 102.

One of the criteria the court or tribunal must take into account in making an order under this section is the extent to which persons not party to the proceedings would otherwise be adversely affected. The Lord Advocate and any other appropriate Law Officer must be given notice of an intention to make such an order and the opportunity to be party to the proceedings as they relate to the order.

CHALLENGING LEGISLATION AND MINISTERIAL ACTIONS – BEYOND THE COURTS

The preceding paragraphs have looked at ways in which legal proceedings can be raised to challenge the Parliament's legislation, and also the actions of Scottish Ministers. Those are not the only ways, however, in which that legislation and those actions can be questioned. The Scottish Parliament has established a range of other institutions that allow those with concerns about something which the Parliament or Scottish Ministers (and, indeed, other public bodies in Scotland) has done, or failed to do, to raise those concerns without using the courts to do so, at least in the first instance. The roles of three of these institutions are now considered. The Scottish Public Services Ombudsman also offers another, and important, avenue by which the actions of Scottish public bodies can be challenged, and is considered in Chapter 4 above.

Scottish Human Rights Commission

The Scottish Human Rights Commission ('SHRC') was brought into being by the Scottish Commission for Human Rights Act 2006. It started work in December 2008. Its general duty is specified in section 2 of that Act, as follows:

2 General duty to promote human rights
(1) The Commission's general duty is, through the exercise of its functions under this Act, to promote human rights and, in particular, to encourage best practice in relation to human rights.
(2) In this Act, '*human rights*' means:
(a) the Convention rights within the meaning of section 1 of the Human Rights Act 1998 (c.42), and
(b) other human rights contained in any international convention, treaty or other international instrument ratified by the United Kingdom.
(3) In this section, '*promote*', in relation to human rights, means promote awareness and understanding of, and respect for, those rights.
(4) In deciding what action to take under this Act in pursuance of its general duty, the Commission must have regard, in particular, to the importance of exercising its functions under this Act in relation to:
(a) the Convention rights, and

(b) human rights of those groups in society whose human rights are not, in the Commission's opinion, otherwise being sufficiently promoted.

'Convention rights' are explained in more detail in Chapter 11 below, which includes a listing of the Convention rights referred to in the Human Rights Act.[9] It will be noted that, although its duty includes the promotion of 'Convention rights', namely the rights incorporated into UK law by the Human Rights Act 1998, the SHRC is not restricted to the promotion of those rights but is also given a broader remit to promote other internationally recognised human rights. It should also be noted that it has been given a responsibility for promoting the human rights of marginalised groups in society.

The chair of the SHRC is appointed by the Queen, on the nomination of the Scottish Parliamentary Corporate Body (SPCB), and its other members are appointed by the SPCB.[10] Its independence from the Crown, the Parliament, the Scottish Government and the SPCB is laid down by statute, however.[11]. It should be noted that many aspects of human rights law and practice in Scotland remain a responsibility of the Equality and Human Rights Commission which works across Great Britain.[12]

The SHRC is authorised[13] to publish and disseminate information or ideas; provide advice or guidance; conduct research; and provide education or training, in order to fulfil its duty.

The SHRC is also able to influence human rights law and practice in Scotland in other ways. That is because it has been given the power[14] to review and recommend changes to: (a) any area of the law of Scotland, or (b) any policies or practices of any Scottish public authorities.

These powers are qualified by the restriction placed upon the SHRC requiring it to consult the Scottish Law Commission before undertaking such a review of the law, and also requiring it to seek to ensure, so far as practicable, that any activity undertaken by it under this Act does not duplicate unnecessarily any activity undertaken by any other person under any other enactment.

Notwithstanding those qualifications, it is clear that the SHRC has the potential to use its powers in such a way as to have wide influence over the law and practice relating to human rights in Scotland.

As well as a general power to review and recommend changes to law, practice, or policies, it has the power[15] to conduct an inquiry (subject to certain restrictions)[16] into the policies or practices of a particular Scottish public authority, or all or some of them. In support of such inquiries, it has powers to obtain evidence in support of that enquiry[17] and to enter 'places of detention'.[18]

The SHRC is not allowed to provide assistance (which includes assistance in the form of advice, guidance and grants) to persons involved in any claim or legal proceedings. However, although it is unable to support, in legal actions, persons who have human rights issues which they want to bring to court by giving them assistance, it does have the power to intervene in civil proceedings before a court, except children's hearing proceedings (with leave of, or at the invitation of, the court) where it considers that such an intervention would be relevant to its duties and would be in the public interest.[19] It can therefore ensure that it can provide its input to questions of wider relevance to human rights in a particular case even though it cannot directly support the individual who has raised the proceedings.

The Scottish Information Commissioner

The office of Scottish Information Commissioner was established by section 42 of the Freedom of Information (Scotland) Act 2002. The commissioner is appointed by the Queen, on nomination by the Parliament. The commissioner's primary function is to ensure that the public right to information from Scottish public authorities is complied with by such authorities. There is a general entitlement for members of the public who request such information to be given it by the authority, subject to some important exemptions.[20]

In addition, the commissioner also has a duty to promote good practice by Scottish public authorities on freedom of information, to publicise the right of access to information, and to make recommendations to Scottish Ministers on whether there should be changes to the list of public authorities in Scotland subject to the rule on freedom of information.[21]

There are several laws dealing with access to information which apply in Scotland. The Scottish Information Commissioner is responsible for enforcing and promoting three of these, which are as follows:

- The *Freedom of Information (Scotland) Act 2002* is an Act of the Scottish Parliament which gives everyone the right to ask for any information held by a Scottish public authority.
- The *Environmental Information (Scotland) Regulations 2004* which are derived from a European directive on access to environmental information.

- The *INSPIRE (Scotland) Regulations 2009*, also derived from a European directive, and create a right to discover and view spatial datasets (for example, map data) held by Scottish public authorities.

There are also some UK-wide laws on freedom of information which apply to Scotland, and these are enforced by the UK Information Commissioner. These are: the Freedom of Information Act 2000 which applies to UK-wide public authorities, some of which operate in Scotland, such as the BBC and the Ministry of Defence; and the Data Protection Act 1998 which governs access to personal information and also applies to the whole of the UK.

The Children and Young People's Commissioner Scotland

The Queen also appoints, on the nomination of the Parliament, the Commissioner for Children and Young People in Scotland. That post was established by the Commissioner for Children and Young People (Scotland) Act 2003.

The commissioner's general function is to promote and safeguard the rights of children and young people. In exercising that general function, the commissioner must: (a) promote awareness and understanding of the rights of children and young people; (b) keep under review the law, policy, and practice relating to the rights of children and young people with a view to assessing the adequacy and effectiveness of such law, policy and practice; (c) promote best practice by service providers; and (d) promote, commission, undertake and publish research on matters relating to the rights of children and young people.[22]

The commissioner can carry out investigations and take measures to secure evidence.[23]

Similar offices exist in England, Northern Ireland and Wales.

SUMMARY

The Scottish Parliament is not the first experiment in devolution in the UK. After the partition of Ireland, a Northern Ireland Parliament was established in 1921 and continued in existence until 1972. By and large the members of that Parliament were content with the powers that had been conferred. They tried to avoid constitutional tension by seeking the co-operation of the UK Parliament and generally found co-operation there. The courts were rarely called upon to resolve disputes. Though a number of challenges were made, only one had much success.[24] To date, there have been only four successful challenges to the competency of Acts of the Scottish Parliament, and no such challenge has been made at the instance of either members of the Scottish Parliament or the Scottish Government. In that respect, therefore, the Scottish experience has been similar to that of Northern Ireland. The frequency of challenges, however, almost invariably on 'human rights' grounds, to the competence of actions of the Scottish Government and, in particular, the Lord Advocate, has kept the Scottish courts very busy considering the terms of the SA 1998, particularly prior to the changes introduced by SA 2012 described above. Though successful challenges have been few and far between, those that have been successful have sometimes had significant consequences, as the cases described in the next chapter show.

NOTES

1. Section 36(4).
2. Section 36.
3. Section 57(3).
4. See Chapter 9, p. 183.
5. SA 1998, section 129(2).
6. Section 27A, Court of Session Act 1988.
7. For the Court of Session, these are set out in Act of Sederunt (Devolution Issues Rules) 1999, SI 1999/1345, amended by Act of Sederunt (Rules of the Court of Session Amendment No. 7) (Devolution Issues) SSI 2007/360, Act of Sederunt (Devolution Issues) (Appeals and References to the Supreme Court) SSI 2009/323, and the Wales Act 2014, section 4(4)(a). The rules can be found in consolidated form in Chapter 25A of the Rules of the Court of Session. These rules can be found in the Parliament House Book, with annotations on procedure and practice on devolution issues in the Court of Session. For civil proceedings in the sheriff court, the relevant rules can be found in the Act of Sederunt (Proceedings for Determination of Devolution Issues Rules) 1999, SI 1999/1347, amended by the Act of Sederunt (Proceedings for Determination of Devolution Issues Rules) Amendment 2007/362 and the Act of Sederunt (Devolution Issues) (Appeals and References to the Supreme Court) SSI 2009/323.

   The rules of procedure for appeals and references to the Supreme Court are set out in the Rules of the Supreme Court, SI 2009/1603.

   For criminal matters, the rules can be found in the Act of Adjournal (Devolution Issues Rules) 1999, SI 1999/1346.
8. See section 288ZZ and following sections of the Criminal Procedure (Scotland) Act 1995.

9. See p. 246.
10. Scottish Commission for Human Rights Act, Schedule 1, paragraph 1. For more details of the SPCB, see p. 81.
11. Ibid. Schedule 1, paragraphs 2 and 3.
12. See https://www.equalityhumanrights.com/en/commission-scotland/our-work-scotland (last accessed 10 April 2017).
13. Ibid. section 3.
14. Ibid. section 4.
15. Ibid. section 8.
16. Ibid. section 9.
17. Ibid. section 10.
18. Ibid. section 11.
19. Ibid. section 12.
20. Freedom of Information (Scotland) Act 2002, sections 1 and 2.
21. Ibid. section 43.
22. Commissioner for Children and Young People (Scotland) Act 2003, section 4.
23. Ibid. sections 7 and 9.
24. *Ulster Transport Authority* v. *James Brown & Son Ltd* [1953] NI 79.

CHAPTER NINE

Legal Challenges in Practice

Previous chapters have described the legislative powers of the Scottish Parliament, and how it makes laws.[1] The preceding chapter has set out the means by which a person or body aggrieved at some such legislation, or at an action of Scottish Ministers can challenge that legislation or act as having no legal foundation in the powers set out in the Scotland Act 1998. This chapter now looks at the challenges that have been made since the Parliament was established, the extent to which they have been successful, and the principles that the courts have applied in considering how to deal with such challenges.

CHALLENGES TO LEGISLATION

To date, there has been a limited number of challenges to the validity of Acts of the Scottish Parliament or Scottish ministers which have gone as far as cases disputed in court. This is not to be unexpected, given the provisions of Section 31 of the Scotland Act 1998 which require both a statement from the person in charge of a proposed bill that it is within the Parliament's legislative competence and a statement from the Presiding Officer as to whether or not it is within its legislative competence.[2]

None of these challenges has arisen because the UK or Scottish Government has challenged proposed legislation as being beyond the Scottish Parliament's powers. (This is in contrast with the position in Wales where questions as to the competence of legislation have been raised on a number of occasions by government Law Officers.)[3]

The challenges which have gone ahead have all been made following the enactment of the legislation in question but, in some cases, before it has actually come into effect.[4] Given the potentially heavy legal costs of such challenges, which by their very nature have a high possibility of being argued not just in the Outer House of the Court of Session[5] but also thereafter on appeal to the Inner House, and potentially again to the UK Supreme Court, it is not surprising that those raising such challenges have mostly been major commercial entities or large non-governmental organisations though, in some cases, individuals have been joined as parties in such challenges.

Although infrequent, challenges to the validity of Acts of the Scottish Parliament began to be made as soon as it started to legislate. Its very first Act, the *Mental Health (Public Safety and Appeals) (Scotland) Act 1999*, was subject to challenge on the grounds that its Section 1, allowing for the continued detention of mentally disordered patients on grounds of public safety, was incompatible with the right to liberty and security provided for by Article 5 of the European Convention on Human Rights (ECHR), in the case of *Anderson & Ors* v. *Scottish Ministers and Another* [2001] UKPC D5, [2003] 2AC 602. That challenge was ultimately unsuccessful before the Judicial Committee of the Privy Council.[6]

Another early provision in Scottish Parliament legislation which was challenged as being incompatible with Convention rights was paragraph 13 of the schedule to the Convention Rights (Compliance) (Scotland) Act 2001. This amended certain provisions in the Prisoners and Criminal Proceedings (Scotland) Act 1993 regarding the punishment part of a life sentence. It was claimed the measure was incompatible with numerous Convention rights, namely those set out in Articles 5, 6, 7, 14, 17, 53. Once again, the challenge was unsuccessful in *Flynn (Patrick Anthony)* v. *HM Advocate (No 1)*, 2004 S.C. (P.C.) 1.

High-profile challenges were made soon thereafter to the Protection of Wild Mammals (Scotland) Act 2002. This Act was directed primarily at prohibiting hunting with dogs, and had been brought forward as a Members' Bill by Lord Watson of Invergowrie, MSP. The first challenge was made in *Adams* v. *Scottish Ministers*, 2004 SC 665 in which it was claimed that the Act was incompatible with a number of Convention rights, viz. Articles 8 (Right to respect for private and family life), 11 (Freedom of assembly and association), and Article 1 of the First Protocol (Protection of Property). The challenge was made after the Act had become law but before the date on which it was due to come into effect. The Court of Session held that the Act was not incompatible with Convention rights and was therefore within devolved competence.

A second challenge to this Act was made by two petitioners, in the cases of *Friend* v. *Lord Advocate* and *Whaley* v. *Lord Advocate*.[7] The challenge was again based on the grounds that it was incompatible with Convention rights. In this case, it was claimed that the Act was incompatible with Articles 8, 9, 10, 11, 14, 17 and 53. The petitioners were unsuccessful in the Outer House of the Court of Session, and again in their subsequent appeals to the Inner House and to the House of Lords (2007 UKHL 53, 2008 SC (HL) 107). Finally, Mr Friend took his case to the European Court of Human Rights but was unsuccessful there too, *Friend* v. *UK*, (2010) 50 EHRR SE6.

The next significant challenge was made to another item of legislation passed by the Scottish Parliament in the same year, namely the Sexual Offences (Procedure and Evidence) (Scotland) Act 2002. In *DS* v. *HMA*, 2007 SC (PC) 1. It was argued that Section 10 (which inserted section 275A into the Criminal Procedure (Scotland) Act 1995, requiring the prosecutor in certain circumstances to place before the presiding judge any previous relevant conviction of the accused) was incompatible with Article 6 of the Convention (Right to a fair trial). The Judicial Committee held that it was compatible but required to be construed and applied in a substantially restricted manner (including the insertion of a comma at an important point in the section) for it to be so.

Challenges to the validity of Scottish Parliament legislation have tended to arise shortly after the legislation has become law. That is not always the case, however, as can be seen from one of the very few successful challenges so far to Acts of the Scottish Parliament. That was the case of *Salvesen* v. *Riddell* [2013] UKSC 22; 2013 SC (UKSC) 236 in which the validity of Section 72(10) of the Agricultural Holdings (Scotland) Act 2003 was challenged some years after the legislation in question was passed. This provision affected the rights of limited partners to serve dissolution notices on general partners where a landlord (normally the limited partner) had granted a tenancy of a relevant agricultural holding to a limited partnership during a certain period. It was held by the Supreme Court that the relevant section was incompatible with the Convention rights regarding the protection of property (Article 1 of the First Protocol) and therefore unlawful. To allow the legislation to be amended, however, the court suspended the effect of its order quashing the provision for twelve months or such shorter period as might be required for the defect to be corrected. The Salvesen case is considered in more detail below.

By contrast, another challenge, made some time after the relevant enactment, was unsuccessful in the case of *S* v. *L*, [2012] UKSC 30; 2013 SC (UKSC) 20; 2002 S.C. (P.C.) 63. In that case, Section 31(3) (d) of the Adoption and Children (Scotland) Act 2007 was challenged on the grounds that it allowed a court in certain cases to dispense with a parent's consent to an order for adoption, and was therefore incompatible with the Article 8 Convention right to respect for private and family life. It was not successful. The court did, however, make it clear that the exercise of the powers in that section should be done in a way which was compliant with Article 8.

Another challenge which was made some time after the legislation in question became law was in the case of *I* v. *Dunn*, 2012 HCJAC 108; 2013 JC 82. Here, certain provisions of the Vulnerable Witnesses (Scotland) Act 2004 were challenged as being incompatible with the Article 6 Convention right to a fair trial. In this case, again, the challenge was unsuccessful. This challenge arose during the course of criminal proceedings and, as questions of compatibility with Convention rights in such cases will necessarily arise when they are relied upon by persons when they are accused, that has also meant that challenges of this type have been made some time after the legislation has been enacted. For example, in the case of *Martin* v. *Most* [2010] UKSC 10; 2010 SC (UKSC) 40, the legislation under scrutiny was Section 45 of the Criminal Proceedings etc. (Reform) (Scotland) Act 2007, in which the sheriff's sentencing powers for offences of driving while disqualified were increased. It was argued, unsuccessfully, that this change 'related to a reserved matter within the meaning of Schedule 4 paragraph (2)(3) of the Scotland Act 1998. For that reason, it was not beyond the competence of the Scottish Parliament for it to have enacted that provision.

Another recent case in which it was argued that certain provisions of Scottish Parliament legislation were incompatible with the Article 6 right to a fair trial was that of *Barclay (John)* v. *HM Advocate* [2012] HCJAC 47; 2013 JC 40, in which it was argued that the requirement introduced by Section 124 of the Criminal Justice and Licensing (Scotland) Act 2010 for a defence statement to be lodged was incompatible with that right. The court did not accept the argument.

Mention can also be made here of another recent unsuccessful challenge to the validity of Scottish Parliament legislation which, in this case, was disposed of much more rapidly because of the urgency of the matter. In this case, two serving prisoners argued that the provisions of Section 2 and Section 3 of the Scottish Independence Referendum (Franchise) Act 2013, which prevented them from voting in that referendum, breached their Convention rights, were unlawful at common law, and failed to comply with other obligations of the United Kingdom under international laws. They were, however, unsuccessful on all these grounds, *Moohan, Petitioner*, 2015 SC 1; 2014 SLT 755.

It can be seen that, for more than ten years after it was established, Scottish Parliament legislation successfully resisted challenge in the courts. There has been a small number of cases more recently, however, where challenges had more success. These cases are now considered in more detail, together with some other challenges which, though unsuccessful, deserve special mention.

Cameron v. Cottam

The case of *Cameron* v. *Cottam*, [2012] HCJAC 19, 2013 J.C. 12 saw the first occasion when a provision in the Parliament's legislation was held not be lawful. In this case, it was argued that Section 58 of the Criminal Justice & Licensing (Scotland) Act 2010, which amended Section 245A of the Criminal Procedure (Scotland) Act 1995 to the effect that new standard conditions of bail requiring an accused person to participate in an identification procedure, and to allow any print, impression, or sample to be taken from that person, when reasonably instructed to do so, were incompatible with the Article 5 Convention right (Right to Liberty and Security) because the new provision gave no opportunity for judicial discretion and supervision. The High Court of Justiciary accordingly found the relevant provision to be unlawful as being beyond devolved competence.

In Cottam, the court also considered whether it would be possible to interpret the relevant provision of the legislation in such a way that it would be compatible with the European Convention on Human Rights. If the court could do that, then it would not have needed to hold the legislation as being unlawful. The court came to the view, however, that any such interpretation would be equivalent in all respects to discounting the substance of the section in question. It therefore felt that it was 'constrained to the view that the [provision] is not compatible with the requirements of Article 5 ECHR and should be declared . . . to be 'not law'.[8]

Salvesen v. Riddell

The case of Salvesen was briefly described above. In that case, the Supreme Court found that the difference of treatment in the relevant legislation between different categories of landlords had

> no logical justification. It is unfair and disproportionate. It is no answer to this criticism to say that there was an urgent need to meet the problem that had been identified. The legislation was intended to have an effect which was permanent and irrevocable. [It] does not pursue an aim that is reasonably related to the aim of the legislation as a whole.[9]

That being so, the retrospective application of the relevant provision imposed an unreasonable burden on one category of affected landlords, and thereby failed to strike a fair balance between their interests on the one hand and preserving the integrity of the legislation on the other.

Having concluded that the relevant legislative provision did raise a question of compatibility with Convention rights, Lord Hope then considered the approach that the court should take to resolve that question:

> Section 101(2) of the Scotland Act provides that a provision of an Act of the Scottish Parliament is to be read as narrowly as is required for it to be within competence, if such a reading is possible, and to be given effect accordingly. But as we are concerned in this case with an issue about compatibility with a Convention right, the proper starting point is to construe the legislation as required by sec 3(1) of the Human Rights Act 1998 (cap 42) (*DS* v. *HM* Advocate, para 24). The obligation to construe a provision in an Act of the Scottish Parliament so far as it is possible to do so is a strong one, and the court must prefer compatibility to incompatibility. But any sec 3 interpretation must, as Lord Rodger of Earlsferry said in *Ghaidan* v. *Godin-Mendoza* (para 121), go with the grain of the legislation (see also Lord Nicholls of Birkenhead, para 33). It is not for the court to go against the underlying thrust of what it provides for, as to do this would be to trespass on the province of the legislature.[10]

Lord Hope concluded that the relevant legislative provision could not be 'read down' in a way that was compatible with Convention rights:

> It is plain that the whole section needs to be looked at again, as does its relationship with sec 73. This is not just a matter of redrafting in order to ensure that all its provisions are compatible with the Convention rights. There are important issues of policy too which the court must leave to the democratic process. But the finding of incompatibility ought not to extend any further than is necessary to deal with the facts of this case . . .[11]

The 'Named Person' Case

The third case in which Scottish Parliament legislation has been successfully overturned so far was that of *The Christian Institute & Ors* v. *The Lord Advocate* [2016] UKSC 51, 2016 S.L.T. 805. Its lawfulness was challenged, without success, on a number of grounds in the Court of Session. The case was eventually appealed to the UK Supreme Court. The challenge concerned the competency of the information-sharing provisions of Part 4 of the Children and Young People (Scotland) Act 2014 regarding the appointment of a 'named person' for children and young persons.

It was argued before the Supreme Court that the legislation impinged upon reserved matters, namely the Data Protection Act 1988, and EC Directive 95/46/EC.[12] This argument was unsuccessful.

The appellants also argued, however, that certain provisions of Part IV of the Act were incompatible with Article 8 Convention rights (Right to respect for private and family life). Here they were successful on the grounds that the provisions were 'not in accordance with the law' in the terms required by Article 8, in essence because of 'serious difficulties in accessing the relevant legal rules' and 'the lack of safeguards that would enable the proportionality of an interference with article 8 rights to be adequately examined'.[13] (The appellants' challenge based on European Union law grounds was held by the court to be unsuccessful insofar as any incompatibility with EU law went beyond Article 8 grounds.)

The court then went on to consider how it could remedy the defects which it had identified, and decided it could not remedy the defect by reading down the provisions under Section 101 of the Scotland Act 1998. It therefore concluded that the information-sharing provisions of Part 4 of the Act are not within the legislative competence of the Scottish Parliament[14] and therefore unlawful. It said[15] that

> . . . it would not be appropriate for this court to propose particular legislative solutions to remedy the defect, but nevertheless went as far as to state that changes are needed both to improve the accessibility of the legal rules and to provide safeguards so that the proportionality of an interference can be challenged and assessed.

Thereafter,[16] the court stated that it was of the view that it should consider making an order under section 102(2)(b) of the Scotland Act 1998 but delayed making an order to give parties an opportunity to make submissions on the period of suspension and any conditions that should be attached. In the event, the court was not required to make an order as the Scottish Government announced it would introduce an order to pause commencement of the relevant sections. Later it brought forward the Children and Young People (Information Sharing) (Scotland) Bill in an effort to address the concerns of the court.

AB v. HM Advocate

The most recent successful challenge to the Parliament's legislation came in the case of *AB* v. *HM Advocate*, [2017] UKSC 25. In this case, a challenge was raised, as a 'compatibility issue'[17] to the legality of the provision of section 39(2) of the Sexual Offences (Scotland) Act 2009. Section 39(1) of that Act allows a person charged with various sexual offences against older children to rely on the defence of having 'reasonably believed' that the victim had attained the age of sixteen. That defence cannot be used, however, in certain circumstances, one of which (in Section 39(2)(a)(i)) is if the accused person has been charged by the police with a relevant sexual offence. (The rationale for not being able to use that defence is that the previous charge should be regarded as a warning against committing such an offence against a child under sixteen.) In the *AB* case, the Supreme Court held that this provision was incompatible with Convention rights in its application to *AB* because it interfered disproportionately with his right under Article 8 of the ECHR. In the circumstance of this case, the charge could not have been considered to have constituted sufficient warning. Lord Hodge further observed[18] that section 39(2)(a)(i)) would be likely to breach those rights in all other cases where the prior charge required did not objectively give the relevant warning. The court further concluded that the problem with the provision could not be resolved by interpreting the legislation narrowly but could only be resolved with further legislation.[19]

The AXA General Insurance and Imperial Tobacco Cases

In many cases, challenges to the competence of the Parliament's legislation have been based on a number of different grounds, comprehending both alleged breaches of Convention rights and other grounds too. Two notable examples of such cases were *AXA General Insurance Ltd, Petitioners*, [2011] UKSC 46; 2012 S.C. (UKSC) 122; 2011 SLT 1061, and *Imperial Tobacco Ltd* v. *Lord Advocate* [2012] UKSC 61; [2013] SC (UKSC) 153. Though both challenges were ultimately unsuccessful, they raised important issues. In the AXA General Insurance Ltd case, a major insurer claimed that the Damages (Asbestos-related Conditions) (Scotland) Act 2009 (which enabled those suffering from pleural plaques to sue former employers) was invalid on the grounds that it was incompatible with the Convention right to enjoyment of property (Article 1, First Protocol) and also that it was subject to judicial review on common law grounds. In this case, the UK Supreme Court upheld the Inner

House decision that the Act was within devolved competence, and also laid down the important principle that an Act of the Scottish Parliament cannot be susceptible to judicial review on the common law grounds that it has exercised its legislative authority in an unreasonable, irrational, or arbitrary manner.[20] This principle is set out by Lord Hope at paragraph 52:

> As for the appellants' common law case, I would hold, in agreement with the judges in the Inner House (para 88), that Acts of the Scottish Parliament are not subject to judicial review at common law on the grounds of irrationality, unreasonableness or arbitrariness. This is not needed, as there is already a statutory limit on the Parliament's legislative competence if a provision is incompatible with any of the Convention rights (Scotland Act, sec 29(2)(d)). But it would also be quite wrong for the judges to substitute their views on these issues for the considered judgment of a democratically elected legislature unless authorised to do so, as in the case of the Convention rights, by the constitutional framework laid down by the UK Parliament.

Lord Reed did, however, suggest[21] that the court might have the power to intervene in exceptional circumstances, for example, if it were shown that legislation offended against fundamental rights or the rule of law, but that was not the position in this case.

In the case of *Imperial Tobacco Ltd* v. *Lord Advocate* [2012] UKSC 61; [2013] SC (UKSC) 153, the tobacco company argued that Sections 1 and 9 of the Tobacco and Primary Medical Services (Scotland) Act 2010 were beyond devolved competence (the sections prohibit the sale of tobacco products at point of sale, and the use of vending machines for their sale). This, they claimed, was because those provisions related to the regulation of the sale and supply of goods to consumers, and to product safety. Both of these matters are ones reserved to the UK Parliament by Schedule 5 Part II of the *Scotland Act 1998* (in paragraphs C7(a) and C8 respectively). Furthermore, as a consequence, the changes to the criminal law made to implement the prohibitions were claimed to relate to reserved matters, and were accordingly beyond devolved competence as a result of the terms of Schedule 4, paragraph 2 of the *Scotland Act 1998*. Imperial Tobacco Ltd also argued that the provisions of the Act related to freedom of trade within the UK and, as such, were beyond devolved competence because Schedule 4, paragraph 1 of the *Scotland Act 1998* provides that the Scottish Parliament cannot make legislation which modifies the *Union of England Act* 1707 Section 6 and the *Act of Union* 1706 Article IV in so far as those articles related to freedom of trade. Notwithstanding the wide scope of their challenge, however, the company was unsuccessful in their argument that the 2010 Act was beyond devolved competence.

A challenge was also raised to the same legislation, this time in respect only of the measures prohibiting the sale of tobacco products in vending machines, in the case of *Sinclair Collis Ltd* v. *Lord Advocate* [2012] CSIH 80, 2013 S.C. 221. In this case, the challenge was firstly, that the legislative provision was incompatible with the Convention rights (under Article 1 of the First Protocol) of tobacco machine vendors, and secondly, that it breached European Union law, as constituting a quantitative restriction on imports and accordingly was contrary to Article 34 of the *Treaty on the Functioning of the European Union*. Both challenges were unsuccessful.

The 'Minimum Pricing' Case

A further notable case was that of *Scotch Whisky Association* v. *Lord Advocate* in which the Scotch Whisky Association and a number of other trade associations challenged the lawfulness of the *Alcohol (Minimum Pricing) (Scotland) Act 2012* and the *Alcohol (Minimum Pricing per Unit) (Scotland) Order 2013*, which together sought to set a minimum unit price ('MUP') for alcohol sold to a consumer. The challenge was unsuccessful in the Outer House of the Court of Session.[22] The petitioners appealed to the Inner House. One of the grounds for challenge in the Outer House was that the legislation breached the Acts of Union between Scotland and England but this was not argued before the Inner House of the Court of Session. The other ground which was maintained before the Inner House, however, was that the legislation was beyond devolved competence because it infringed European Union law on free trade.[23] The case was referred to the Court of Justice of the European Union for a preliminary ruling.

In a complex judgment, that court found[24] that Articles 34 and 36 of the *Treaty on the Functioning of the European Union*

> must be interpreted as precluding a member state choosing, in order to pursue the objective of the protection of human life and health by means of increasing the price of the consumption of alcohol, the option of legislation, such as that at issue, which imposes an MUP for the retail selling of alcoholic drinks, and rejecting a measure,

such as increased excise duties, that may be less restrictive of trade and competition within the European Union. It is for the referring court to determine whether that is indeed the case, having regard to a detailed analysis of all the relevant factors in the case before it. The fact that the latter measure may bring additional benefits and be a broader response to the objective of combating alcohol misuse cannot, in itself, justify the rejection of that measure.[25]

It was therefore left to the Scottish courts to decide how to answer that question and to the Scottish Government on whether they should amend their legislation with the aim of ensuring that it complied with European Union law. The case accordingly returned to the Inner House of the Court of Session which decided[26] that the judge in the original Outer House proceedings had directed himself correctly on European Union law and applied it accurately to the facts which he found demonstrated by the material before him. The Inner House accordingly refused the petition originally raised by the Scotch Whisky Association, and the challenge to the legislation was therefore unsuccessful. The Scotch Whisky Association, however, then appealed to the Supreme Court against the decision of the Inner House. That appeal was ultimately rejected in November 2017, when a seven-member bench of the Supreme Court unanimously upheld the decision of the Court of Session. This case is notable not just for the complexity of the arguments advanced but also for the way in which it illustrates how lengthy proceedings can be if a challenge is made to the competency of the Parliament's legislation when that involves a question of the interpretation of European Law. Such a question may require a reference to the Court of Justice of the European Union which, when decided, in turn needs to be applied by the relevant Scottish court. In this case, the initial legislation was passed in 2012 and yet a final decision on its legality was still outstanding five years later.

CHALLENGES TO THE ACTIONS OF SCOTTISH MINISTERS

The provisions of the Scotland Act 1998 mean that it is not only Acts of the Parliament that can be challenged as being beyond the powers given to the Parliament in that Act. The Scottish Ministers are also unable to act beyond the competence given to them by that Act and, if they do act in such a way, such actions can be declared unlawful.[27] Questions as to whether such actions are within devolved competence are also regarded as 'devolution issues'.

As is pointed out in the previous chapter, the largest number of cases challenging the competence of actions by Scottish Ministers were directed at the Lord Advocate, in his role as the head of the prosecution service in Scotland, on the grounds that an action taken by him or her, or someone under their direction, breached Convention rights and was thus incompetent. A notable example where this argument was successfully made was in *Starrs* v. *Ruxton* 2000 JC 208, 2000 SLT 42, where an appeal was successful on the basis that: (1) a prosecution by a procurator fiscal constituted an act of the Lord Advocate; and (2) that the Lord Advocate had an important role in the making, recall and renewal of appointments of temporary sheriffs, and the allocation of work to temporary sheriffs. It was argued that a trial before a temporary sheriff in such circumstances breached the Convention right to an 'independent and impartial tribunal', as provided for by Article 6(1) of the European Convention on Human Rights, because to do so would be contrary to the principles of judicial independence. The basis for this proposition was that the judge's appointment was dependent to a significant extent upon the same person, the Lord Advocate, who was also ultimately responsible for the prosecution. The consequence of this decision was that substantial changes were made to the conditions of appointment and service of temporary sheriffs to emphasise their independence from the prosecuting authorities.

Attempts to make similar arguments were unsuccessful, however, in *Robbie the Pict* v. *Wylie* 2007 JC 101 (regarding the independence of the clerk to a district court in a case involving a speeding offence where the clerk was employed by a local authority that was a member of a partnership maintaining speed cameras in its area), and in *Kearney* v. *HM Advocate*, 2006 SC (PC) 1, 2006 SLT 499 (regarding a trial, at the instance of the Lord Advocate, before a temporary judge on whose appointment the Lord Advocate had been consulted). Following the amendments made by SA 2012,[28] challenges to acts of the Lord Advocate can no longer be raised as 'devolution issues'.

Though most of the challenges to acts of the Scottish Ministers have been challenges to acts of the Lord Advocate, however, it is, of course, possible to challenge other types of action by them, and a number of such challenges has been made, without much success.

THE PRINCIPLES APPLIED BY THE COURTS

It can be seen that the number of challenges to the validity of Scottish Parliament legislation has been extremely limited. The number of successful challenges has been even more limited, being four in total so far (now that the *Scotch Whisky Association* has been finally determined by the Supreme Court). All the successful challenges have been founded on incompatibility with Convention rights. No cases have yet been successful based purely on the grounds that the Scottish Parliament legislation impinged on the matters reserved to the UK Parliament as a result of the provisions of Schedules 4 or 5 of the *Scotland Act 1998*. Nevertheless, even though the challenges have been few in number, it is still possible to draw out some general principles that the United Kingdom courts will apply in deciding whether or not a provision of Scottish Parliament legislation is outside devolved competence.

Firstly, a challenge to a legislative provision as relating to reserved matters[29] will not succeed if there is only a 'loose or consequential connection' with the reserved legislation under criticism. In the *Christian Institute* case[30] the Supreme Court endorsed the approach taken in *Martin v. Most* [2010] UKSC 10; 2010 SC (UKSC) 40 where Lord Walker said that the expression 'relates to' was 'familiar in this type of context, indicating more than a loose or consequential connection, and the language of section 29(3), referring to a provision's purpose and effect, reinforces that'. Such an approach was endorsed by Lord Hope in the *Imperial Tobacco* case. The court also agreed with[31] the approach, in relation to similar provisions in the Government of Wales Act 2006, which was taken in the case of *In re Agricultural Sector (Wales) Bill* [2014] UKSC 43; 1 WLR 2622, where it was stated:[32]

> As Lord Walker of Gestingthorpe JSC observed in *Martin v. Most* 2010 SC (UKSC) 40, paragraph 49, the expression 'relates to' indicates more than a loose or consequential connection. The issue as to whether a provision relates to a subject is to be determined ... by reference to the purpose of the provision, having regard (among other things) to its effect in all the circumstances.

As the section requires the purpose of the provision to be examined, it is necessary to look not merely at what can be discerned from an objective consideration of the effect of its terms. The clearest indication of its purpose may be found in a report that gave rise to the legislation, or in the report of an assembly committee; or its purpose may be clear from its context: *Imperial Tobacco Ltd* v. *Lord Advocate* 2013 SC (UKSC) 153, paragraph 16.

Looking at a provision's purpose and effect, however, is not the same as applying the 'pith and substance' test developed to resolve problems in a number of federal systems. The Inner House of the Court of Session was wrong when it used that 'pith and substance' test to decide whether or not any of the provisions of the 2014 Act relate to the reserved matters of DPA (Data Protection Act) and Directive 95/46/EC in *The Christian Institute* case.[33] The intention of the Scotland Act 1998 is that it is to the Act itself that one should look for guidance, not how the problem was handled in other jurisdictions. It is to the rules that the 1998 Act lays down that the court must address its attention.[34]

Moreover, if a provision has a number of purposes, and only one of them relates to a reserved matter, it will nevertheless be outside devolved competence unless that purpose can be regarded as consequential only, as can be seen from Lord Hope's comments in the Imperial Tobacco case:

> I do not see this as a case which gives rise to the problem which may need to be dealt with if the provision in question has two or more purposes, one of which relates to a reserved matter. In such a situation, the fact that one of its purposes relates to a reserved matter will mean that the provision is outside competence, unless the purpose can be regarded as consequential and thus of no real significance when regard is had to what the provision overall seeks to achieve.[35]

Secondly, although the rules of the 1998 Act are what the court should turn to when there is question of interpretation of Scottish legislation, the courts will give considerable weight to the rule in the 1998 Act that legislation (which could be read as being outside competence) should be read as narrowly as is required for it to be within competence, if that is at all possible.[36] The courts have, in a number of cases, relied on that provision to allow it to draw back from deciding that a particular provision is unlawful. They have recognised that 'the obligation to construe a provision in an Act of the Scottish Parliament so far as it is possible to do so is a strong one, and the court must prefer compatibility to incompatibility'.[37] It is certainly possible to draw from the limited case law so far that the courts have been reluctant to go as far as striking down Acts of the Scottish Parliament. When they have done so, they have, correctly, limited the effect of their decision, and have also used their powers under Section 102 of the 1998 Act to allow the legislature reasonable opportunities to correct the defect in question.

Thirdly, when it comes to challenges to Scottish Parliament legislation based on traditional judicial review grounds, then the courts are likely only to intervene in the most exceptional circumstances. The Supreme Court has recognised, as Lord Hope has explained,[38] "that the Scottish Parliament is nevertheless a body to which decision making powers have been delegated. And it does not enjoy the sovereignty of the Crown in Parliament that, as Lord Bingham of Cornhill said in Jackson, paragraph 9, is the bedrock of the British constitution. Sovereignty remains with the United Kingdom Parliament. The Scottish Parliament's power to legislate is not unconstrained. It cannot make or unmake any law it wishes."[39]

There being no provision in the Scotland Act which excludes the possibility of Acts of the Scottish Parliament being subject to judicial review on common law grounds, in principle Acts of the Scottish Parliament are amenable to the supervisory jurisdiction of the Court of Session at common law. The question is, of course, in what way should the Court of Session be prepared to exercise that supervisory jurisdiction. Lord Hope analyses that question from fundamental principles:

> The dominant characteristic of the Scottish Parliament is its firm rooting in the traditions of a universal democracy. It draws its strength from the electorate. While the judges, who are not elected, are best placed to protect the rights of the individual, including those who are ignored or despised by the majority, the elected members of a legislature of this kind are best placed to judge what is in the country's best interests as a whole. A sovereign Parliament is, according to the traditional view, immune from judicial scrutiny because it is protected by the principle of sovereignty. But it shares with the devolved legislatures, which are not sovereign, the advantages that flow from the depth and width of the experience of its elected members and the mandate that has been given to them by the electorate. This suggests that the judges should intervene, if at all, only in the most exceptional circumstances. As Lord Bingham of Cornhill said in R (Countryside Alliance) v. Attorney General [2008] 1 AC 719, paragraph 45, 'the democratic process is liable to be subverted if, on a question of political or moral judgment, opponents of an Act achieve through the courts what they could not achieve through Parliament'.[40]

Lord Hope agreed with the view of the Inner House that Acts of the Scottish Parliament are not subject to judicial review at common law on the grounds of irrationality, unreasonableness or arbitrariness. He pointed out that this was not needed, as there was already a statutory limit on the Parliament's legislative competence if a provision is incompatible with any of the Convention rights: Section 29(2)(d) of the Scotland Act 1998.

Moreover, 'it would also be quite wrong for the judges to substitute their views on these issues for the considered judgment of a democratically elected legislature unless authorised to do so, as in the case of the Convention rights, by the constitutional framework laid down by the United Kingdom Parliament'.

CONCLUSION

The history of the challenges which have been made to legislation made by the Scottish Parliament, whether because of claims that it was beyond devolved competence, or on common law grounds of judicial review, demonstrate the courts' unwillingness to interfere with the democratic will of the Scottish people expressed through the Scottish Parliament. If there is a clear case of legislation being beyond devolved competence, the courts will intervene but are likely to try to find a way of avoiding a direct challenge to the legislature if they can do so. Furthermore, so long as the Scottish Parliament is required to legislate in a way which is compliant with Convention rights, the courts are likely to strike down Acts of the Scottish Parliament on common law grounds only in the most extreme of cases.

NOTES

1. See Chapters 2 and 5.
2. See p. 66 for more discussion on the role of the Presiding Officer.
3. In Wales, following the transfer of limited powers to the National Assembly for Wales under the Government of Wales Act 2006, there has been a number of challenges by government Law Officers to its legislation. See the cases of *Attorney General* v. *National Assembly for Wales* [2013] 1 AC 792; In re Agricultural Sector (Wales) Bill [2014] UKSC 43, [2014] 1 W.L.R. 2622; and Re Recovery of Medical Costs for Asbestos Diseases (Wales) Bill, [2015] UKSC 3; [2015] A.C. 1016.

4. See, for example, the *Christian Institute* case discussed elsewhere in this chapter.
5. Judicial review proceedings in any matter can be raised only in the Court of Session, *Brown* v. *Hamilton District Council*, 1983 S.C. (H.L.) 1.
6. Prior to 1 October 2009, the jurisdiction of the UK Supreme Court on devolution issues, which it acquired under section 40(4)(b) of, and Schedule 9 to, the Constitutional Reform Act 2005 (cap 4), had been exercised by the Judicial Committee of the Privy Council.
7. Mr Whaley had previously attempted, unsuccessfully, to interdict Lord Watson from introducing or promoting his bill on the ground that, by receiving assistance from a campaign group, he was in breach of Article 6 of the Scotland Act 1998 (Members' Interests) Order 1999. *Whaley* v. *Lord Watson of Invergowrie*, 2000 SC 340.
8. Paragraph 20.
9. *Salvesen* v. *Riddell* [2013] UKSC 22; 2013 SC (UKSC) 236, paragraph 44.
10. Ibid. paragraph 46.
11. Ibid. paragraph 51.
12. As set out in section B2 of Part II of Schedule 5 to the Scotland Act 1998.
13. *The Christian Institute & Ors* v. *The Lord Advocate* [2016] UKSC 51, 2016 S.L.T. 805, paragraphs 83 and 84.
14. Ibid. paragraph 107.
15. Ibid. paragraph 107.
16. Ibid. paragraph 108.
17. See the previous chapter for the procedure to be used for challenges raised as 'compatibility issues'.
18. *AB* v. *HM Advocate*, [2017] UKSC 25, paragraph 47.
19. Ibid. paragraph 66.
20. *AXA General Insurance Ltd, Petitioners*, [2011] UKSC 46; 2012 S.C. (UKSC) 122; 2011 SLT 1061, paragraph 52.
21. Ibid. paragraph 153.
22. *Scotch Whisky Association* v. *Lord Advocate*, [2013] CSOH 70, 2013 SLT 776.
23. *Scotch Whisky Association* v. *Lord Advocate*, [2014] CSIH 38, 2013 SLT 776 [2013] 3 CMLR 34.
24. *Scotch Whisky Association* v. *Lord Advocate* (C-333/14).
25. Ibid. paragraph 50, Judgment of Court.
26. [2016] SLT 1141, paragraph 207.
27. Section 54 of SA 1998 is in the following terms:
    'section 54 Devolved competence
    (1) References in this Act to the exercise of a function being within or outside devolved competence are to be read in accordance with this section.
    (2) It is outside devolved competence:

(a) to make any provision by subordinate legislation which would be outside the legislative competence of the Parliament if it were included in an Act of the Scottish Parliament, or

(b) to confirm or approve any subordinate legislation containing such provision.

(3) In the case of any function other than a function of making, confirming or approving subordinate legislation, it is outside devolved competence to exercise the function (or exercise it in any way) so far as a provision of an Act of the Scottish Parliament conferring the function (or, as the case may be, conferring it so as to be exercisable in that way) would be outside the legislative competence of the Parliament.'

28. See p. 169.
29. Under sections 28 and 29(3) of the Scotland Act 1998.
30. Paragraph 29.
31. Paragraph 30.
32. Paragraph 50.
33. Paragraph 32.
34. Lord Hope at paragraph 13 in Imperial Tobacco case. Endorsed by the court in *The Christian Institute* case at paragraph 32.
35. Paragraph 43, *Imperial Tobacco* case. The court in *The Christian Institute* case quotes that passage in paragraph 31.
36. section 101, 1998 Act.
37. Lord Hope in *Salvesen* v. *Riddell*, paragraph 46, quoted above in this chapter.
38. Paragraph 46, *Axa General Insurance* case.
39. Paragraph 46, *Axa General Insurance* case.
40. Paragraph 49, *Axa General Insurance* case.

CHAPTER TEN

Finance

INTRODUCTION

The principal sources of finance for the Scottish Parliament and the Scottish Government are the 'block grant' allocated to it by the UK Government and Parliament; income tax; part of the VAT raised in Scotland; and certain 'devolved taxes'. Originally, when established in 1999, the Scottish Parliament had no powers over VAT or any devolved taxes, and its power over income tax was limited to a power to vary, up or down, the standard rate of tax by a maximum of 3 pence in the pound. In fact, as described later in this chapter, that power to vary the rate of income tax was never used and was actually allowed to lapse. The Calman Commission, however, recommended further devolution of tax-raising powers to the Scottish Parliament which were put into effect by the SA 2012. These powers were further enhanced by the provisions of the SA 2016, putting into effect the recommendations of the Smith Commission.

The Smith Commission Report,[1] at paragraph 95, set out a number of principles that it considered should govern the future financial relationship between the UK and Scottish Governments. It recommended that the Scottish Government would continue to receive a block grant from the UK Government and that this would continue to be determined via the operation of the Barnett Formula which is explained below. The revised funding framework should, however, result in the devolved Scottish budget benefiting in full from policy decisions by the Scottish Government that increase revenues or reduce expenditure, and the devolved Scottish budget bearing the full costs of policy decisions that reduce revenues or increase expenditure. For example, if the Scottish Government decided to increase income tax rates in Scotland, it would receive all the extra revenue to spend as it wished. Conversely, if it decided to cut income tax, it would have to reduce its spending to make up for the full amount of income it lost as a result. Another example would be that, if the Scottish Government decided to increase spending on the health service in Scotland, it could do that but it would have to increase Scottish taxes, or cut spending somewhere else, to pay for that extra spending on the health service.

The Smith Commission also recognised that a consequence of the further devolution of tax and spending powers to Scotland would mean that it was likely that there would be occasions when the decisions of either the UK or Scottish Government would affect the tax receipts or expenditure of the other. It therefore also recommended that, where either the UK or the Scottish Governments made policy decisions which affect those tax receipts or expenditure of the other, the government that made such a decision would reimburse the other if there was an additional cost, or receive a transfer from the other if there was a saving. The intention was that changes to taxes in the rest of the United Kingdom, for which the equivalent tax power in Scotland has been devolved, should affect public spending only in the rest of the United Kingdom. Equally, changes to devolved taxes in Scotland should affect public spending only in Scotland. Perhaps somewhat optimistically, the Smith Commission was also of the view that, once a revised funding framework had been agreed, its effective operation should not require frequent ongoing negotiation. It did recommend, however, that the arrangements should be reviewed periodically to ensure that they continue to be seen as fair, transparent, and effective.

These principles for the future fiscal arrangement between the UK and Scottish Governments were incorporated into an agreement reached between the two governments in March 2016.[2]

The various sources of finance available to the Scottish Government following the changes introduced after the reports of the Calman and Smith Commissions are now considered.

THE BLOCK GRANT AND THE BARNETT FORMULA

In 'Scotland's Parliament',[3] the UK Government made it clear that it envisaged that the main source of finance for the Parliament would be the block grant. The block grant is a grant paid by the UK Treasury, prior to devolution, to the Scottish Office, and, since then, to the Scottish Government. Notwithstanding the changes made by the SA 2012 and SA 2016 as a consequence of the Calman and Smith Commission reports, the block grant still remains the single most important element of the

Scottish Government's income but its relative significance has reduced substantially since the further devolution introduced by those two Acts.

The level of the block grant is decided from year to year in accordance with a formula that decides the balance of government spending between Scotland, England and Wales. This is known as the 'Barnett formula', named after the Chief Secretary to the Treasury in 1978 when the formula was devised to take account of the plans for devolution at that time. The Barnett formula took account of the fact that, at the time it was devised, government spending was relatively higher in Scotland (and Wales) than in England.[4] The formula aimed, at least in theory, to bring about a gradual convergence between the relative levels of government spending in Scotland, Wales, and England. In fact, for many years, primarily due to the fact that Scotland's share of the total population of Great Britain is declining, it appeared that convergence might never actually take place. The substantial increases in public expenditure introduced by the Labour Government after 1997, however, particularly in the 2002 Spending Round, meant that, in theory at least, convergence might have been achieved within a decade or two. Though there was, indeed, some convergence between 2002–3 and 2004–5, however, since then the gap has widened again as a result of those continuing long-term population trends.[5]

A significant change was made in the block grant arrangements as a result of the changes brought about by the Calman Commission and Smith Commission, and these are now described.

THE BLOCK GRANT AFTER THE SMITH COMMISSION

The Smith Commission laid down the principles under which the funding arrangements for the block grant would operate as a result of further devolution. It recommended that the initial devolution of tax receipts to the Scottish Government should be accompanied by a reduction in the block grant equivalent to the revenue lost by the UK Government because of the transfer of the tax receipts to the Scottish Government. That reduction in the block grant should be indexed appropriately so that it would increase or reduce each year in line with changes in the rate of inflation or deflation. Similarly, the initial devolution of further spending powers should be accompanied by an increase in the block grant equivalent to the existing level of Scottish expenditure by the UK Government. That is because the UK Government would no longer be delivering the item of expenditure in question, so the Scottish Government would receive the funds which had previously been spent by the UK Government on that item.

In addition, the increase in the block grant would include sums to cover any identified administrative savings arising to the UK Government from no longer delivering the devolved activity. The block grant would also give the Scottish Government additional funding to cover a share of the associated implementation and running costs in the policy area being devolved which would be sufficient to support the functions being transferred to the Scottish Parliament at the time that they were transferred. This future growth in the addition to the block grant, arising for this reason, should also be indexed appropriately. The consequence of these changes is that the block grant, which is still recalculated each year by the use of the Barnett formula, is to be adjusted annually to take account of the further devolution of tax and spending powers to Scotland.

The way that the revised system now works, with effect from the 2017/8 tax year, is as follows. The starting point is that the block grant in any particular year is made up of the previous year's block grant plus or minus sums described as 'Barnett consequentials'. These 'consequentials' arise when the UK Government decides to increase or reduce its spending in areas which are devolved to Scotland. When this happens, the Barnett formula is used to calculate how much would be the increase or reduction in spending in Scotland if that change were also applied to Scotland. The block grant is then reduced or increased accordingly. This reduction or increase is added to, or deducted from, the block grant as a lump sum. The Scottish Government is under no obligation to change its own spending in the areas which are the direct parallel in Scotland to the areas where spending levels have changed in England. For example, the UK Government could decide to increase or reduce its spending on health in England. The Scottish Government would then receive or lose an appropriate sum as a 'consequential', worked out by means of applying the Barnett formula. The Scottish Government could choose to reduce or increase its spending on health in Scotland too. If it wished, though, it could apply that change entirely or in part to another area of its budget such as transport or housing. It could also reduce or increase taxes to reflect, entirely or in part, the sums which it had received or lost as a result of 'Barnett consequentials'. In practice, when there have been increases in the block grant as a result of 'Barnett consequentials', the Scottish Government has frequently used the extra funds it has received for a different purpose from that on which spending has been increased in England.

The principle of the Scottish Government receiving either an increase or reduction in its grant as a consequence of the UK Government increasing or reducing its spending for the UK as a whole on functions of government which are undertaken by the Scottish Government in Scotland is not new. It was used to work out adjustments to the block grant prior to the further devolution of tax and spending powers in the SA 2012 and 2016.

What is new as a result of that further devolution, however, is the way that, in addition to the block grant figure being revised to take account of 'Barnett consequentials', 'block grant adjustments' ('BGAs') are calculated for each tax or benefit that is now devolved to Scotland. BGAs linked to the devolved or assigned taxes are now to be deducted from the block grant to reflect the fact that revenue from these taxes now flows to the Scottish Government. BGAs linked to the devolved benefits will be added to the block grant to reflect the fact that this spending on social security, which had previously been paid from the UK Treasury, will now be paid to the Scottish Government. The baseline on which BGAs are calculated are tax revenues in Scotland in the year prior to devolution of the tax or the benefit spend the year prior to devolution of the benefit.[6] The BGAs are indexed so that they increase or reduce each year. The change each year, as a result of indexation, is based on the annual growth or reduction in comparable revenue or expenditure in the rest of the United Kingdom. (Special arrangements are made for the calculation of the BGAs relating to the devolution of the Scottish assets and revenues of the Crown Estate to the Scottish Government.)[7]

The significance of these changes for the overall Scottish Government budget can be seen from the fact that the gross block grant of £30,274 million in 2016–17 was reduced by a BGA of £5,500 million. In 2017–18, when tax rates and bands were fully devolved, the gross block grant of £30,936 million was reduced by £12,450 million, a drop of more than 40 per cent. That drop therefore required the Scottish Government and Parliament to make its own tax and spending decisions to compensate for the reduction in the block grant.

THE FUTURE OF THE BLOCK GRANT AND THE BARNETT FORMULA

Though there have been suggestions from time to time that there should be some independent method of deciding the appropriate level of government grant to Scotland in relation to that of other parts of the United

Kingdom, no such provision has been adopted, and it is to be noted that every UK Government to date has committed itself to the continuing use of the Barnett formula. This was included in the 2015 Conservative Party election manifesto.[8] This restatement was made notwithstanding pressure over the years for a change to the method by which the block grant should be allocated, including a number of calls for expenditure per head in Scotland to be reduced to the average for the United Kingdom as a whole.[9] It should be noted that the SA 1998 has nothing to say about the level of the block grant or how the level of government expenditure in Scotland should relate to that of the rest of the United Kingdom. That being so, the UK Government could change the funding support mechanism for the Scottish Government without requiring either its approval or changes to the SA 1998. Given that there are no current indications that it intends to do so, it appears to be reasonable to assume that the current block grant system, incorporating the adjustments made after the SA 2012 and SA 2016, will continue to be the largest single constituent of the finance available to the new Parliament and the Scottish Government.

As the level of grant and the formula are left to the UK Government and Parliament, the SA 1998 needed to make only limited provision to allow the current system to be applied to the new Parliament. It simply establishes a Scottish Consolidated Fund and gives to the Secretary of State the powers to make payments into that fund 'out of money provided by [the UK] Parliament of such amounts as he may determine'.[10]

INCOME TAX

In contrast to the limited number of provisions allowing a block grant to be paid to the new Scottish Government, the provisions set out in the SA 1998, to allow the Parliament to raise its own taxes, are comprehensive. That arises from the fact that the power to levy taxes is one of the powers that are otherwise reserved to the UK Parliament, and many aspects of income tax are still reserved. This results in there being a considerable complexity in the way that the legislation has had to distinguish those aspects of income taxation that have been devolved from those that have not.[11]

The power to raise taxes is contained in Part IV of the Act. In its original version, the SA 1998 gave only the limited power to the Parliament to increase or decrease the basic rate of UK tax for 'Scottish taxpayers' by up to 3 pence in the pound. That power was never used. From the earliest days after the Parliament had been established, however, there were arguments that this tax power was insufficient and, moreover, that, by its predominant dependence on the 'block grant', the Parliament was able to spend tax without being accountable to the electorate who paid that tax. A classic early expression of that view can be found in the speech given in 2003 by David Steel shortly after he had completed his term as the first Presiding Officer of the Scottish Parliament where he said:

> no self-respecting parliament should expect to exist perma-
> nently on 100% handouts determined by another parliament, nor
> should it be responsible for massive public expenditure without
> any responsibility for raising revenue in a manner accountable to
> the electorate.[12]

No doubt partly as a result of these and similar views, the Parliament now has much more extensive powers over income tax. Following the implementation of the recommendations of the Smith Commission, the Parliament now has the power to set the rates of income tax for Scottish taxpayers, including the power to set different rates of tax for different bands and the thresholds at which they start. This power excludes the power to set rates and bands for savings and dividend income of Scottish tax payers. This, like all other aspects of income tax, remains reserved to the UK Parliament. The UK Parliament therefore retains power over the imposition of the annual charge to income tax, the level of personal allowances, the ability to introduce and amend tax reliefs, and the definition of income, as well as the taxation of savings and dividend income.

As the Scottish Government is to receive all income tax paid by Scottish tax payers on their non-savings and non-dividend income, a corresponding adjustment is made to the block grant received by it from the UK Government in the manner described earlier in this chapter.

In order to levy income tax, the Parliament must pass a 'Scottish rate resolution' for each year that it wishes to do so.[13] During the period when the Parliament had only the limited power to vary the basic tax rate by 3 pence in the pound, such a resolution was never passed. Since the Parliament's tax-raising powers were extended by the SA 2012, however. it has passed such a resolution every year since they came into effect for the 2016–17 financial year. If it had not done so, the finances of the Scottish Government would have been severely affected because part of the further devolution arrangements introduced after the Calman and Smith Commission reports was a reduction in the block grant to allow for the fact that the Scottish Parliament had been given extended tax-raising powers. If the Scottish Parliament had not levied a Scottish rate, the block grant would not have been increased to make up for the sum lost.

SCOTTISH TAXPAYERS

It will be seen that the tax-varying power applies only to 'Scottish taxpayers'. Accordingly, the SA 1998 requires to define such a person, and does so in a complex set of provisions set out in section 80D and subsequent sections. The Act should be referred to for its precise provisions but the basic definition is that a Scottish taxpayer is an individual who, in the relevant year, is resident for income tax purposes in the United Kingdom and also meets one or more of the following criteria:

1. having a close connection with Scotland;
2. spending more days of the relevant year in Scotland than in any other part of the United Kingdom, if he or she does not have a close connection with England, Wales, or Northern Ireland;
3. he or she is an MSP, an MP for a Scottish constituency, or an MEP for Scotland.

Section 80E defines the meaning of a 'close connection', and section 80F defines 'days spent' for the purposes of s 80D.[14]

The purpose of the definition is to ensure that all those who might reasonably be regarded as Scottish taxpayers are liable to the tax without also catching more transient persons, such as the occasional holiday visitor. It seeks to deal with some of the possible anomalies which might arise if the Scottish Parliament exercises its powers to vary the basic tax rate from that levied in England. For example, a person who lives in Dumfries, but who travels every day to work in Carlisle, will normally be a Scottish taxpayer (although that person's colleagues may well be paying a different tax rate if they live in Carlisle). A person who lives in Edinburgh, but commutes each week to work (and stays overnight) in London from Monday to Friday, will also still be regarded usually as a Scottish taxpayer as long as that person's home in Scotland can be regarded as his or her main place of residence. A person who normally resides outside Scotland, however, but who has a holiday home in Scotland, will, in most situations, not qualify as a Scottish taxpayer.

There is a number of other important features to note about the arrangements made in the Act for the use of the power to vary income tax:

- 'Scottish taxpayer' is defined as being an individual;[15]
- income from savings and distributions, as defined in section 73 of the SA 1998, is excluded from income to which the tax-varying power applies (so that any such income will not be liable to any increase in tax if a Scottish Parliament uses its power to raise taxes);[16]
- a proposal that the tax-varying power should be used can be put to the Parliament only by a member of the Scottish Government (so the power could not be used at the instigation of an opposition party, a committee of the Parliament, or an individual backbench MSP).[17]

THE USE OF THE INCOME TAX POWERS

Though the Parliament was given substantial devolution of tax and spending powers by the SA 2012 and SA 2016, it has not used its powers in such a way as to make major changes from the previous UK tax regime. In the first year that it used the powers under the SA 2012 (2016–17), it levied a Scottish rate of income tax at the same rate as the UK income tax rate applied for that year. In the 2017–18 financial year, when it was given full powers over income tax rates and bands, the Scottish Government again proposed to keep the tax rates the same as those levied by the UK Government for the rest of the United Kingdom. It did, however, take a slightly different approach to the UK Government in that it proposed to increase the threshold for payment of the higher rate of tax by Scottish taxpayers from £43,000 a year to £43,430 which was lower than the threshold proposed for the rest of the United Kingdom, namely £45,000. As a result of this proposal, the sum raised by income tax in Scotland would have been slightly higher, at £79 million, than if the UK threshold had been adopted.

The Scottish Government faced criticism that its budget proposals would have led to cuts in certain areas of public expenditure, particularly in support for local authority spending. Being a minority government after the 2016 Parliament elections, the SNP was forced to negotiate with the other political parties to get enough support to pass its budget. Eventually, it made a deal with the Scottish Green Party, as a result of which the threshold mentioned above was kept at £43,000 a year. This was estimated to increase by a further £29 million in 2017–18 (on top of the extra £79 million originally proposed by the SNP) the sum that the Scottish Government would receive by income tax as compared to what

Table 10.1

Scottish Income Tax Rates	Scottish Bands
Scottish Basic Rate 20 per cent	Over £11,500*–£43,000
Scottish Higher Rate 40 per cent	Over £43,000–£150,000
Scottish Additional Rate 45 per cent	Over £150,000**

* applies if individual taxpayer receives Standard UK Personal Allowance
** people earning more than £100,000 will have their personal allowance reduced by £1 for every £2 they earn above £100,000

it would have received if it had adopted the threshold for the point at which higher rate tax would apply[18] which it had originally proposed. Table 10.1 shows the Scottish income tax rates and bands for 2017–18.

VALUE ADDED TAX

The Smith Commission also recommended that the Scottish Government would receive a proportion of Value Added Tax (VAT) raised from Scotland. It proposed that the receipts raised in Scotland by the first 10 percentage points of the standard rate of VAT, and by the first 2.5 percentage points of the reduced rate of VAT, should be assigned to the Scottish Government's budget. The method of calculation of the relevant sums was to be agreed between the UK and Scottish Governments, and the sums received by the Scottish Government from the block grant would be reduced accordingly. The recommendation was incorporated into the SA 1998 by provisions in the SA 2016.[19] The Fiscal Framework states that VAT assignment will be implemented in 2019–20.

DEVOLVED TAXES

The SA 2012 and SA 2016 together gave the Scottish Parliament the power to levy certain specific taxes which are described as 'devolved taxes'. Four such devolved taxes are specified, and the power to levy these taxes is transferred from the UK to the Scottish Parliament by the changes made in the SA 2012 and SA 2016. These taxes are the following:

- **taxes on transactions involving interests in land.**[20] A different system of land taxation was introduced in Scotland by the Land and Buildings Transaction Tax (Scotland) Act 2013, replacing, for Scotland, Stamp Duty Land Tax which was previously levied across the UK. The first use of this power was for the 2016–17 financial year when it was expected that £538 million would be raised from that tax.

- **taxes on disposals of waste to landfill.**[21] The Landfill Tax (Scotland) Act 2014 replaced the previous UK Landfill Tax by a Scottish Landfill Tax. This also came into effect for the 2016–17 financial year in which it was expected to raise £133 million.
- **taxes on the carriage of passengers by air from airports in Scotland.**[22] The Scottish Government proposed that Air Departure Tax will replace the UK Air Passenger Duty tax from 1 April 2018, with a lower rate of tax to apply in Scotland than currently applies across the United Kingdom.[23] It has budgeted for a revenue of £326 million in the first financial year of its operation but its introduction has been deferred.
- **taxes on commercial exploitation of aggregate (except where it is used for fuel).**[24] No date for implementation of the devolution of this taxation power has been announced at the time of writing.

In addition, the Scottish Parliament can also be given the power by the UK Government to levy additional devolved taxes or to amend existing devolved taxes.[25] The Scottish Government has not yet given any firm indication, however, that it wishes to make use of this power. Its budget proposals for the period up to 2019–20 do not make provisions for any tax income to come from any other devolved tax.[26]

INCOME FROM FINES, FORFEITURES AND PENALTIES

A further source of potential income for the Scottish Government arises from the power given to the Secretary of State to make, with the consent of the Treasury, regulations requiring the sums raised from fines, forfeitures or fixed penalties to be paid into the Scottish Consolidated Fund.[27] This was envisaged by the Smith Commission as applying to such penalties imposed by courts and tribunals in Scotland, as well as sums recovered under Proceeds of Crime legislation. In this case also, the Scottish Government's block grant is adjusted to take account of the fact that these sums are now to be retained in Scotland.[28] By definition, the sums raised from these sources cannot be predicted with any certainty but have tended to be in the region of £35 million each year.[29]

BORROWING POWER

SA 1998 in its original form gave the Scottish Government limited powers to borrow money. The SA 2012 and SA 2016, however, extended those borrowing powers substantially. Scottish Ministers now have power to borrow from the Secretary of State for the following purposes:[30]

- to cover a temporary shortfall in the Scottish Consolidated Fund or to provide a working balance in that fund;
- to cover shortfall in receipts from devolved taxes, income tax from the Scottish rate of income tax, or from VAT raised in Scotland;
- to cover any shortfall arising from an excess of welfare payments from the Scottish budget over forecast welfare payments, and
- to cover any sums required to meet current expenditure because of a Scotland-specific negative economic shock.

The provision giving the Scottish Government power to borrow to cover shortfalls in tax receipts, or excess of welfare payments, is to allow for the fact that actual tax receipts or welfare spending in any period may obviously vary from the sum predicted to be raised or spent. The power to borrow as a consequence of a 'negative economic shock' is defined in the Fiscal Framework agreement as being triggered when onshore Scottish gross domestic product (GDP) growth is below 1 per cent in absolute terms on a rolling four-quarter basis and 1 percentage point below UK GDP growth over the same period.[31]

The total sum outstanding at any time in respect of the principal of sums borrowed from the Secretary of State for these purposes must not exceed £1.75 billion (though this limit can be increased by order).[32]

The Scottish Ministers can also, with the approval of the Treasury, borrow money by taking out loans, or by the issue of bonds,[33] to meet capital expenditure. In this case, the aggregate at any time outstanding in respect of the principal of sums must not exceed £3 billion (though this limit can also be increased by order).[34]

If Scottish Ministers wish to borrow money in any other ways, they can do so only under the authority of an Act of the UK Parliament.[35]

The SA 1998 also contains a transitional provision which applies in cases where the Secretary of State has lent funds from the UK National Loans Fund prior to the establishment of the Parliament. If the power under which the Secretary of State had made such loans has been transferred to the Scottish Ministers, any repayment of capital or interest on the loan is now paid to the Scottish Ministers and the Scottish

Consolidated Fund, with a matching adjustment made in the sums payable by the Secretary of State to the Scottish Ministers.[36]

ACCOUNTABILITY, SCRUTINY AND COLLECTION

As one would expect, the SA 1998 also contains a number of arrangements to ensure that the Scottish Parliament and Government use the finances available to them in a proper manner. Money may only be paid out of the Scottish Consolidated Fund for expenditure for which the Act or other legislation gives authority.[37] The SA 1998 obliged the Scottish Parliament to introduce legislation requiring the Scottish Ministers to prepare accounts of their income and expenditure and to lay accounts and report on them before the Parliament. Legislation to that effect – the Public Finance and Accountability (Scotland) Act 2000, which received the Royal Assent on 17 January 2000 – was passed early in the life of the Parliament. Its provisions include the establishment of Audit Scotland which provides a single public-sector audit service comprising existing staff of the Accounts Commission for Scotland and the Scottish staff of the National Audit Office.

The SA 1998[38] also provided for the appointment by the Crown, on the nomination of the Scottish Parliament, of an Auditor General for Scotland with duties that include the responsibility to examine and report on the accounts of income and expenditure of the Scottish Government. The Auditor General for Scotland also has a duty to examine the 'economy, efficiency, and effectiveness' with which the Scottish Ministers, the Lord Advocate, or any other person or organisation which has received money from the Scottish Consolidated Fund, have used the funds available to them.[39]

Accordingly, the Public Finance and Accountability (Scotland) Act 2000 gave the Auditor General for Scotland the power to commission financial-audit and value-for-money studies across much of the public sector in Scotland. The audit of local authorities, however, will continue to be supervised by the Accounts Commission for Scotland, and their audit reports will not be submitted to the Parliament. (The Accounts Commission uses the services of Audit Scotland to carry out this supervisory function.)

In line with a recommendation from the Smith Commission that the Scottish Parliament should seek to expand and strengthen the independent scrutiny of public finances, because the further devolution of tax and spending powers would be likely to lead to greater variability and uncertainty for the public finances,[40] the existing obligation on Scottish Ministers to provide information to the Treasury when required[41] has been supplemented with a provision giving the UK Office for Budget Responsibility a right of access to Scottish public services information.[42]

THE SCOTTISH FISCAL COMMISSION

The Scottish Government has also established the 'Scottish Fiscal Commission'[43] to provide independent scrutiny of Scottish Government forecasts of receipts and economic determinants from taxes devolved to Scotland. It was initially set up in June 2014 as a non-statutory body but, under the Fiscal Framework agreed by the Scottish and UK Governments to accompany the Scotland Act 2016, its remit was changed to give it a statutory responsibility for the production of such forecasts from April 2017.

The duties of the commission are set out in the Scottish Fiscal Commission Act 2016. Its key roles for draft Scottish Government budgets from 2018–19 are the following:

- to prepare independent forecasts of all revenue from fully devolved taxes including Land and Buildings Transaction Tax and Scottish Landfill Tax, and Non-Domestic Rate income;
- to prepare independent forecasts of income tax receipts arising from the rate-setting powers devolved to the Scottish Parliament;
- to lay before the Scottish Parliament a report on its forecasts at the same time as the Scottish Government publishes and lays before the Scottish Parliament its Draft Scottish Budget;
- to set out the commission's assessment of the reasonableness of Scottish Ministers' projections as to their borrowing requirements;
- to conduct its business independently and within the bounds of relevant legislation as defined by the Scottish Fiscal Commission Act 2016.

In the future, it is expected that the commission will also be given the responsibility to forecast onshore GDP in Scotland, demand-led devolved social security expenditure in Scotland, and other taxes as and when they are devolved, including the Scottish replacement for Air Passenger Duty and Aggregates Levy.

The Fiscal Framework agreement contains more measures aimed at ensuring that the new arrangements following on from further devolution of tax and spending powers work smoothly. It states that both governments will report to the UK and Scottish Parliaments on the finance, functions and duties arising from the SA 2016. The implementation, operation and review of the new fiscal framework as a whole will be governed by the Joint Exchequer Committee.[44] The fiscal framework sets up a dispute-resolution mechanism although the Memorandum of Understanding Procedure is still likely to have a role to play in resolving disputes over financial and fiscal questions between the two governments.[45] The arrangements set out in the Fiscal Framework will be reviewed following the UK and Scottish Parliament elections in 2020 and 2021 respectively.[46]

TAX COLLECTION

The UK government taxation authority, HM Revenue & Customs, (HMRC), will continue to have the responsibility to collect income tax in Scotland even though most aspects of it have been devolved. It will also continue to collect VAT in Scotland, notwithstanding the assignment of part of the revenue raised by that. A separate Scottish authority, however, Revenue Scotland, has been established by the Scottish Government with the responsibility to administer and collect devolved taxes, currently Land and Buildings Transaction Tax (LBTT) and Scottish Landfill Tax (SLfT). In due course, it will also have the responsibility to administer and collect other devolved taxes as and when they are introduced, including Scottish equivalents for Air Passenger Duty and the Aggregates Levy.[47]

OTHER SOURCES OF FINANCE

The SA 1998 places no general restrictions on the Scottish Parliament from introducing charges for services provided by the Scottish Government or by other bodies on its behalf. Accordingly, it has the power to raise finance in this way as long as the activity to be supported is one which falls within its general remit.

One source of funding, which has become of significant importance in a number of areas of government activity, that, in general, fall within the remit of the Scottish Parliament is the National Lottery. 'Betting, gaming, and lotteries' are matters reserved to the UK Parliament (with one minor exception)[48] so the Scottish Parliament and Government cannot legislate to establish a Scottish lottery. The National Lotteries

Act 2006,[49] however, introduced a number of provisions requiring the UK Secretary of State to consult with Scottish Ministers on a number of issues concerning the apportionment, allocation, and distribution of lottery funds and, in certain cases, transfers the power to issue directions to Scottish Ministers. Therefore, though the Scottish Government cannot vary Scotland's share of the total funds raised by the Lottery, it does have powers to ensure that the substantial funds available to the lottery-distribution bodies are allocated within Scotland in such a way as to reflect its general policy priorities.

An important source of finance for public-authority capital projects in Scotland over many years was 'Public–Private Partnerships' (PPP) (previously Private Finance Initiative [PFI] projects) where the projects, such as schools or hospitals, are built and, in some cases, operated by private companies which are then repaid over a lengthy period. Though a large number of capital projects have been undertaken through PPP/PFI, the financing mechanism is controversial in some quarters (not least because it is argued that the long-term costs of the finance can be excessive) and the SNP opposed its use. After it came to power in 2007, new PPP/PFI projects were dropped and, instead, the Scottish Government sought to develop a different means of involving private-sector capital in the financing of public-sector projects through a 'Non-Profit-Distributing (NPD)' programme delivered by a 'Scottish Futures Trust'. This faced a number of initial difficulties but is now well established as a means of funding for projects for the public sector. Both PPP/PFI and NPD projects ultimately depend on the principle that the private sector takes on board responsibility for the delivery of a project, funded by payments from the public sector over a long period, in such a way that the projects delivered by such methods do not have to be treated as public-sector capital projects and so are not constrained by public-sector spending controls at the time of construction. Of course, under all these types of arrangement, the public purse eventually has to pay the private sector, and it has been argued that the ultimate price paid by governments for projects taken forward in this way has been more expensive that it would have been if they had taken forward by conventional methods of funding public-sector capital projects. In addition, these arrangements have at times attracted critical attention from public-spending regulators on the basis that they were not genuinely private-sector projects. One such example was when, following new European Union accounting guidance[50] which came into effect in 2014, a number of NPD projects, which had been previously classified as private-sector projects, now had to be reclassified as public-sector projects. This was a significant change, as the total value of these projects was more than £1.5 billion.

As there are no specific reservations in the SA 1998, preventing the Scottish Government from obtaining grant aid for its activities, there is presumably no reason why it should not also seek grants from any source that might be prepared to finance its activities.

LOCAL TAXATION AND THE PARLIAMENT

As mentioned earlier in this chapter, the scheme of devolution set out in Schedule 5 to the SA 1998 provides that taxes and excise duties are, in general, reserved to the UK Parliament.[51] There are now several exceptions to that reservation, however, which give the Scottish Parliament considerable tax-raising devolution. In addition, there is an exception to the general reservation of taxation powers which allows the Scottish Parliament to legislate on the system of local taxation.[52] Council tax and non-domestic rates are given as specific examples of such local taxation on which the Parliament is able to legislate.

The Parliament therefore has wide powers to reform local taxation if it so wishes. It has the power to make fundamental reforms to the system of local government finance and calls for such reforms have been frequently made since the Parliament was established. Among the proposals have been the introduction of a land-value tax, a steeply progressive property tax, a reformed, proportionate Council Tax[53] and the introduction of a local tourist tax.[54] It can make changes to the way that the present system is administered, for example, by changing the banding system for council tax. It can decide whether to retain its current powers to set a level for the non-domestic rate (the 'business rate') on a Scotland-wide basis, or to allow local councils to determine the level of business taxation in their area as used to be the case. The Parliament can also decide whether to impose any 'cap' on the spending of local councils. Such a cap has, in fact, been in place since 2008. However, it was not imposed by legislation but by a decision of the Scottish Government to give additional financial support to local authorities which complied with a council tax freeze. As the effect of refusing to comply with the Scottish Government's wishes would have had serious financial consequences for a local authority which did not, local authorities accepted the freeze though, in most cases, reluctantly. All councils complied with the freeze until it was lifted in 2017.

From time to time, it has also been suggested that the Scottish Parliament should introduce new forms of local taxation such as local income tax or local sales tax and, indeed, the SNP Scottish Government sought to introduce a local income tax after it took power in 2007. The SNP continues to have a policy in favour of the introduction of a local income tax in principle. In practice, however, such changes would need the consent of the UK Parliament (or at least the agreement of the UK Government) because they would be practicable only if the UK sales and income taxes systems were modified to make the collection of such a tax possible. Practical difficulties of this type were among the reasons (along with political opposition) why the SNP eventually dropped the proposal and, to date, no significant changes to the system of local taxation have been made since the establishment of the Scottish Parliament. In fact, as we have seen, far from change in the system of local government finance, the first ten years of the SNP Scottish Government saw the imposition of a council tax freeze. Only in 2017 did the Scottish Government relax the freeze to a limited extent by allowing councils to increase council tax for all properties by up to 3 per cent and by imposing a mandatory graduated increase for all higher-value domestic properties.[55]

The only other changes to the local-taxation system so far have been minor changes to the business rate for local government, introduced in 2003, with a small business-rate relief scheme which provided for reductions in rates paid by smaller businesses, funded by increases in rates for larger businesses. This was replaced in 2008 with a small-business bonus scheme, still funded partly by higher rates for larger businesses. A revaluation of businesses' liability for rates was undertaken to take effect for the 2017–18 financial year. Though many businesses had a reduced rates liability as a result of the revaluation, many others which had to pay substantially increased rates protested and, as a result, the Scottish Government introduced extra measures of transitional relief aimed at such businesses.[56] This had the effect of delaying the full impact of the revaluation.

THE INTERRELATIONSHIP BETWEEN LOCAL AUTHORITY SPENDING AND SCOTTISH GOVERNMENT SPENDING

As a substantial proportion of the resources provided either by the block grant or by the use of its own tax-raising powers is then passed on to local government to support the services that it provides, the possibility exists that the Scottish Government could increase the real resources available to it by the device of reducing the sums it pays to local government. As a result, it would be able to retain a bigger share of the resources available to it, and local councils would have to meet the shortfall in resources either by cutting services or increasing local taxation. Some might well argue that such circumstances applied in the case of the council-tax freeze just described, though the Scottish Government view was that it adequately compensated local authorities for the cost of the freeze by adjusting the funds it made available to local government. By such means, the Scottish Parliament could, in effect, increase its tax-raising powers by making use, in an indirect manner, of the taxation powers available to local government. Though there are no specific provisions in the SA 1998 to meet such an eventuality, however, the government clearly had in mind, when it launched its proposals for Scottish devolution, that some controls over local-government expenditure might be required.

Consequently, it is stated in Scotland's Parliament[57] that, if there were to be growth in the 'self-financed' expenditure of local councils which could be considered 'excessive and were such as to threaten targets set for public expenditure . . . it would be open to the UK Government to take the excess into account in considering the level of their support for expenditure in Scotland' if the Scottish Parliament chose not to take steps to reduce that growth in expenditure. In blunt terms, that would mean that, if local councils increased local taxes, either because of their own decisions or as a result of reduction in grant support from the Scottish Parliament, the UK Government might well reduce the block grant payable to the Parliament. Such a threat was presumably meant to serve as a powerful incentive to encourage the Scottish Parliament to restrain local-government expenditure.

Such draconian action has never been taken by any UK Government against the Scottish Government, however, and, indeed, any action of such a nature would appear to conflict with the principles set out in the Smith Commission report which, as we have seen, are aimed at giving the Scottish Parliament extensive fiscal autonomy.

The activities of local government could have an indirect effect on the financial arrangements for a devolved Scotland in another way. At present, central government provides the bulk of the funding for the payments made by local councils as council tax benefit, housing benefit, and universal credit. This is likely to continue even with the devolution of some further powers over welfare benefits which was introduced in the SA 2016. Under present arrangements, if local councils in Scotland were substantially to increase their levels of council tax and/or housing rent, the effect would be to increase the level of funding from central government. Scotland's Parliament made it clear that the resources for these benefits will be included, after devolution, within the block grant so that, if expenditure on these benefits increases as a result of decisions taken by Scottish local councils, it will be the Scottish Parliament that will have to find the extra money.[58]

It should be noted that, although there are potential mechanisms to allow the UK Government to recoup any additional expenditure incurred by it as an indirect result of actions by the Scottish Government or local authorities in Scotland, there are no formal mechanisms (other than through negotiating an increase in block grant) to reimburse funds to the Scottish Government if the UK Government saves money as a result of a decision by the former. This apparent imbalance was highlighted in 2001 when the then Scottish Executive decided to fund free personal care for the elderly in Scotland. The Scottish Executive argued that, as a result, the UK Government would need to spend £23 million less on social-security payments in Scotland, and asked the UK Government to transfer that sum of money to the Scottish Executive to help it meet the cost of providing free personal care. The UK Government refused to give the Scottish Executive the additional funds, requiring the Scottish Executive to meet the additional cost from within the block grant it receives from the UK Government (which, admittedly, would begin to increase substantially at the time that the new costs for personal care would be incurred).

As described above, however, one of the principles set out by the Smith Commission was that, where either the UK or the Scottish Governments makes policy decisions affecting the tax receipts or expenditure of the other, the decision-making government will reimburse the other if there is an additional cost or receive a transfer from the other if there is saving. If that principle had been agreed and implemented at the time of the dispute concerning the cost of social-security payments in Scotland, the Scottish Government would have received an appropriate payment from the UK Government reflecting the sum that the latter had saved as a result of the Scottish Government's decision.

Since the SNP formed its first government in 2007, there has been a substantial increase in the number of disputes between the Scottish Government and the UK Government on aspects of the financial settlement between the former and latter. It may be, however, that, given the substantially increased devolution of tax and spending powers introduced by the SA 2012 and SA 2016, such disputes may reduce. The potential for conflict is always there, however, given that the Scottish Government still relies heavily on a block grant, calculated each year in accordance with the Barnett Formula. As a result, if UK fiscal decisions result in an overall reduction in spending at UK level, that is also likely to be reflected in reductions in the block grant paid by the UK Government to the Scottish and the other devolved administrations in the UK.

THE FUTURE

The Scottish Parliament has come a long way from its original status as a body which combined extensive powers to legislate and spend along with limited autonomy over its ability to raise finance, autonomy which was moreover never exercised. As a result of the reforms introduced to implement the recommendations of the Calman and Smith Commissions, the Scottish Government will have its own financial resources to meet approximately half of its current budget, once those reforms are fully implemented. With the exception of the share of VAT assigned to the Scottish Government, it will, in conjunction with the Scottish Parliament, have the power to increase, reduce, or amend a wide range of taxes raised in Scotland.

There remain significant taxes raised in Scotland which are decided, raised, and allocated at UK level. These include corporation tax and a substantial portion of VAT. There are those who would like to see these and other taxes devolved to the Scottish Parliament. Some would even argue that all taxes raised in Scotland should be paid to the Scottish Government, and that the Scottish Government would then make payment to the UK Government for an appropriate share of expenditure on UK-wide and international functions. Nevertheless, notwithstanding such calls, there is no doubt that the Scottish Parliament can no longer be regarded as an institution where the link between financial accountability for the raising of expenditure is almost entirely unconnected with decisions on how to spend the money raised. With the ability to make its own decisions over how it raises much of its finance, and how the funds raised are spent, the Scottish Parliament now has the power and the necessity to decide its own spending priorities over wide areas of government activity in Scotland, along with the financial autonomy to decided how those priorities should be paid for.

NOTES

1. The Smith Commission: Report of the Smith Commission for further devolution of powers to the Scottish Parliament, 27 November 2014, paragraph 95.

2. Scottish Government and UK Government (2016): The agreement between the Scottish Government and the United Kingdom Government on the Scottish Government's fiscal framework ('the Fiscal Framework).

3. Scottish Office, *Scotland's Parliament* (1997), Cm 3658.

4. After the 1992 general election, the formula was revised to a limited extent by Michael Portillo (then Chief Secretary to the Treasury).

5. See IPPR report 'Fair Shares? Barnett and the politics of public expenditure', July 2008. (See Table 4.1, p. 16.)

6. Except for Cold Weather Payments where the initial baseline addition will be an average of the UK Government's spending in Scotland on this benefit from 2008–09 to the year prior to devolution of the legislative power over Cold Weather Payments. (Fiscal Framework, paragraph 13).

7. See Scottish Parliament Information Centre (SPICe) briefing, 16/88, p. 14.

8. Conservative Party election manifesto, p. 70.

9. See, for example, the report of the House of Lords Select Committee on the Barnett Formula (First Report, ordered to be printed 9 July 2009, and some of the evidence given to it.)

10. SA 1998, section 64.

11. SA 1998, Schedule 5, Part II, section A1.

12. Lord Steel of Aikwood, Donald Dewar Memorial Lecture (Edinburgh International Book Festival), 2003 (quoted in Alan Page, *Constitutional Law of Scotland*, Edinburgh, 2015, p. 227, paragraph 14–06).

13. Section 80C, SA 1998. See also sections 14 and 15 of SA 2016 for details of amendments to the Income Tax Act 2007 and Finance Act 2014 required to give effect to the extended tax-raising powers.

14. SA 1998 also includes a provision, section 80DA, that specifies when a Scottish Parliamentarian, who is also a Welsh Parliamentarian, is regarded as a Scottish taxpayer. It can be envisaged that this provision is unlikely to apply to many individuals, if ever.

15. So sole traders and partners in firms would be liable to pay the varied rate of tax but bodies such as companies and trusts will not.

16. Among the types of income that will normally be covered are wages and salaries from employment, most pensions, the profits of a trade or profession, and the profits from land.

17. SA 1998, section 80C (8).

18. See Scottish Government: Scotland's Budget: Draft Budget 2017–18.

19. Section 64A of SA 1998.

20. 80I, SA 1998.

21. Section 80K, SA 1998.

22. Section 80L, SA 1998.

23. Details of the proposed bill and the related consultation process can be found at http://www.parliament.scot/parliamentarybusiness/Bills/102778.aspx (last accessed 10 April 2017).

24. Section 80M, SA 1998.

25. By section 80B, SA 1998.
26. Scottish Government: Scotland's Budget: Draft Budget 2017–18, Table 1.01.
27. S 65A, SA 1998.
28. The Smith Commission: Report of the Smith Commission for further devolution of powers to the Scottish Parliament, 27 November 2014, paragraph 96(6).
29. In both 2013–14 and 2014–15 (years before this income was devolved), the total raised each year was a little over £35 million. See SPICe Briefing, 16/88, p. 10.
30. Section 66, SA 1998.
31. Explanatory Notes, SA 2016, paragraph 166.
32. SA 1998, section 67(1), (2), (3), (3A).
33. Except bonds transferable by delivery, section 66(1A).
34. SA 1998, section 67A.
35. SA 1988, section 66(4).
36. SA 1998, section 71.
37. SA 1998, section 65.
38. SA 1998, section 69.
39. SA 1998, section 70.
40. 'The Smith Commission: Report of the Smith Commission for further devolution of powers to the Scottish Parliament', 27 November 2014, paragraph 95(7).
41. SA 1998, section 96.
42. SA 1998, section 96A.
43. See http://fiscal.scot (last accessed 10 April 2017) for more details of the Scottish Fiscal Commission.
44. One of the Joint Ministerial Committees. See Chapter 7.
45. Ibid.
46. Scottish Government and UK Government (2016): The agreement between the Scottish Government and the United Kingdom Government on the Scottish Government's fiscal framework, paragraph 21.
47. See https://www.revenue.scot (last accessed 10 April 2017) for more information about Revenue Scotland.
48. Under Schedule 5, Part II, B9 'Betting, gaming and lotteries' is a reserved matter, except for the authorisation, in off-track premises, of the number of gaming machines authorised for which the maximum charge for use is more than £10 (or whether such machines are authorised).
49. See National Lotteries Act 2006, sections 7, 8, 15 and 36E.
50. The 'European System of Accounts 2010 (ESA 2010)'. See SPICe research briefing 16/103, p. 12 for details of the accounting change, and also the projects affected.
51. SA 1998, Schedule 5, Part II, section A1.
52. SA 1998, Schedule 5, Part II, section A1.

53. These were the options for a reformed local taxation system given most consideration by the Commission on Local Tax Reform. See SPICe (Scottish Parliamentary Information Centre) briefing 16/28, 15 March 2016, p. 6.

54. There has been an extensive (though to date unsuccessful) campaign by Edinburgh City Council, supported by various business organisations, for the Scottish Government to allow the council to impose a 'bed tax' to be paid by tourists staying in hotels in the city. See http://www.scotsman.com/news/poll-should-edinburgh-have-a-tourist-tax-1-4343839 (last accessed 10 April 2017). Arguably, such a tax might in any event be considered a local tax and, therefore, the power to allow a local authority to charge such a tax might fall within the existing devolved competence that the Scottish Parliament has had since 1999.

55. The mandatory increase was imposed on all properties valued in Bands E to H inclusive, starting at 7.5 per cent for Band E properties and increasing in steps for each band up to an increase of 22.5 per cent for Band H properties.

56. See http://www.gov.scot/Topics/Government/local-government/17999/11199/FactSheet-MrMackayStatement21022017/busrates21feb17 (last accessed 10 April 2017).

57. Scottish Office, *Scotland's Parliament* (1997), Cm 3658, paragraph 7.24.

58. Ibid., paragraph 7.25.

CHAPTER ELEVEN

The European and International Dimensions

INTRODUCTION

On 23 June 2016, in a referendum across the United Kingdom, a majority of voters decided that the UK should leave the European Union. That referendum was not binding upon the UK Government or Parliament but the then Prime Minister, David Cameron, made it clear immediately after the referendum that his government would accept the decision. Initially the UK Government intended to begin the process of terminating the UK's EU membership by notifying the European Union of the intention to withdraw through ministerial action alone by the use of the royal prerogative. Legal proceedings were raised to challenge the UK Government's power to do that, however, and, in January 2017, the Supreme Court ruled that notification of that intention could only be given by the UK Government with the authority of an Act of Parliament.[1] The UK Government accordingly introduced a bill into Parliament to give it that authority, and that Act of Parliament, the European Union (Notification of Withdrawal) Act 2017, was enacted on 16 March 2017. Using that authority, the Prime Minister, Theresa May, formally notified the European Union on 29 March 2017 of the UK's intention to leave the European Union.

The process by which any member state leaves the European Union is governed by Article 50 of the Treaty on European Union (TEU). That provides that a member state will leave the EU two years after notice to leave is given unless agreement is reached between the European Union and the member state that it should leave on a different date or, alternatively, that the two-year notice period should be extended. As part of the United Kingdom, Scotland will therefore leave the EU along with the rest of the UK unless, of course, Scotland negotiates its own agreement to allow it to continue to remain in the European Union as an independent member state after the UK's departure. It is clear, however, that, because of the complex negotiations that will be required to give effect to the UK's withdrawal from the EU, it is likely that the United Kingdom will remain in the European Union until some date in 2019, and perhaps later. Even after departure from the EU, the UK Government has recognised that some form of 'implementation' or transitional arrangements is likely to be required after the date of departure. These could last for several years after that date. The current constitutional position of Scotland in relation to the European Union and EU law may therefore continue to apply in certain areas for some time. Relationships with the EU, and EU law, are likely to remain of considerable importance for Scotland and, indeed, for the rest of the United Kingdom.

In this chapter, therefore, we set out the way in which the constitutional arrangements for devolution ensure that Scottish Parliament legislation is consistent with the principles of the UK's current membership of the European Union, and how disputes about those matters are resolved. We also describe the mechanisms established by the Scottish Parliament to consider European issues, both in legislating but also on wider policy issues, and briefly consider the relationship between Scotland and the Council of Europe and with the European Court of Human Rights in particular. These are not institutions of the European Union. Finally, we consider questions as to how the UK's departure from the EU will affect the future role and activities of the Scottish Parliament. We also look briefly at Scottish Parliament and Government links with the wider world outside Europe.

As regards to the question of the Scottish Parliament's relationship with the European Union, the issue of how the establishment of a Scottish Parliament would affect relationships with European institutions, and the European Union in particular, is one that was considered in the final report of the Scottish Constitutional Convention, and the government made various proposals regarding the relationship with the European Union in the White Paper: *Scotland's Parliament*.[2]

The issue is important because the European Union makes legislation that is binding in all member states or that member states are obliged to implement. If a member state has devolved certain of its powers to a devolved legislature (such as the Parliament), a mechanism must be put in place to ensure that such a devolved legislature both implements European legislation which the member state is obliged to implement and also does not seek to make legislation that would contravene existing European law. Such a mechanism is important, not least because the member state could, in the last analysis, be fined by the Court of Justice of the European Union or be required to pay compensation to anyone whose interests had been damaged by a failure of a devolved legislature to comply with European law.

The reverse side of the coin is that it is only the member states that participate in the Council of Ministers which plays the most important part in the legislative process of the European Union (the only possible mechanism for formal participation in that legislative activity by devolved legislatures being through the minimal consultative rights given to regions in the Committee of the Regions). Thus, a devolved legislature finds itself being required to implement European legislation in the adoption of which it has had no direct say. It can readily be seen that such a situation, though perfectly feasible in terms of constitutional arrangements, is one that might present political difficulties both for the devolved legislature and for the sovereign legislature of the state concerned.

The devolution scheme for Scotland addressed these issues in two ways. First, the legislative arrangements for devolution include mechanisms to ensure that the Scottish Parliament complies with European legislation and other obligations where these concerned devolved matters. Second, the UK Government agreed to give the Scottish Parliament and Government some role in the European legislative and policymaking process even though it is the United Kingdom which, as the member state, is the entity that has the legal right to take part in that process.

THE LEGISLATIVE PROVISIONS

The Scotland Act 1998 (SA 1998) sought to ensure, by means of a few simple mechanisms, that the Parliament does not breach the UK's European obligations.

First, it provides that any Act of the Scottish Parliament which is incompatible with the 'Convention rights' enshrined in UK law by the Human Rights Act 1998, or with EU law, is outside the legislative competence of the Parliament and cannot become law.[3]

Second, it provides that a member of the Scottish Government cannot make any subordinate legislation, or do anything else, which is incompatible with the Convention rights or with EU law (subject to a reservation in respect of certain acts by the Lord Advocate relating to the prosecution of crime).[4]

Third, UK Ministers continue to be able to implement EU obligations by means of secondary legislation even where it covers matters that are devolved to the Scottish Parliament.[5]

Fourth, the UK Parliament retains a general right to legislate for Scotland, even over devolved matters, and clearly this power could be used to ensure compliance by the Scottish Government and Parliament with the UK's obligations under EU law.

Moreover, in the White Paper, *Scotland's Parliament*,[6] it was envisaged that there might be cases where (with the agreement of the Scottish Government) implementation of EU obligations affecting devolved matters might be achieved by UK (or GB) legislation rather than by specifically Scottish legislation, and this has happened on a number of occasions.[7] Furthermore, where EU obligations are to be implemented by separate legislation in the Scottish Parliament, it is stated that 'there will be arrangements with the UK Government to ensure that differences of approach are compatible with the need for consistency of effect, and to avoid the risk of financial penalties falling on the UK'. It can be seen, therefore, that, if any concerns arising from such differences of approach cannot be resolved by agreement between the UK Government and the Scottish Government, the UK Government has reserved powers that it can use to legislate on devolved matters to resolve the dispute as it sees fit, though, in fact, it has never chosen to take that course of action.

Accordingly, the legislation contains mechanisms to deal with any eventuality that might arise if the Scottish Parliament or Government fails to comply with obligations under EU law. An attempt to pass legislation or do anything which conflicts with such obligations is unlawful. If the Scottish Parliament or Government refuses to legislate to take account of changing European obligations and, as a result, by an act of omission places itself in contravention of such obligations, the UK Government can enforce compliance by passing both primary and secondary legislation in appropriate terms. In addition, of course, the allocation of block grant is a matter entirely for the UK Government and Parliament, so no doubt any financial penalty falling on the United Kingdom as a result of such a breach of obligation could be compensated by a commensurate reduction in the grant paid to the Scottish Government. (Furthermore, the concordat on EU policy issues, which is considered in the following section, commits the Scottish Government to meeting the costs of any financial penalties imposed on the UK as a result of a failure on the part of the Scottish Administration to implement EU obligations in devolved matters.)

CONSULTATIVE ARRANGEMENTS

The requirement of the devolved Parliament and Executive to comply with European obligations was therefore clearly a cornerstone of the SA 1998. The Scottish Parliament and Government, however, were not given any statutory rights in the Act to participate in the decision-making process that eventually results in European legislation. This is in contrast with some other European countries where devolved or federal regions and states have, in some cases, been given a legal right under these countries' own constitutional arrangements to take part, to some degree at least, in the process whereby the member state takes part in the European decision-making and legislative process.[8]

Instead, the UK Government proposed that a number of consultative, but non-statutory, methods should be established to allow the Scottish Parliament and the then Executive to play a part in those aspects of European business that affect devolved areas. This statement of intent was put into effect in one of the concordats agreed between the UK Government and the various devolved administrations after their establishment. The Concordat on Co-ordination of European Union Policy Issues[9] states that it is the UK Government's wish to involve the Scottish Ministers as directly and fully as possible in decision making on EU matters that touch on devolved areas (including non-devolved matters which would have an important impact on Scotland). It emphasises that such involvement by the Scottish Ministers would be subject to 'mutual respect for the confidentiality of discussions and adherence by the Scottish Ministers to the resulting UK line'. It indicates that, without such respect and adherence, it would be impossible to maintain close working relationships, presumably implying that a Scottish Government which refused to be bound by such conditions would be at risk of losing its right to participate in decision-making on EU matters. That concordat is still in force and was incorporated in the latest restatement of the Memorandum of Understanding and Supplementary Agreements between the UK Government and the devolved administrations which was presented to the four Parliaments and Assemblies in October 2013.

The concordat established a number of mechanisms to facilitate the involvement by the Scottish Executive in such EU issues. These mechanisms consist of the following:

- a commitment by the UK Government to provide the Scottish Government with full and comprehensive information, as early as possible, on all business within the EU which appears likely to be of interest to it, with a reciprocal requirement on the Scottish Government to provide information to the UK Government on such issues in its turn;

- access by officials of the Scottish Government to the same relevant papers on EU issues as their Whitehall counterparts;
- reference of matters to the Joint Ministerial Committee for discussion when differences between the Scottish and UK Governments cannot be resolved by more informal contact;
- the possibility of Ministers from the Scottish Government attending meetings of the Council of Ministers on relevant matters, although it would be up to the relevant UK Minister to decide whether or not such attendance was appropriate. In certain cases, the Scottish Minister could speak for the United Kingdom as a whole although the UK 'lead minister' will retain overall responsibility for negotiations (similar arrangements would apply to allow participation in EU meetings at official level);
- the right of the Scottish Government to establish an office in Brussels for the purpose of assisting direct relationships with other European regional governments and with the institutions of the European Communities. Such an office is restricted, however, to dealing with matters that are within the competence of the Scottish Parliament and Government, and is required to work closely with, and in a complementary manner to, the UK representation in Brussels. This qualification is clearly intended to prevent such an office turning into a 'Scottish embassy' or something similar, as advocated from time to time by the SNP;
- the delegation to the Scottish Government of the appointment of the Scottish members of the UK representation on the Committee of the Regions, and the Economic and Social Committee;
- a commitment that the relevant Whitehall department would keep the Scottish Government informed of EU legislative proposals in order that the Scottish Parliament can, if it wishes, scrutinise such matters and let the UK Government have its views on such proposals;
- detailed arrangements for ensuring that new EU obligations are implemented in Scotland, as and when they arise, and for the co-ordination of the UK response to any proceedings taken against the UK for alleged breach of an EU obligation concerning a devolved matter.

There are also parts of the separate 'Concordat on Financial Assistance to Industry'[10] which have a bearing on Scotland's relations with Europe. Among other things, it provides that Ministers and officials of the devolved administration will be fully involved in discussions within the United Kingdom about the UK's policy position on all issues that touch on financial assistance to industry where this relates to the European Union. There will also be consultation with the devolved administrations on proposals that the UK makes to the EU regarding the designation of assisted area.

The experience of the first two sessions of the devolved arrangements, from 1999 to May 2007, suggests that these mechanisms indeed worked reasonably smoothly and more or less in the manner envisaged when they were set up. Scottish Ministers do participate reasonably frequently in the Council of Ministers as part of the UK delegation and, on a few occasions, a Scottish Minister has taken the lead on behalf of the UK as a whole.[11] Since the change of political control from Labour/Liberal Democrat to SNP in 2007, however, there have been some complaints from Scottish MSPs that they are not involved in international discussions and delegations as often as they feel they should be. For example, the Scottish Ministers were denied a place on the UK Government's delegation to the United Nations Conference on Climate Change in Copenhagen in 2009, although they were included in the UK delegation to the subsequent major United Nations climate change conference in Paris in 2015.[12]

The Scottish Executive established a European office very soon after devolution, in October 1999, sharing Scotland House with Scotland Europa, an umbrella body representing public-, private-, and voluntary-sector interests, which had already operated a Brussels office for a number of years. This office works very closely with the UKRep office in Brussels.[13] Working relationships have also been set up between the Scottish Government and UK departments to deal with questions of whether European obligations affecting devolved issues should be applied in Scotland by the Scottish Government or by means of a UK/ GB statutory instrument.[14]

During the eight-year period of Labour/Liberal Democrat coalitions, the Scottish Executive declared itself generally satisfied with the way in which these mechanisms, aimed at promoting co-operation between the UK and Scottish levels of government, worked in practice. The Joint Ministerial Committee on Europe met on a few occasions to discuss EU issues and to review the co-ordination arrangements, and it proved unnecessary for the committee to act as the formal forum for resolving any differences between the Scottish and UK Governments that could not be resolved informally because both the UK and Scottish Governments were Labour led.[15]

With the change of political control, however, and the establishment of an SNP-led minority administration in 2007, intergovernmental relationships with the UK on many issues became less cordial. One matter of contention was the infrequency of meetings of the Joint Ministerial Committee on Europe. The committee now meets more frequently.

THE SCOTTISH PARLIAMENT AND EUROPEAN ISSUES

It is, of course, not just the Scottish Government that has had a role to play in European matters as far as devolved issues are concerned. Alongside the Scottish Government's mainly informal role in the development of UK policy on EU matters has to be set the Scottish Parliament's role in this area. Given its legislative powers, the Scottish Parliament can decide how EU legislation is implemented in devolved matters (except in the unusual case of being overruled by the UK Parliament's reserved power of legislation). Moreover, although, as we have seen, it is ultimately the UK Government that decides what input there will be from the United Kingdom into decision-making and legislation within the European Union, the Scottish Parliament decided from the start that it would take the opportunity offered to it of scrutinising EU legislative proposals in advance. To deal with such matters, the Parliament established a European (from 2003, a European and External Relations) Committee[16] with the primary function of undertaking detailed scrutiny of draft EU legislation and its implementation within Scotland. The committee's current remit extends beyond European and external affairs, and now has the remit to cover culture and tourism as well, reflecting the reorganisation of the ministerial structure of the Scottish Government carried out by the SNP after it formed an administration in 2007. The committee is therefore now known as the 'Culture, Tourism, European and External Affairs Committee'.

As well as its role in the scrutiny of EU legislation, the committee was also given a remit to deal with 'any European Communities or European Union issue' and, since it was redefined to include external relations more generally, the international activities of the Scottish Government concerning both the European Union and anywhere else in the world. The committee therefore has the ability to fulfil both the specialist function of scrutinising EU legislation and also the role of a generalist committee on European affairs. The committee has enthusiastically taken up the latter opportunity, undertaking a wide range of activities, ranging from major inquiries into aspects of European policy as relating to Scotland, the organisation of major public conferences, and the development of links with similar devolved Parliamentary assemblies in other parts of Europe. It has also developed links with similar committees at Westminster and the Assemblies in Northern Ireland and Wales, particularly between the officials of the various bodies, with Members of the European Parliament from Scotland, and with the European Commission. The committee has therefore developed an interest both in wider European issues and contacts as well as in specific European legislation although its extended remit into the fields of culture and tourism has meant that it has also had to devote considerable time to those areas of policy. Not surprisingly, since the EU referendum in June 2016, the future status of Scotland after Brexit has been a major focus of its interest since that date.

From time to time, the committee also refers matters as appropriate to other committees or to the full Parliament. Rule 6.2 of the Parliament's standing orders allow any committee 'to consider any European Union legislation or any international conventions or agreements or any drafts which relate to or affect any competent matter'. Much of the Parliament's work in the implementation of European legislation therefore falls to individual 'subject' committees of the Parliament. In addition, an important role in the process of implementing EU legislation is played by the Delegated Powers and Law Reform Committee, as subordinate legislation made by members of the Scottish Executive is often the mechanism by which such legislation is put into effect in Scotland.

Overall, the arrangements made by both the Scottish Government and Parliament for dealing with European business appear to be working in a satisfactory manner given the parameters of the devolution settlement. Certainly, it appears that the Scottish Parliament Culture, Tourism, European and External Affairs Committee is able to carry out a much more detailed and comprehensive scrutiny of proposed and actual EU legislation, as well as consider wider European issues, than its Westminster counterparts (which do, of course, have a much broader field to cover than that to which the Scottish Parliament is limited).

THE COUNCIL OF EUROPE

The European Union is not the only European institution of which the United Kingdom has been a member. The United Kingdom is also a member of the Council of Europe,[17] founded in 1949, with forty-seven European states in membership. With permanent headquarters in Strasbourg, the Council of Europe has an institutional structure consisting of a secretary general, a committee of Ministers from member states, and a Parliamentary assembly made up of Parliamentarians from those member states.

The Scottish Government and Parliament play no formal role in the institutions of the Council of Europe but the Council of Europe has established the Congress of Local and Regional Authorities of Europe which is a forum to promote co-operation among European local and regional governments and to encourage local democracy. It includes representatives from the devolved UK Administrations, including the Scottish Parliament.[18]

Unlike the case with the European Union, the member states of the Council of Europe have not transferred parts of their legislative and executive competence to that body and, as a result, it does not have the power to make laws binding on its members. Rather, it aims to achieve its objectives by encouraging its member states to enter into international conventions and treaties with which they are obliged to comply under international law. It also pursues its objectives by promoting voluntary co-operation among its member states on the basis of common values and common political decisions. Many provisions in treaties and conventions promoted by the Council of Europe have also been incorporated directly into EU law by EU legislation and, in those circumstances, will be binding on EU member states in the same way as any other legislation. Assuming that the United Kingdom, including Scotland, ceases to be a member of the European Union, it will still nevertheless be bound in international law to those Council of Europe covenants and treaties. That may be significant for legal proceedings because of the principle adopted by the UK courts that it is to be presumed that the UK Parliament intends both primary and secondary legislation to comply with the international obligations of the United Kingdom. This principle, the 'compliance presumption', was set out by Lord Diplock in the following terms, in the case of *Salomon* v. *Commissioners of Custom & Excise*:[19]

> But if the terms of the legislation are not clear but are reasonably capable of more than one meaning, the treaty itself becomes

relevant, for there is a prima facie presumption that Parliament does not intend to act in breach of international law, including therein specific treaty obligations; and if one of the meanings which can reasonably be ascribed to the legislation is consonant with the treaty obligations and another or others are not, the meaning which is consonant is to be preferred. Thus, in case of lack of clarity in the words used in the legislation, the terms of the treaty are relevant to enable the court to make its choice between the possible meanings of these words by applying this presumption.

These principles have been applied in many other cases but, given that EU law is binding upon member states anyway, it has often not been necessary to turn to international treaties and conventions to interpret the provisions of domestic legislation.

It should be emphasised, however, that the 'compliance presumption' comes into play only in circumstances where the 'terms of the legislation are not clear but are reasonably capable of more than one meaning' [in the words of Lord Diplock quoted above]. Where that is not the case, that 'compliance presumption' has no application because it is also settled law that the fact that the United Kingdom has entered into international treaty obligations does not give rights under domestic law unless those treaties have been given effect in domestic legislation.

Having said that, it is true that the UK courts have also recognised that 'judges can take into account rules of international law which are binding on the United Kingdom when interpreting statutes and in developing the common law'.[20] In the words of Lord Sumption in the case of *R. (Chester)* v. *Secretary of State for Justice*; *McGeoch* v. *Lord President of the Council* [2014] AC 271, paragraph 121:

> The courts have for many years interpreted statutes and developed the common law so as to achieve consistency between the domestic law of the United Kingdom and its international obligations, so far as they are free to do so.

Lord Hodge, it should be noted, in the Moohan case emphasised, in quoting those words of Lord Sumption, that: 'In my view the concluding words [that is, "so far as they are free to do so"] are an important limitation'.[21]

In addition, the courts have been prepared to recognise that, by ratifying an international treaty, the UK Government can bind itself to take certain steps to implement its terms, that gives a person a right which they can seek to have enforced in domestic courts.[22] Furthermore, in questions as to how Convention rights should be applied in legal proceedings before UK courts, courts may look to other international treaties and conventions as assistance in interpreting the extent of those Convention rights which are legally enforceable rights in the UK because of HRA 1998.

Exactly how the UK courts may make use of Council of Europe conventions and treaties in applying domestic law after UK departure from the EU cannot be predicted within any certainty. It is reasonable to suggest, however, that they may become more significant sources than previously, particularly in situations where it can be argued that such conventions and treaties have created or stated rules of international law.

THE EUROPEAN CONVENTION ON HUMAN RIGHTS

One of the most important institutions of the Council of Europe is the European Court of Human Rights.[23] This was set up by the European Convention on Human Rights (ECHR) which was adopted in 1950. It is an entirely separate body from the Court of Justice of the European Union (CJEU). The European Court of Human Rights started business in 1959, and member states, including the UK, nominate judges to sit in the court. The ECHR is of particular importance to the devolution settlement for Scotland, as SA 1998 requires the Scottish Parliament and Government to act in a manner that is compatible with ECHR.

The method by which SA 1998 seeks to ensure that the Scottish Parliament and Government comply with the ECHR is by its provision that any Act of the Scottish Parliament which is not compatible with 'Convention rights' does not become law. These are the rights laid down in the ECHR which the Human Rights Act 1998 (HRA 1998) enshrined for the first time in UK law. The Convention rights are set out in a number of Articles. These are given on pages 246–9.

Reference should be made to the HRA 1998 for the full extent of these rights, and how they can be enforced in the United Kingdom, but there are many devolved matters where it is easy to see how the Convention rights may have major implications both for the Parliament and for the Scottish Government. (As mentioned above, the HRA 1998 is one of the Acts of the UK Parliament which the Scottish Parliament is specifically prohibited from modifying.)[24] For example, the criminal and civil

legal systems of Scotland must be consistent with the right to liberty
and security and the right to a fair trial, and must ensure that there is
no punishment without law (which last provision prohibits, in general,
retrospective legislation). Social policy must comply with the right to
respect for private and family life. Scotland already has experience of
parents turning to the ECHR to vindicate their right to education in
conformity with their own religious and philosophical convictions. Land
reform must respect the Convention rights relating to the protection of
property. This list of illustrative examples by no means exhausts the list
of possible implications of the Convention rights for legislation by the
Parliament and activity by the Scottish Government.

As legislation by the Parliament is outside its competence if it is
incompatible with Convention rights, the existence of such rights can
give rise to challenges to its legislation both prior to Royal Assent and
thereafter. Similar challenges can be made to actions of the Scottish
Government if they are incompatible with Convention rights. As discussed above,[25] the Convention rights were brought into effect for
devolved matters in advance of their general implementation within the
UK under the HRA 1998. By the end of 2002, there had been a large
number of legal challenges made to actions of the Scottish Executive
(and a few to Acts of the Scottish Parliament), the majority relating to
the actions of the prosecution authorities, and usually relying on a claim
that the Convention right to a fair trial had been breached. Most were
unsuccessful but some succeeded, occasionally with major consequences
for the criminal justice system. The method by which challenges can
be made to Scottish Parliament legislation, and to actions of Scottish
Ministers, on the basis that they breach 'Convention rights' is considered
in more detail in Chapter 8 above. Chapter 9 gives more, detail of some
of the challenges that have so far been successful, and the principles the
courts apply in considering such challenges.

SCOTLAND'S EUROPEAN LINKS AND THE LABOUR/LIBERAL DEMOCRAT COALITION, 1999–2007

The Labour/Liberal Democrat coalitions, which formed the Scottish
Executives after the elections in 1999 and 2003, were relatively content
with the current arrangements for participation by the Scottish
Parliament and Executive in European issues. In essence, the objective of these Administrations was to seek to ensure that Scotland's

interests were represented within the global United Kingdom position in Europe by use of the various consultative mechanisms available to it. In addition, they sought an increase in its own direct representation within the European Union. This included the establishment of a direct Scottish presence in Brussels, as described above, and the development of direct political links with a number of similar devolved administrations.

The Scottish Executive also decided that, when the power to nominate Scotland's representatives on the European Committee of the Regions was transferred to it, it would share the places between itself and Scottish local government which had previously held all the places.

THE SCOTTISH NATIONAL PARTY AND THE EUROPEAN UNION

The fundamental aim of the Scottish National Party is to achieve independence for Scotland but its stated policy for many years has been that Scotland should be a full member of the European Union. Whether either aim will be fulfilled remains to be seen, particularly in the light of the uncertainty following the 2016 referendum on UK membership of the European Union and a possible further referendum on Scottish independence from the UK. The future relationship between Scotland and the rest of the European Union will therefore depend on a number of factors: the eventual terms of UK departure from the EU, on the assumption that that will take place; whether Scotland would be able to retain and, in effect, 'take over' the UK's membership of the EU if it became independent before the date of the UK's departure; and whether, and when, Scotland would be able, or wish, to rejoin the European Union or the European Economic Area (EEA) if it were to become independent after the United Kingdom had left the European Union.

The EEA consists of the EU member states and three of the four members of EFTA[26] (the European Free Trade Area) which are brought together into a single market. All members of the EEA accept the four fundamental freedoms of EU law: the free movement of goods, services, persons, and capital. They also co-operate in other areas, such as research and development, education, social policy, the environment, consumer protection, and tourism and culture, Citizens and businesses of all EEA states are guaranteed equal rights and obligations within its single market. A number of important areas of EU policy are not, however, included within the EEA agreement.[27]

Until the implementation, however, of any final agreement between the United Kingdom and the rest of the European Union on their relations after a departure by the UK, the current position, namely that Scotland is recognised as one of the many regions within the EU and must rely on the UK Government to represent its interests, remains. The SNP Government has seen this as a serious limitation on its ability to represent Scotland's interests but has had to accept that, under the current constitutional arrangements, EU affairs are part of foreign policy and are therefore reserved. Thus, at the Council of Ministers, Scottish Ministers can attend only as part of the UK delegation and with the permission of the UK Government. SNP Scottish Ministers find this unsatisfactory but they attend Council meetings.

Officials in the Scottish Government's EU office in Brussels work closely with the UK Permanent Representation in Europe (UKRep) and identify other member states with similar policy interests and build relations with them to strengthen Scotland's position in EU discussions.

Scottish Ministers also meet with EU commissioners, both in Brussels and in Scotland, and sometimes respond to commission consultations with a separate Scottish response.

As has been mentioned above, there has been frustration at the infrequency of meetings of the Joint Ministerial Committee on Europe, and the meetings of this body now take place more regularly because, with the change in political control in Scotland, it is no longer possible to resolve issues informally.

It would be wrong to suggest, however, that there has been a significant change in the relationships between the Scottish Government and the EU since the SNP formed its minority administration in 2007. Rather, they have so far taken a pragmatic approach and work within the constraints of the current constitutional arrangements, albeit with a distinctive Scottish flavour.

SCOTLAND AND EUROPE AFTER 'BREXIT'

If the United Kingdom does eventually proceed to leave the European Union, as seems likely given that Prime Minister Theresa May has now used the authority given to her by Act of Parliament to invoke Article 50 of the TEU to commence the procedure by which the UK terminates its EU membership, the relationship between Scotland and the EU will inevitably change fundamentally. Unlike the result for the United Kingdom as a whole, Scotland was, by a considerable majority, in favour of the UK remaining in the EU in the 2016 referendum. Of the votes cast, 62 per cent were in favour of 'remain', with majorities for that in every single local authority area in Scotland. This has inevitably led to questions as to whether Scotland should seek some form of different relationship with the European Union from that which is likely to be the case for the rest of the United Kingdom (or, at least, for England and Wales, Northern Ireland having also voted to remain in the EU, though by a smaller majority than in Scotland).

First Minister Nicola Sturgeon has stated[28] that, although her government's preference remains that Scotland should ultimately become an independent state, its immediate preference would be that the United Kingdom as a whole should remain within the European Single Market – through the European Economic Area (EEA) – and within the EU Customs Union, failing which that Scotland should remain a member of the European Single Market and retain some key benefits of EU membership even if the rest of the UK decides to leave.

If none of these options is accepted by the UK Government, however, the First Minister has stated that the Scottish Government will seek to hold a further referendum on Scottish independence and has made it clear that, if there were to be a vote in favour of that, it would want to see Scotland retaining close relationships with the European Union. It has not, however, given a clear statement that it would want to see Scotland retain or acquire membership of the European Union if it became independent. Though that would appear to be the preferred option of most leading members of the SNP, there are some who have suggested that it would be better for Scotland to seek membership of the European Economic Area rather than the EU, either for the long term or as a transitional step towards joining the European Union at a later date. Membership of the European Union would, of course, require the agreement of the rest of the EU but, If that were to be the eventual constitutional outcome, then it would follow that Scotland would secure the rights to participate in EU institutions as do current member states, including the UK, and would also continue to have to ensure that its legislation was compatible with EU law, and to accept the supremacy of the CJEU in matters concerning the interpretation and application of EU law. Membership of the EEA would place fewer obligations upon Scotland but it would still have to ensure that its legislation complied with the EU 'four freedoms' described above. Scottish membership of the EEA would have to be approved by the other EEA member states and by the European Union.

On the basis that the UK Government had not given the assurances that it seeks regarding Scotland's access to the European Union after Brexit, the Scottish Government placed a motion before the Scottish Parliament asking for the transfer of powers to it to allow for the holding of such a referendum. That motion was carried at the end of March 2017 with the backing of the SNP and the Scottish Green Party, with the other parties represented at Holyrood all voting against. The Scottish Government has indicated that it would wish to hold that referendum before the United Kingdom (and therefore Scotland) has left the European Union but at a date at the end of the UK's negotiations with the EU. However, the SNP's enthusiasm for a referendum seems to have declined following its losses in the 2017 general election.

The possibility of Scottish independence is one that has been firmly rejected by the UK Government. It has stated that 'now is not the time' for such a referendum (leaving open the question as to whether there would ever be such a time). It has also made clear that it will not accept any arrangements whereby Scotland could obtain some form of 'partial membership' of either the EU or the EEA while still remaining in the United Kingdom. Scotland, therefore, along with the rest of the UK, would leave the European Union. Moreover, the conditions that the UK has laid down for its future relationship with the rest of the EU are such that it seems unlikely that it could take the form of UK membership of the EEA, or a similar type of special status for the UK.

If that is the eventual outcome of negotiations, it would follow that Scotland, like the rest of the UK, would no longer be bound by EU law or by decisions of the CJEU.

THE IMPACT OF BREXIT ON THE LAW AND THE COURTS

EU law, and perhaps even the CJEU, however, would be likely to have an impact on the law and legislation for many years to come after UK departure from the EU. Firstly, this is because it may be that any agreement between the United Kingdom and the European Union to put in place transitional arrangements after Brexit might give some role to the CJEU in the determination of matters of dispute between the UK, and its citizens and businesses, and the EU, and the remaining member states of the EU (and their citizens and businesses as well).

Secondly, because the UK Government has stated in its White Paper setting out its negotiating objectives for Brexit[29] that it would initially want to enact legislation which would incorporate most existing EU law at the time of Brexit into domestic legislation, it is therefore very likely that UK courts, including those of Scotland, will need to interpret and apply the original terms and intent of EU legislation until and unless such legislation is amended or repealed for the United Kingdom. The UK Government's own White Paper[30] on what it has termed a 'Great Repeal Bill' makes it clear that the EU treaties may assist in the interpretation of the EU laws preserved within EU law. It is also proposing that any question as to the meaning of EU-derived law will be determined in the UK courts by reference to the CJEU's case law as it exists on the day that the United Kingdom leaves the European Union. It is also reasonable to assume that, even after Brexit, the UK courts would give considerable weight to CJEU reasoning on the proper interpretation of EU-derived law and legislation as a court with the experience and judicial competence in those matters even in cases which were decided by the CJEU after UK departure from the EU.

There may also be an indirect influence on UK law from international treaties which the EU had a major role in formulating, depending on the way in which UK courts, including Scottish courts, will adopt the 'compliance presumption' described earlier in this chapter.

The UK Government's White Paper on exiting the European Union also suggests that there will need to be 'dispute resolution mechanisms'[31] to deal with disputes between the European Union and the United Kingdom arising from any future agreement between the EU and the UK. These might give corporate bodies and individuals a ground to raise proceedings in UK courts.

In its White Paper,[32] the UK Government has also declared its intention that the devolved administrations will be able to contribute to the process whereby the United Kingdom leaves the European Union, and has established a Joint Ministerial Committee on EU Negotiations for that purpose. That committee has considered proposals from the Scottish and Welsh devolved administrations for their countries' future relationships with the EU,[33] though it has to be said that the UK Government has so far given a cool response to those proposals.

Of longer-term significance, the UK Government has accepted in that White Paper that some of the responsibilities currently resting with the European Union may well be transferred to the devolved administrations after Brexit. It has not, however, accepted the premise that areas of government activity currently within EU competence, and which are not specifically reserved to the UK under SA 1998, will automatically be devolved to the Scottish Parliament and Government. All that it has stated is that

> as the powers . . . are repatriated to the UK from the EU, we have an opportunity to determine the level best placed to make new laws and policies on these issues, ensuring power sits closer to the people of the UK than ever before. We have already committed that no decisions currently taken by the devolved administrations will be removed from them and we will use the opportunity of bringing decision making back to the UK to ensure that more decisions are devolved.[34]

If there is a further devolution of powers to Scotland as a result of the Brexit process, that will require a further amendment of SA 1998 to give effect to that devolution. A further amendment will, in any event, be required if Scotland does, indeed, leave the European Union along with the rest of the UK, to provide that legislation of the Scottish Parliament would no longer be required to be compatible with EU law. The European Union (Withdrawal Bill) contains a number of provisions to that effect.

No doubt the Scottish Parliament would continue to wish to have an input into European policy and the Scottish Government's ongoing relationship with the EU even if that was now informal rather than founded on the UK's obligations under the various EU treaties. It can also be expected that it would seek to establish additional mechanisms to scrutinise closely the way that the Scottish Government decided to make any amendments to existing EU legislation in areas of previous EU competence which had now become devolved to Scotland. It would presumably ensure that its committee structure was modified, if it was felt necessary to do so, to allow it to fulfil these functions.

Of course, any prediction of the future relationship between Scotland and the European Union will depend on political decisions and lengthy negotiations whose direction is unclear. It is clear, however, that Scotland's departure from the EU is likely to mean fundamental changes for the powers of both the Scottish Parliament and Scottish Government. At the same time, however, the effects of EU law and judgments of the CJEU are likely to be significant for Scottish courts and lawyers for many years to come.

If Scotland were to become an independent member state of the European Union, it is likely that the Scottish Parliament would want to ensure that its committee structure was able to take account of the need to scrutinise all proposed EU legislation and to hold the Scottish

Government to account in the role it would now play in the institutions of the EU.

BEYOND EUROPE

Scotland's membership, through the United Kingdom, of the European Union has been of considerable importance during the period since the Scottish Parliament was established. The requirement that the Parliament's legislation is compatible both with EU law and the rights derived from the ECHR is at the centre of the devolution scheme set up by the SA 1998.

The relationships with the European Union and with the Council of Europe (from which the ECHR derives) are not the only connections that Scotland's government institutions have with the wider world outside the United Kingdom. The Scottish Government's interest in international relations was recognised in one of the initial concordats agreed with the UK Government shortly after the Parliament was established.[35]

That concordat emphasised that the UK Government is responsible for international relations and that the UK Foreign Secretary is responsible for the UK's foreign policy, including concluding treaties and ensuring compliance with the UK's EU and other international obligations. It is stated, however, that the UK Government recognises that the devolved administrations will have an interest in international policy-making in relation to devolved matters and also in obligations touching on devolved matters that the United Kingdom may agree as a result of it concluding international agreements (including United Nations conventions). The concordat points out that, under the devolution arrangements, Scottish Ministers are responsible for observing and implementing the international obligations that relate to the functions of the Scottish Government.

The concordat therefore sets out arrangements for how all the devolved administrations in the United Kingdom (including Scotland) will be able to become involved in international relations.[36] It covers the following issues:

- exchange of information;
- formulation of UK policy and conduct of international negotiations;
- implementation of international obligations;
- co-operation over legal proceedings;
- representation overseas;

- secondments and training co-operation;
- visits;
- public diplomacy, the British Council and BBC world service;
- trade and investment promotion; and
- diplomatic and consular relations.

Among the provisions of the concordat are the following:

- a recognition that, as an inherent part of the Belfast Agreement,[37] the UK's devolved administrations (on matters within their competence) can hold discussions and make arrangements with the Irish Government in the context of the British–Irish Council;
- a commitment that, where international obligations bear directly on devolved matters, it may be appropriate for Ministers or officials from the devolved administrations to form part of a UK negotiating team;
- a commitment to consult with the devolved administrations on how to split a quantitative international obligation, such as a quota, between the United Kingdom and the devolved administrations;
- confirmation that the devolved administrations may establish offices overseas 'within the framework of their responsibility for devolved matters', including for the provision of information on devolved matters to the public, regional governments and institutions, and promotion of trade and inward investment. This is to be done in consultation with the FCO and, where appropriate, such representation might form part of a UK diplomatic or consular mission;
- a commitment that the British Council will continue to promote the United Kingdom and all its constituent parts, and will maintain operational links with the devolved administrations through its offices in Belfast, Edinburgh, and Cardiff.

As with the other concordats, there is a mechanism under the overarching Memorandum of Understanding for regular review and dispute resolution.

Though this concordat, along with the concordat on European Union Policy issues, is an agreement between the UK and Scottish Governments, rather than between the two Parliaments, the Scottish Parliament, through its committees, has taken a close interest in the work of Scottish Ministers on wider international issues beyond EU matters. Ministers will report to the Parliament on their international activities, and MSPs themselves take part in the activities of a number of international bodies, such as the Commonwealth Parliamentary Association.

Human Rights Act, 1998

Schedule 1 THE ARTICLES

Part I THE CONVENTION

Article 2: Right to Life

1. Everyone's right to life shall be protected by law. No one shall be deprived of his life intentionally save in the execution of a sentence of a court following his conviction of a crime for which this penalty is provided by law.

2. Deprivation of life shall not be regarded as inflicted in contravention of this Article when it results from the use of force which is no more than absolutely necessary:

(a) in defence of any person from unlawful violence;

(b) in order to effect a lawful arrest or to prevent the escape of a person lawfully detained;

(c) in action lawfully taken for the purpose of quelling a riot or insurrection.

Article 3: Prohibition of torture

No one shall be subjected to torture or to inhuman or degrading treatment or punishment.

Article 4: Prohibition of slavery and forced labour

1. No one shall be held in slavery or servitude.

2. No one shall be required to perform forced or compulsory labour.

3. For the purpose of this Article the term '*forced or compulsory labour*' shall not include:

(a) any work required to be done in the ordinary course of detention imposed according to the provisions of Article 5 of this Convention or during conditional release from such detention;

(b) any service of a military character or, in case of conscientious objectors in countries where they are recognised, service exacted instead of compulsory military service;

(c) any service exacted in case of an emergency or calamity threatening the life or well-being of the community;

(d) any work or service which forms part of normal civic obligations.

Article 5: Right to liberty and security

1. Everyone has the right to liberty and security of person. No one shall be deprived of his liberty save in the following cases and in accordance with a procedure prescribed by law:

(a) the lawful detention of a person after conviction by a competent court;

(b) the lawful arrest or detention of a person for non-compliance with the lawful order of a court or in order to secure the fulfilment of any obligation prescribed by law;

(c) the lawful arrest or detention of a person effected for the purpose of bringing him before the competent legal authority on reasonable suspicion of having committed an offence or when it is reasonably considered necessary to prevent his committing an offence or fleeing after having done so;

(d) the detention of a minor by lawful order for the purpose of educational supervision or his lawful detention for the purpose of bringing him before the competent legal authority;

(e) the lawful detention of persons for the prevention of the spreading of infectious diseases, of persons of unsound mind, alcoholics or drug addicts or vagrants;

(f) the lawful arrest or detention of a person to prevent his effecting an unauthorised entry into the country or of a person against whom action is being taken with a view to deportation or extradition.

2. Everyone who is arrested shall be informed promptly, in a language which he understands, of the reasons for his arrest and of any charge against him.

3. Everyone arrested or detained in accordance with the provisions of paragraph 1.(c) of this Article shall be brought promptly before a judge or other officer authorised by law to exercise judicial power and shall be entitled to trial within a reasonable time or to release pending trial. Release may be conditioned by guarantees to appear for trial.

4. Everyone who is deprived of his liberty by arrest or detention shall be entitled to take proceedings by which the lawfulness of his detention shall be decided speedily by a court and his release ordered if the detention is not lawful.

5. Everyone who has been the victim of arrest or detention in contravention of the provisions of this Article shall have an enforceable right to compensation.

Article 6: Right to a fair trial

1. In the determination of his civil rights and obligations or of any criminal charge against him, everyone is entitled to a fair and public hearing within a reasonable time by an independent and impartial tribunal established by law. Judgment shall be pronounced publicly but the press and public may be excluded from all or part of the trial in the interest of morals, public order or national security in a democratic society, where the interests of juveniles or the protection of the private life of the parties so require, or to the extent strictly necessary in the opinion of the court in special circumstances where publicity would prejudice the interests of justice.

2. Everyone charged with a criminal offence shall be presumed innocent until proved guilty according to law.

3. Everyone charged with a criminal offence has the following minimum rights:

(a) to be informed promptly, in a language which he understands and in detail, of the nature and cause of the accusation against him;

(b) to have adequate time and facilities for the preparation of his defence;

(c) to defend himself in person or through legal assistance of his own choosing or, if he has not sufficient means to pay for legal assistance, to be given it free when the interests of justice so require;

(d) to examine or have examined witnesses against him and to obtain the attendance and examination of witnesses on his behalf under the same conditions as witnesses against him;

(e) to have the free assistance of an interpreter if he cannot understand or speak the language used in court.

Article 7: No punishment without law

1. No one shall be held guilty of any criminal offence on account of any act or omission which did not constitute a criminal offence under national or international law at the time when it was committed. Nor shall a heavier penalty be imposed than the one that was applicable at the time the criminal offence was committed.

2. This Article shall not prejudice the trial and punishment of any person for any act or omission which, at the time when it was committed, was criminal according to the general principles of law recognised by civilised nations.

Article 8: Right to respect for private and family life

1. Everyone has the right to respect for his private and family life, his home and his correspondence.

2. There shall be no interference by a public authority with the exercise of this right except such as is in accordance with the law and is necessary in a democratic society in the interests of national security, public safety or the economic well-being of the country, for the prevention of disorder or crime, for the protection of health or morals, or for the protection of the rights and freedoms of others.

Article 9: Freedom of thought, conscience and religion

1. Everyone has the right to freedom of thought, conscience and religion; this right includes freedom to change his religion or belief and freedom, either alone or in community with others and in public or private, to manifest his religion or belief, in worship, teaching, practice and observance.

2. Freedom to manifest one's religion or beliefs shall be subject only to such limitations as are prescribed by law and are necessary in a democratic society in the interests of public safety, for the protection of public order, health or morals, or for the protection of the rights and freedoms of others.

Article 10: Freedom of expression

1. Everyone has the right to freedom of expression. This right shall include freedom to hold opinions and to receive and impart information and ideas without interference by public authority and regardless of frontiers. This Article shall not prevent States from requiring the licensing of broadcasting, television or cinema enterprises.

2. The exercise of these freedoms, since it carries with it duties and responsibilities, may be subject to such formalities, conditions, restrictions or penalties as are prescribed by law and are necessary in a democratic society, in the interests of national security, territorial integrity or public safety, for the prevention of disorder or crime, for the protection of health or morals, for the protection of the reputation or rights of others, for preventing the disclosure of information received in confidence, or for maintaining the authority and impartiality of the judiciary.

Article 11: Freedom of assembly and association

1. Everyone has the right to freedom of peaceful assembly and to freedom of association with others, including the right to form and to join trade unions for the protection of his interests.

2. No restrictions shall be placed on the exercise of these rights other than such as are prescribed by law and are necessary in a democratic society in the interests of national security or public safety, for the prevention of disorder or crime, for the protection of health or morals or for the protection of the rights and freedoms of others. This Article shall not prevent the imposition of lawful restrictions on the exercise of these rights by members of the armed forces, of the police or of the administration of the State.

Article 12: Right to marry

Men and women of marriageable age have the right to marry and to found a family, according to the national laws governing the exercise of this right.

Article 14: Prohibition of discrimination

The enjoyment of the rights and freedoms set forth in this Convention shall be secured without discrimination on any ground such as sex, race, colour, language, religion, political or other opinion, national or social origin, association with a national minority, property, birth or other status.

Article 16: Restrictions on political activity of aliens

Nothing in Articles 10, 11 and 14 shall be regarded as preventing the High Contracting Parties from imposing restrictions on the political activity of aliens.

Article 17: Prohibition of abuse of rights

Nothing in this Convention may be interpreted as implying for any State, group or person any right to engage in any activity or perform any act aimed at the destruction of any of the rights and freedoms set forth herein or at their limitation to a greater extent than is provided for in the Convention.

Article 18: Limitation on use of restrictions on rights

The restrictions permitted under this Convention to the said rights and freedoms shall not be applied for any purpose other than those for which they have been prescribed.

Part II THE FIRST PROTOCOL

Article 1: Protection of property

Every natural or legal person is entitled to the peaceful enjoyment of his possessions. No one shall be deprived of his possessions except in the public interest and subject to the conditions provided for by law and by the general principles of international law. The preceding provisions shall not, however, in any way impair the right of a State to enforce such laws as it deems necessary to control the use of property in accordance with the general interest or to secure the payment of taxes or other contributions or penalties.

Article 2: Right to education

No person shall be denied the right to education. In the exercise of any functions which it assumes in relation to education and to teaching, the State shall respect the right of parents to ensure such education and teaching in conformity with their own religious and philosophical convictions.

Article 3: Right to free elections

The High Contracting Parties undertake to hold free elections at reasonable intervals by secret ballot, under conditions which will ensure the free expression of the opinion of the people in the choice of the legislature.

Part III ARTICLE 1 OF THE THIRTEENTH PROTOCOL

Abolition of the death penalty

The death penalty shall be abolished. No one shall be condemned to such penalty or executed.

NOTES

1. *R. (on the application of Miller)* v. *Secretary of State for Exiting the European Union* [2017] UKSC 5; [2017] 2 W.L.R. 583; [2017].
2. See Chapter 5, Scottish Office, *Scotland's Parliament* (1997), Cm 3658.
3. SA 1998 section 29(2).
4. SA 1998 section 57(2)–(3).
5. SA 1998 section 29(2).
6. Scottish Office, *Scotland's Parliament* (1997), Cm 3658, paragraph 5.8.
7. To enable the UK Government to do so, the Scottish Parliament has to pass a 'Legislative Consent Motion' or 'Sewel motion'. See Chapter 7.
8. Belgium and Germany, for example.
9. See p. 156 for a fuller discussion on the concordats.
10. See the Memorandum of Understanding; C, p. 39. See p. 165, note 27 for more detail about the memorandum.
11. In the first three years from May 1999, Scottish Ministers had attended twenty-eight European Councils, and taken the lead at three. See oral evidence given by Jim Wallace, MSP, Deputy First Minister, to the House of Lords Select Committee on Devolution at p. 166, paragraph 563.
12. See https://www.holyrood.com/articles/inside-politics/climate-change-and-paris-talks-interview-dr-aileen-mcleod (last accessed 10 April 2017).
13. Indeed, UKRep has been described as having a 'very close, even umbilical, relationship with the offices that the devolved administrations have set up in Brussels' (Oral evidence of Stephen Wall, Head of the European Secretariat in the Cabinet Office: see House of Lords Select Committee Devolution at p. 62, paragraph 205).
14. See, for example, the working arrangements set out by the UK Department for Food, Environment and Rural Affairs in its Memorandum to the House of Lords Select Committee, Devolution pp. 71–2, paragraphs 18–22.
15. See the memorandum submitted by the UK Cabinet Office to the House of Lords Select Committee Devolution at p. 20, paragraph 53, and also the evidence of Jim Wallace, MSP at p. 166, paragraph 562.
16. See Chapter 4 for more information about Scottish Parliament committees.
17. For more details about the Council of Europe, generally, see http://www.coe.int
18. See http://www.coe.int/t/Congress for more information about the congress.
19. [1966] 3 W.L.R. 1223, [1967] 2 Q.B. 116.
20. *Moohan* v. *Lord Advocate* [2014] UKSC 67, [2015] A.C. 901, paragraph 33
21. Ibid.
22. *EK* v. *Secretary of State for the Home Department* [2013] UKUT 313 (IAC), paragraph 60.
23. For more information about the European Court of Human Rights see http://www.echr.coe.int (last accessed 10 April 2017).

24. See p. 32.
25. See p. 170.
26. See www.efta.int (last accessed 10 April 2017); Norway, Liechtenstein, and Iceland are the three EFTA members within the EEA. The fourth, Switzerland, is not and has its own bilateral agreement with the EU.
27. The following are not included within the EEA agreement:
    - Common Agriculture and Fisheries policies (although the agreement contains provisions on various aspects of trade in agricultural and fish products);
    - Customs Union;
    - Common Trade Policy;
    - Common Foreign and Security Policy;
    - Justice and Home Affairs (even though the EFTA countries are part of the Schengen area); or
    - Monetary Union (EMU).
28. *Scotland's Place in Europe*, Scottish Government, 2016.
29. *The United Kingdom's exit from and new partnership with the European Union*, Cm 9417, 2017.
30. *Legislating for the United Kingdom's withdrawal from the European Union*, March 2017, Cm 9446.
31. Paragraphs 2.6–8, Cm 9417.
32. Chapter 3, Cm 9417.
33. Cm 9417, paragraph 3.2.
34. Cm 9417, paragraph 3.5.
35. See Memorandum of Understanding: D: Concordat on International Relations – Scotland. See Chapter 7 above for more details of the concordats between the UK and Scottish Governments.
36. See Concordat on International Relations, p. 52, D4. Ibid.
37. See Command Paper 3883.

CHAPTER TWELVE

Reshaping Britain

INTRODUCTION

The rioting in the streets of Glasgow and Edinburgh which greeted the announcement of the terms of the Treaty of Union in 1706 was not exactly followed by dancing in the streets on the passing of the Scotland Act 1998 (SA 1998) on 19 November 1998. Nevertheless, the Scots had turned out in considerable numbers to vote 'Yes/Yes' in the two-question referendum in September 1997. The turnout in the referendum was 60 per cent and the turnout for the first elections on 6 May 1999 was a respectable 58.2 per cent. These figures were not as high as in the immediately preceding UK general election where the turnout had been 71.4 per cent but much higher than the turnout for local elections which rarely reaches 50 per cent and, on some occasions in recent years, has fallen to as low as 20 per cent in by-elections.

Perhaps not surprisingly, as the idealistic hopes of the supporters of a Scottish Parliament prior to its establishment were replaced by the experience of the raw politics of the new institutions, the initial enthusiasm for devolution waned somewhat in the years after 1999. Turnout in subsequent Scottish Parliamentary general elections has been smaller. In 2003, 49.4 per cent of the electorate voted while, in 2007, the percentage rose marginally to 51.8, to the disappointment of supporters of devolution (and to the glee of some of its detractors). It should be borne in mind, however, that the fall of just under 10 per cent in turnout between the 1999 and 2003 elections was actually smaller than the drop in turnout between the 1997 and 2001 United Kingdom general elections. Similarly, in the 2005 UK general election and the 2007 Scottish Parliamentary election, there was only a modest increase in turnout of around 2 per cent. In the 2011 Scottish Parliament election the turnout was 50.7 per cent and, in 2016, it increased to 55.6 per cent. The percentage increase in 2016, however, may be partly due to the lowering to sixteen of the voting age for Scottish Parliament and local government elections and the decline in the total Scottish electorate of around 100,000 (2.5 per cent) in that year. That may have occurred as a result of more intensive efforts to ensure the accuracy of the register, including the introduction of individual voter registration. There is, therefore, a strong case to be made that the relatively small drop in turnout in the Scottish elections is more to do with a wider decline in participation in the electoral process (not restricted to the United Kingdom) rather than any special features of either Scottish politics or the record of the Scottish Parliament and Government.[1]

What can fairly be said is that there is little doubt that the Scottish Parliament is here to stay. All the political parties in Scotland now accept the fact of devolution to Scotland, even the Conservative Party which had steadfastly opposed it under the premierships of Margaret Thatcher and John Major. Indeed, some have argued that the arrival of the Scottish Parliament helped save the Scottish Conservative Party from extinction, with the Parliament's proportional electoral system allowing it to elect a significant block of members, thus giving it a profile that it had lost as a result of its loss of all its Scottish MPs in the 1997 UK general election. Few would have predicted then that, less than twenty years later, the Scottish Conservative Party would have found itself the principal opposition party in Scotland, with a substantially higher share of Scottish Parliament seats (if not of votes) than the Scottish Labour Party. Meanwhile, the Scottish National Party, which decided to work within the devolved Scottish Parliament, now forms the Scottish Government while retaining ambitions for its longer-term goal, that of independence for Scotland, despite losing the independence referendum held in 2014.

Devolution to Scotland should be seen not in isolation but as part of the deliberate policy of the Labour Government which was elected in 1997. Its policy of decentralisation of government was part of a wide-ranging programme of constitutional reform. The pace of reform slowed after the early years of the 1997–2010 Labour Government but that programme of reform has already had major repercussions for the way in which the United Kingdom is governed, and is likely to continue to do so for many years to come. This chapter looks at that programme to date and how reform has been taken forward under the coalition majority Conservative Governments since then. It also examines what the future may hold.

DECENTRALISATION OF GOVERNMENT

The Labour Government's programme of decentralisation following the 1997 UK general election was originally envisaged as extending to the whole of the United Kingdom, not just to Scotland.

Wales

The Government of Wales Act 1998 established a directly elected National Assembly for Wales as a corporate body with the Executive as a committee of the Assembly and operating as one with the legislature. The Assembly assumed most of the responsibilities of the Secretary of State for Wales.[2] Unlike the Scottish Parliament, the Assembly did not initially have the power to introduce primary legislation. Its powers were mainly administrative but there was a statutory duty placed on the Secretary of State for Wales to consult the Assembly on the government's legislative programme for Wales.[3] The Welsh Executive and the various subject committees did, however, have the power to prepare secondary legislation for submission to the Assembly for debate and approval,[4] and this is a power which the assembly frequently exercised.

However, in 2002, the Welsh Assembly Government set up a Commission on the Powers and Electoral Arrangements of the National Assembly for Wales (the Richard Commission) which considered, among other issues, whether the powers of the Assembly should be extended. The Commission reported in 2004 and concluded that the existing devolution arrangements were unsuitable and that the assembly should be given the powers to introduce primary legislation for Wales. It also recommended that the existing assembly should be replaced by two separate bodies – an executive and a legislature. The Government of Wales Act (2006) created a separate Executive with a First Minister, Welsh Ministers to be drawn from the Assembly, in addition to giving the Assembly powers to make laws in certain areas, to be known as Measures of the National Assembly for Wales.

In 2011, a Commission on Devolution to Wales, known as the Silk Commission, was established by the UK Government to look at the future of devolution in Wales. A referendum was held in 2011 to gauge the attitude of the Welsh to the devolution of further law-making powers to the Assembly. The result was two to one in favour. The Wales Act 2014 implemented a number of recommendations made by the Silk Commission, including various tax-raising powers, full law-making powers in certain areas, and formally changing the Welsh Assembly Government's name to the Welsh Government.

In 2017 another Wales Act was passed by the UK Parliament. One of its most important provisions moves Wales from a transferring or conferring model to a retaining model similar to the model of the Scotland Act 1998. In sections 1 and 2 there are also provisions which declare that the National Assembly and the Welsh Government are to be regarded as permanent parts of the UK's constitutional arrangement and statutory recognition of a legislative consent convention (based on the Sewel Convention in the Scottish Parliament) similar to the provisions for Scotland in the Scotland Act 2016.

Northern Ireland

In the case of Northern Ireland, the Northern Ireland Act 1998 established (albeit rather precariously) a Northern Ireland Assembly. This Assembly has legislative and administrative powers. Like the SA 1998, the Northern Ireland Act 1998 adopts the retaining model for the distribution of legislative powers. In the case of Northern Ireland, however, in addition to matters reserved to the UK Parliament,[5] there are matters that are excepted from the Assembly's legislative competence.[6] As a result of the religious and political circumstances of Northern Ireland, there are special provisions to ensure cross-community support for various measures, such as the appointment of the First Minister and Deputy First Minister. Cross-community support requires set percentages of designated Unionists and designated Nationalists to vote in favour of an issue.

Furthermore, as a result of the political agreement, which established the Northern Ireland Assembly and Executive,[7] a number of institutions were established which provide for links between and among both the UK (and Irish) Governments and the devolved institutions within the United Kingdom. A British–Irish Council was set up which is composed of representatives of the United Kingdom and Irish Governments, the Scottish Government, the Welsh Government, the Northern Ireland Assembly Executive, the Isle of Man Government and the Bailiwicks of Guernsey and Jersey. The Council can meet at summit level and also in special sectoral formats (which can be at ministerial or officer level) to deal with specific areas of policy. The council meets at summit level twice a year and on other occasions when appropriate. Its members exchange information, discuss, consult and endeavour to reach agreement on co-operation in matters of mutual interest within the competence of the relevant Parliaments and assemblies. The elected institutions are also encouraged by the Belfast Agreement to develop inter-parliamentary links. Other institutions, established as a result of the Agreement, are the North–South Ministerial Council to develop consultation, co-operation and action within the Island of Ireland. The degree to which these provisions have been taken up varies. The Belfast Agreement (Strand 3.3) envisaged that the British–Irish Council would meet twice a year and at other times when appropriate. In fact, it has only met about once a year and, up to November 2016, there had been only twenty-eight meetings at ministerial level. There also appears to have been very little activity undertaken to develop the inter-parliamentary links envisaged in the agreement (Strand 3.11). In contrast, by the end of November 2016, there had been more than sixty sectoral meetings held under the auspices of the North–South Ministerial Council.[8] Another related constitutional development was the Disqualifications Act 2000, the provisions of which allow members of the legislature of the Republic of Ireland to sit in the House of Commons and in the Northern Ireland Assembly. Interestingly, the provisions also allow them to sit in the Scottish Parliament and the National Assembly of Wales. (Such members must still, of course, be qualified under UK law to stand for election to any of those bodies.)

The Northern Ireland Assembly, established by the NI Act 1998, has had a somewhat turbulent existence.[9] Unfortunately, because of major disagreements between the Unionists and the Nationalists over the decommissioning of arms, the UK Government had to rush on to the statute book the Northern Ireland Act 2000 which gave it the power to suspend the Northern Ireland Assembly and Executive. The powers were used to suspend these institutions from 11 February 2000 to 29 May 2000. The UK Government has used these powers to suspend the institutions on three further occasions. Two of these were for one day only but, on 14 October 2002, as a result of the search of Sinn Fein's Parliamentary offices and the arrest of three Sinn Fein members on spying charges, a further suspension began which lasted until 2007.

In 2006, following the St Andrews Agreement between the political parties, the Northern Ireland (St Andrews Agreement) Act 2006 set out a timetable for restoring devolution in Northern Ireland. Elections were held in March 2007 and full power was restored to the Assembly in May 2007.

This lasted until January 2017 when the Deputy First Minister resigned over concerns about an alleged financial scandal. A replacement for him was not put forward within seven days and this triggered an election for the Northern Ireland Assembly which was held in March 2017.

Following the election there was a period of three weeks during which time the two main political parties, Sinn Fein and the Democratic Unionists, should have come to an agreement about power-sharing. At the end of that period, no agreement had been reached. In such a situation, the UK Secretary of State for Northern Ireland has the option of calling another election or imposing direct rule from Westminster but, at the time of writing, he has given the parties more time to come to an agreement. In the meantime, a senior Northern Ireland civil servant has been appointed to control the budget and the allocation of resources to public services.

The situation is made more complicated by the UK Government's decision to trigger Article 50 of the Treaty on European Union following the Brexit referendum in June 2016 in which a majority in Northern Ireland voted to remain in the EU. If the United Kingdom leaves the European Union, there is the possibility of a 'hard border' between Northern Ireland and the Republic of Ireland. That could mean the reintroduction of border controls between Northern Ireland and the Republic of Ireland and potential obstructions to trade between the two if they are no longer part of the same customs union and single market. Sinn Fein has called for a border poll (referendum) on the question of the unification of Ireland to be held. This will be resisted by the UK Government and even more strongly so by the unionist political parties in Northern Ireland

England

England did not escape the government's decentralising zeal. The Regional Development Agencies Act 1998 established nine regional agencies in England, all of which, except for London, were operational by 1999. They had powers to further the economic development and regeneration of their areas and to promote business efficiency and employment in both urban and rural areas.[10] These agencies were quangos, their members being appointed by a Government Minister, not directly elected, and they were abolished in 2012.

In London, an elected Greater London Authority, with a directly elected mayor and assembly, was established.[11] The Greater London Authority does not have its own tax-raising powers but does raise revenue from precepts, road tolls and parking fees. The Mayor has the power to promote economic and social development in London, as well as transport and economic development bodies, and has the responsibility for attracting new investment, job creation and the regeneration of run-down urban areas. He/she also has responsibilities relating to the police and fire services for London, and the GLA Act 2007 gave the Mayor additional powers in the fields of planning, housing, health and the environment.

The constitutional developments in Scotland, Wales and Northern Ireland acted as a stimulus for debate in England and, in May 2002, the then Labour Government set out proposals for the establishment of elected regional assemblies, with executive and advisory powers, in those English regions where voters wished to have them. The Government proposed assemblies for North East England, North West England and Yorkshire and the Humber, with referendums to be held to determine whether to proceed with the proposals. However, only the North East referendum took place (in 2004) where the proposals were soundly rejected by the electorate. As a result, the Government subsequently announced that it would not proceed with its proposals for the remaining two regions. This defeat was widely considered to have killed off plans for further devolution in England and no further steps were taken by the Labour Government during its term in office to establish elected regional assembles for England. However, it did continue until 2010 to maintain indirectly appointed regional chambers along with regional leaders' boards which performed certain advisory and co-ordination functions.

The Conservative Party had opposed the introduction of regional assemblies in England and was sceptical about English regional government in general. Very shortly after the formation of the Conservative–Liberal Democrat Coalition Government in 2010, it announced the abolition of Regional Development Agencies and the Regional Strategies, the ending of funding for the regional leaders' boards, and the closure of the Government Office for London. However, although it was opposed to the form of regional government which had been half-heartedly pursued under Labour, the coalition government did take steps to encourage local authorities to form, on a voluntary basis, 'combined authorities' (under legislation introduced by the previous government) to co-ordinate transport and economic development policies. Many of these authorities covered very wide areas of England, such as West Midlands, North East, and Greater Manchester, and, in effect, created a type of regional government in large parts of the country. Although the membership of the governing bodies of these combined authorities was initially appointed indirectly, the Conservative Government decided that it would allow the introduction of directly elected mayors to combined authorities in England and Wales with powers over housing, transport, planning and policing. That measure was introduced by the Cities and

Local Government Devolution Act 2016. Having initially been hostile to any form of regional government after it returned to power in 2010, by 2016 the Conservative Party had, in effect, gone a long way towards the establishment of a form of elected regional government in much of England.

However, such moves did not do anything to tackle what many MPs representing constituencies in England considered to be a major problem with the devolution arrangements set up by the Labour Government. That was the issue of the West Lothian Question which is discussed earlier in this book.[12] Despite the reduction in the number of MPs representing constituencies in Scotland, these MPs could vote and therefore influence bills dealing with matters devolved to Scotland which applied only to England, while the MPs for English constituencies had no influence on Scottish Parliament bills. Responding to such complaints, the Government announced in 2012 the establishment of a commission to examine the consequences of devolution for the House of Commons (the McKay Commission). A proposal which emerged became known as EVEL – English Votes for English Laws – whereby MPs for English constituencies would be able to vote on and veto certain legislative provisions which apply only to England.

In 2015 the House of Commons adopted new procedures that enable MPs for English or Welsh constituencies to veto certain legislative provisions. The Speaker of the House of Commons must decide whether a bill or parts of a bill apply only to England (or England and Wales) and issue a certificate to that effect. A bill relating only to England must go to a committee consisting solely of MPs for English constituencies. There are a further three new stages which such a bill might go through between the Report Stage and the Third Reading – a consent motion which is considered by a Legislative Grand Committee followed, if necessary, by a Reconsideration and Consequential Consideration Stage. The bill then has to be passed by a vote of all UK MPs, thus allowing MPs from the devolved parts of the country to participate. Many MPs find the procedures baffling, as do most of the public, and they cannot be regarded in any sense as an 'answer' to the West Lothian Question. It remains the case that MPs from across the entire United Kingdom will have the final say on legislation that affects only England (or, as the case may be, England and Wales).

ASYMMETRICAL DEVOLUTION

The UK Government's policy of devolution since 1997 has evolved in different ways and with differing results across each of the nations and regions of the United Kingdom, and has been described as asymmetrical devolution. The debate has shifted towards not just an increase in devolved powers but to the issue of independence in some parts of the United Kingdom.

The Welsh National Assembly has evolved from being a largely administrative body under the auspices of the Secretary of State for Wales to one with legislative powers. Following the 2007 Welsh Assembly elections, a coalition agreement between the Labour and Plaid Cymru Parties contained a commitment to hold a referendum on full law-making powers for the Assembly before the end of the Assembly's term (in 2011), prompting some critics to suggest that this would be used as a staging post towards eventual independence for Wales.

At the 2007 Scottish Parliamentary elections the Scottish National Party emerged as the largest individual political grouping in the Scottish Parliament and, as a result, formed a (minority) Scottish Government. This moved the issue of Scottish independence to the top of the constitutional agenda. In response to this, the other main political groupings in the Scottish Parliament established the Calman Commission charged with looking at ways in which to strengthen the current devolution settlement while retaining the Union. Most of its proposals were put into effect by the Scotland Act 2012 but, by this time, the SNP had formed a majority Scottish Government, elected on a manifesto that included a commitment to hold a referendum on Scottish independence. That referendum was held in 2014 and resulted in a majority choosing to stay in the United Kingdom. Following the referendum, the Smith Commission was set up to consider the devolution of further powers to the Scottish Parliament. This led to the Scotland Act 2016.[13]

In the Scottish general election of 2016, the SNP lost its majority and formed a minority government. In the UK general election of 2017 the SNP lost more than a third of its seat, reducing the number of SNP MPs to thirty-five from the fifty-six it had won in 2015. This fall in support for the SNP may have the effect of delaying the Scottish Government seeking a second referendum on independence for Scotland.

English devolution appears to have fallen off the political radar, at least in the shape of directly elected assemblies covering large regions. The rejection by voters in 2004 of a regional assembly for North East England effectively ended any remaining prospects of English regional government. The discontent among MPs for English constituencies about MPs from Scotland (and also Northern Ireland and Wales) voting on issues at Westminster which were devolved in their own nations appears to have subsided. That may, of course, be due less to the arrangements introduced for 'English votes for English laws' but more to a simple reflection of the fact that the Conservative Government elected in 2015 had an overall majority in the House of Commons. The electoral arithmetic after that election made it much more unlikely that MPs from Scotland would be able to overrule the will of the majority of MPs from England.

At the time of writing, power sharing has broken down in Northern Ireland. The divide between unionists and nationalists has made Northern Ireland unique within the politics of the United Kingdom. The power of the UK Government to suspend home rule and impose direct control from Westminster, as a result of these divisions, has meant that devolution has not been as fully embedded in Northern Ireland as it has been in Scotland and Wales.

CONSTITUTIONAL REFORM

Furthermore, the programme of devolution and decentralisation has to be set in a wider context of constitutional reform, much of which was set out in the Labour Party's manifesto for the 1997 general election, and the governments, after Labour lost power in 2010, have also been active in some aspects of reform.

The European Convention on Human Rights (ECHR) was incorporated into UK law by the Human Rights Act 1998, improving the access of UK citizens to the rights and freedoms guaranteed by the Convention.[14] Although leading Conservatives have talked about abolishing the Human Rights Act, possibly replacing it with a 'British Bill of Rights', and even withdrawal from the ECHR itself, they were not in a position to do so during the term of the coalition government owing to the opposition of their Liberal Democrat partners in government. Since the referendum in 2016 on remaining in or leaving the European Union, the massive task of putting Brexit into effect appears to have dissuaded the Conservative Government from embarking on another complex constitutional reform and, in its White Paper on the 'Great Repeal Bill', has gone as far as to say that it does not intend to withdraw from the ECHR.[15] Whether the Conservative Party revives its enthusiasm for reform of the human rights legislation after the Brexit process is, of course, a question for some years in the future.

Both the UK as a whole and Scotland have seen the passage of legislation giving citizens access to freedom of information in the shape of, respectively, the Freedom of Information Act 2000 and the Freedom of Information (Scotland) Act 2002. In January 1999, the Government issued a White Paper, *Modernising Parliament: Reforming the House of Lords*.[16] The first step was to legislate for the removal of the right of hereditary peers to sit and vote in the House of Lords. Before the year came to an end, legislation was on the statute book. There is now a transitional house in which ninety-two hereditary peers sit on a temporary basis along with the life peers. An independent, non-statutory Appointments Commission, which is responsible for identifying suitable cross-bench nominees and for vetting all the political parties' nominations, has been established. The Government also established a Royal Commission, under the chairmanship of Lord Wakeham, to consider and make recommendations on the role and functions of a second chamber and the methods of its composition. The Royal Commission reported in January 2000.[17] Its preference, in terms of composition, was for a chamber consisting of mainly appointed members with a small number of regional elected members. However, it proved impossible to find a consensus on the Commission's recommendations, and reform of the House of Lords has slipped down the political agenda. It resurfaced for a while during the passage through Parliament of the bill authorising the Prime Minister to 'trigger' UK withdrawal from the European Union. During that process, it appeared possible that the House of Lords would make substantial changes to, or even reject, the Government's plans to notify the European Union that the United Kingdom would be terminating its membership. That led to some of the supporters of 'hard Brexit' to threaten that the House of Lords would be abolished if it acted in such a way. However, little has been heard of that threat since the bill completed its passage.

Even the monarchy has agreed to modernise itself. The rules which governed succession to the Crown meant that male heirs and their children (regardless of sex) took precedence over female heirs, while the Act of Settlement 1700 and the Acts of Union 1706–07 confined succession to members of the Protestant religion and specifically excluded Roman Catholics and those married to Roman Catholics. These rules seemed increasingly out of date in modern Britain and calls for the abolition mounted in recent years. The process of reforming the law relating to the succession to the Crown was complex and required legislation involving the amendment not only of various UK statutes, including the Acts of Union, but also the statutes of the many Commonwealth countries of which the monarch is Head of State. For many years, the UK Government stated that repeal did not come high in its list of priorities. In 2011, however, the Prime Ministers of the sixteen Commonwealth countries, which have the same monarch and the same order of succession as the UK, unanimously agreed to adopt a common approach to amending the rules of succession. This led to the Succession to the Crown Act 2013, an Act of the UK Parliament. Section 1 replaced the rule of male primogeniture with absolute primogeniture which means that a woman who is the first-born child of a monarch can succeed to the throne. In addition, section 2 of the Act ended the disqualification of a person in the line of succession who marries a Catholic. The monarch still remains the Head of the Church of England.

Changes to methods of voting were introduced to increase the turnout at elections. The Representation of the People Act 2000 aims to make it easier for certain people to register and to vote, and allows for pilot projects of innovative electoral procedures in local government elections in England and Wales, and also extended eligibility for postal voting in Scotland[18] as well as in England and Wales. The initial experience was that election turnout could be increased substantially through the use of innovative methods of voting. In the local elections in May 2003, around 6.5 million people were able to vote by digital television, the internet, touch telephone, text message or by post. More recently, however, the turnout in elections has fallen considerably, possibly due to further changes in the way potential voters are registered. A further measure was the reduction to eighteen, in 2006, of the age for standing for election to the parliaments, assemblies and councils within the UK.[19]

Political parties which had previously been almost invisible in statute now require to be registered if they wish to field candidates at elections.[20] Restrictions have also been introduced on the sources of donations, to prohibit foreign and anonymous donors and also on the amount of money a political party can spend in an election campaign and the amount spent by individuals or organisations in support of, or in opposition to, political parties. In addition, shareholder consent has to be obtained before a company can make a donation to a political party or incur political expenditure.[21]An important development was the establishment of the Electoral Commission,[22] which is an independent body charged to oversee elections and the electoral process, and make recommendations for change. It has stated its objective as being to 'gain public confidence and encourage people to take part in the democratic processes within the United Kingdom by modernising the electoral process, promoting public awareness of electoral matters, and regulating political parties'.

There has also been extensive reform of the first-past-the-post voting system. The Scottish Parliament and the National Assembly for Wales are elected by a mixture of the first-past-the-post and party-list systems known as the Additional-Member system (AMS).[23] The members of the Northern Ireland Assembly are elected under the system known as the Single Transferable Vote (STV). The members of the Greater London Authority and the Mayor of London are elected under a system called the supplementary vote while the elections to the European Parliament since 1999 have been on the party list system. All of these, to a greater or lesser degree, produce results in which the number of seats won by each political party is proportional to the number of votes cast for that party. They reduce the likelihood of one party winning an outright majority and, thus, coalition and interparty co-operation become more likely. In Wales, the Richard Commission's review of the devolution settlement recommended that elections to the Welsh Assembly be conducted using the Single Transferable Vote, with Assembly Members (AMs) elected on a multi-member ward basis. However, this was rejected by the Welsh Labour Party in 2004 and reaffirmed in 2005 in the UK Government's White Paper, *Better Governance for Wales*.[24]

In Scotland, changes to the local government electoral system were placed high on the political agenda as a result of the coalition agreement between Labour and the Liberal Democrats following the 2003 Scottish Parliamentary elections. As a result of this agreement, the Local Governance (Scotland) Act 2004 was passed which changed the electoral system to the Single Transferable Vote and, in May 2007, the local government elections were held using this system. This electoral system required the establishment of multi-member wards in place of the long-established single-member wards which enabled smaller parties, such as the Greens, to win seats.

In 2011, as a result of the agreement between the Conservative and Liberal Democrat Parties forming the UK Coalition Government, the Parliamentary Voting System and Constituencies Act 2011 enabled the holding of a referendum on the question of changing the voting system for the House of Commons from the first-past-the-post system to the alternative-vote system (FN). The result of the referendum was rejection of the AV system by 67.9 per cent to 32.1 per cent.

The current UK Government is opposed to any change in the electoral system for elections to the UK Parliament, and there is still no great enthusiasm for any form of proportional representation in the UK Labour Party,

REFERENDA

Recent years have also seen a growth in the use of referenda at both national and local levels. Until recently, referenda were used very sparingly by UK governments. In 1973, a referendum was held in Northern Ireland on the question of continued union with the United Kingdom. In 1975, there was a referendum on the question of the UK's continued membership of the European Communities. The implementation of the Scotland and Wales Acts 1978 was put to the people of Scotland and of Wales in 1979.

After the Labour Government came to power in May 1997, there were as many referenda in less than two years as there had been in the previous twenty-five. In 1997 the people of Scotland were consulted on the establishment of the Scottish Parliament and, separately, on the question of that Parliament having tax-varying powers. In the same year, the Welsh were consulted on the establishment of the National Assembly for Wales. In 1998, the citizens of London were consulted on the question of a directly elected mayor and an elected Greater London Authority, and the people of Northern Ireland were asked to vote on the Belfast Agreement. (The people of the Republic of Ireland were consulted by the Irish Government in a referendum on the same issue). As part of the Government's commitment to devolution to the English regions, referenda were proposed on the subject for three English regions but only one of those (in the North East England region) proceeded.

The Government of Wales Act 2006 contained provisions for a referendum to be held to determine whether to devolve additional law-making powers to Wales, and a referendum to gauge this was held in 2011, while the SNP-led Scottish Government held a referendum in 2014 on independence for Scotland.

Legislation, designed to ensure the fair conduct of referenda, is now in place.[25] It includes provisions for spending limits up to £700,000 for campaign bodies, free mailing of referendum addresses and free air time for referendum campaign expenditure by political parties. It also places restrictions on the publication and distribution of promotional material by central and local government and on referendum-campaign expenditure by political parties. The Electoral Commission is required to be consulted on the terms of referendum questions. A further innovation was the provision the Government introduced (in England and Wales) allowing for local referenda on the introduction of a directly elected mayor in the local areas concerned.[26]

In June 2003, the Labour Government announced that it would be introducing legislation to allow for the holding (at some future date) of a referendum on UK membership of the euro. That referendum did not materialise because that Government, and every government since, decided not to proceed with such a proposal. However, the Conservative Government elected in 2015 promised in its election manifesto to hold a referendum on continued UK membership of the European Union itself.

That referendum, undoubtedly the most controversial referendum to date, was held on 23 June 2016. It was held under the EU Referendum Act 2015. It was widely expected that the majority would be in favour of remaining in the European Union but the result was 48.1 per cent in favour of remaining and 51.9 per cent in favour of leaving the EU. The UK's departure from the European Union has become known as Brexit.

As a result of the doctrine of Parliamentary sovereignty,[27] in legal terms, referendums are advisory only and cannot be considered as legally binding on the Government or Parliament. Nevertheless, governments have regarded the results of the referendums held so far to be morally binding and a mandate for the actions they propose to take. In the case of the Brexit referendum, leaving the European Union was certainly not an action which the Government proposed to take. Such was the controversy and strength of feeling about the result, however, that Prime Minister David Cameron resigned. He was replaced by Theresa May. She felt she was politically bound to accept the result of the referendum. Indeed, she considered that the result of the referendum, even though only advisory, gave her the authority to proceed to give formal notification to the European Union of the UK's intention to leave. This view was challenged, however, and, in the *Miller* case, the Supreme Court ruled that formal notification could be given by the UK Government only if it was authorised to do so. The UK Government secured this authority by the passage of the European Union (Notification of Withdrawal) Act 2017. This matter is considered in more detail in the preceding chapter.

In the case of the Scotland Act 1998, it certainly had an easier passage through Parliament, in particular through the House of Lords, than the last named Act. No doubt that was a result of the overwhelming support for the Scottish Parliament expressed by the Scottish people in the referendum in 1997 meant that there was no serious opposition to the relevant legislation being placed on the statute book. As the British become more used to being consulted by government on major issues, there could, in the longer term, be implications for the sovereignty of Parliament.

CONCLUSION

There is no doubt that, for those who are interested in the constitution, these are exciting times. The establishment of the Scottish Parliament in 1999 led, almost immediately, to major differences in the way in which Scotland is governed. The election of a minority SNP administration in the 2007 Scottish general election, and a majority administration in 2011, led to the debate on independence for Scotland taking centre stage in Scottish politics, culminating in the Scottish independence referendum of 2014. Despite the defeat of the 'Yes' campaign in that referendum, the SNP still maintained a high level of electoral support in the UK general election of 2015 and the Scottish general election in 2016. Although the SNP suffered significant losses in the 2017 UK general election, it remains the most supported political party in Scotland, and opinion polls suggest that the support for independence is broadly at the same levels that it was in 2014. The issue of independence is still likely to continue to be a high-profile issue in Scotland.

For the rest of the United Kingdom, government has in ways that would not have been contemplated twenty or so years ago. Even though the UK governments elected in 2015 and 2017 have displayed much less appetite for domestic constitutional reform than their predecessors, there has been legislation for further devolution for Scotland and Wales in the implementation of reform processes begun under the previous Coalition Government. An increasingly important role has been given to 'city regions', bringing together local authorities across wide areas, which may in turn give greater status and political influence to powerful elected mayors.

Furthermore, as has been discussed above, the UK's departure from the European Union may also have dramatic consequences for the UK's governmental structure. This might occur as a result of the departure from the United Kingdom of Scotland or Northern Ireland or both, possibly leading in the longer term to Wales following suit. Even if those dramatic changes do not come about, the return to the United Kingdom of powers currently exercised by the European Union is likely to lead to some of those powers being further transferred to the devolved administrations. The tensions between the different parts of the United Kingdom, which have been exacerbated by the results of the Brexit referendum, may lead to a greater interest in the possibility of the UK being transformed into a fully federal state.

The constitutional map of the United Kingdom already looks very different from the way it looked in 1997, and it may well look even more radically different in the not too distant future.

NOTES

1. On the fall in turnout in 2001, see Catherine Bromley and John Curtice, 'The Lost Voters of Scotland: Devolution Disillusioned or Westminster Weary?', in *British Elections & Parties Review*, 2003.
2. Government of Wales Act 1998 (GWA 1998), section 22 and Schedule 3.
3. GWA 1998, section 31.
4. GWA 1998, section 22.
5. Northern Ireland Act 1998 (NIA 1998), Schedule 3.
6. For more information, see www.niassembly.gov.uk (last accessed 10 April 2017).
7. The Belfast Agreement, also known as the Good Friday Agreement, made on 10 April 1998 as a result of the multiparty negotiations.
8. For details of the activity of these bodies, see www.british-irish.council.org and www.northsouthministerial.council.org (both last accessed 10 April 2017).
9. For more information, see www.niassembly.gov.uk
10. Regional Development Agencies Act 1998, section 4.
11. Greater London Authority Act 1999.
12. See p. 38.
13. See Chapter 1 for the Calman and Smith Commissions.
14. See previous chapter for more on human rights law and the ECHR.
15. Legislating for the United Kingdom's Withdrawal from the European Union, March 2017, Cm 9446, paragraph 22.
16. 1998, Cm 4183.
17. Report of the Royal Commission on the Reform of the House of Lords: A House for the Future (Cm 4534).
18. Representation of the People Act 2000, Schedule 4.
19. Electoral Administration Act 2006, section 17.
20. Political Parties, Elections and Referendums Act 2000 (PPERA 2000), section 22.
21. PPERA 2000, Parts IV, V, VI, VIII and IX.
22. PPERA 2000, section 6.
23. See electoralcommisson.gov.uk (last accessed 10 April 2017) for further details.
24. Cm 6582, June 2005.
25. PPERA 2000, Part VII.
26. Local Government Act 2000, Part II.
27. See p. 15.

Glossary of Terms

absolute majority: a number of votes which is equivalent to more than half of the total number of seats in the Parliament. The figure in a Parliament with 129 seats is 65 or more.

Advocate General: the Advocate General (for Scotland) is the Law Officer whose task is to advise the UK on matters of law relating to Scottish devolution.

Barnett formula: the formula used to calculate the change to the block grant for each devolved administration when the UK Government increases or decreases its own spending.

block grant: a lump sum payment made every year by the UK Government to each devolved administration.

Brexit: an abbreviation for 'British exit', meaning British (or, more accurately, UK) exit from the European Union.

Cabinet Secretary: the term introduced by the SNP Government in 2007 to describe Ministers in the Scottish Government with a seat in its Cabinet.

Calman Commission: an independent commission set up in 2007 by the Scottish Parliament, and supported by the UK Government to consider possible further devolution for Scotland. It issued its final report in June 2009. Its recommendations were reflected in the Scotland Act 2012.

committee bill: a bill proposed by a committee of the Scottish Parliament (rather than the Scottish Government or an individual MSP).

constituency members: members of the Scottish Parliament who are returned by the first-past-the-post method of election and who represent individual constituencies. There are currently seventy-three constituency members.

Consultative Steering Group (CSG): a group, containing representatives of the main political parties in Scotland and others, which was set up by the UK Government to prepare for the establishment of the Scottish Parliament. Its task was to report on the operational needs and working methods of the Parliament and develop proposals for rules of procedure and **Standing Orders** which the Parliament might adopt (and which, for the most part, it did).

Convener: the person who chairs a committee.

Convention rights: the human rights set out in the European Convention on Human Rights which have been incorporated into UK law by the Human Rights Act 1998 and the Scotland Act 1998. All legislation of the Scottish Parliament must be compatible with these human rights as must, in general, be action taken by Scottish Ministers.

Council of Europe: an international organisation concerned with protecting human rights, democracy, and the rule of law in Europe. It has forty-seven member states. Not to be confused with the European Council which is an institution of the EU.

Court of Justice of the European Union (CJEU): the supreme court of the European Union sits in Luxemburg. It is made up of judges, each one nominated by a different member state of the European Union. Its rulings on matters of EU law are binding on all courts in every member state of the European Union. It consists of two courts, the Court of Justice and the General Court. The former is also known informally as the European Court of Justice.

Court of Session: the highest court of civil jurisdiction in Scotland. Under certain conditions, appeal or reference may be made from it to the UK Supreme Court.

declarator: an order of a Scottish court which declares the rights of a party.

devolved administrations: the informal collective name for the Scottish Government, the Welsh Government, and the Northern Ireland Executive.

ECHR: the European Convention on Human Rights (now incorporated, for the most part, in UK law by the Human Rights Act 1998).

EU: the European Union. The EU is a political and economic community, currently with twenty-eight members including the UK. The principal institutions of the European Union are the European Council, the Council of the European Union (often referred to as the Council of Ministers), the European Parliament, the European Commission, the Court of Justice of the European Union, the European Central Bank, and the European Court of Auditors.

EU law: the law of the EU. It is to be found in EU treaties; regulations, directives, and decisions which are derived from the principles and objectives set out in the treaties; and the case law of the CJEU interpreting and applying those treaties and other legislation.

First Minister: the person who is the head of the Scottish Government, normally (though not automatically) the leader of the political party with the largest number of seats.

Government Bill: a bill proposed by a Minister in the Scottish Government.

High Court of Justiciary: the highest court of criminal jurisdiction in Scotland. A reference, but not an appeal, can be made in certain circumstances from this court to the UK Supreme Court.

interdict: an order from a Scottish court which prohibits conduct.

intra vires: within the powers granted by legislation; for example, the powers of the Scottish Parliament as laid down in the Scotland Act.

junior Scottish Ministers: members of the Scottish Parliament who are appointed to assist the Scottish Ministers and who normally carry out ministerial functions for part of their Minister's brief.

Law Officers: in Scotland these are the Lord Advocate and the Solicitor General. The Lord Advocate is the principal legal adviser to the Scottish Government and is also the head of the system of public prosecution of crime and the investigation of deaths in Scotland. The Solicitor General is the deputy to the Lord Advocate. They are members of the Scottish Government but they need not be elected as MSPs (and none has been since the Parliament was established).

legislative competence: areas within which the Scottish Parliament can make laws as laid down in the Scotland Act 1998.

Legislative Consent Motion: or **LCM**. See **Sewel Convention and Sewel Motions,** below.

MSP: a Member of the Scottish Parliament.

Member's Bill: proposed legislation which is introduced by an individual MSP and not by a Scottish Minister.

Order in Council: a form of secondary legislation, made in a more formal manner than a statutory instrument.

Parliamentary Bureau: the PB consists of the Presiding Officer and a representative of each political party with five or more MSPs. There are also provisions for representation by parties with fewer than five MSPs. Its main functions are the organisation of the business programme of the Parliament and the establishment, remit, and membership of the Parliament's committees and subcommittees.

Presiding Officer: the MSP who chairs the meetings of the full Parliament and is responsible for keeping order during proceedings in Parliament. The role is very similar to that of the Speaker of the House of Commons.

Private Bills/private legislation: legislation promoted through the Parliament, usually by bodies such as local authorities, occasionally by private individuals.

quorum: the minimum number of members who must be present for business to be undertaken.

regional members: members of the Scottish Parliament who are returned from the regional lists drawn up by the political parties or as individual candidates on the regional lists. There are fifty-six regional members at present. The regional members are often described as the 'list members'.

schedule: part of an Act of Parliament which may be found at the end of the sections of an Act. It contains matters of detail which cannot conveniently be included in the body of the Act such as the list of reserved matters in the Scotland Act. Not every Act has a schedule. The Scotland Act 1998 contains nine schedules.

Scotland Act 1998: the Scotland Act 1998 (SA 1998) was passed by the UK Parliament after a referendum in Scotland in 1997 showed substantial support for the UK Government's proposals for an elected Scottish Parliament with tax-raising powers. It has been amended on a number of occasions, most significantly by the Scotland Act 2012 (SA 2012) and the Scotland Act 2016 (SA 2016).

Scottish Administration: this term covers the First Minister and the other members of the Scottish Government, Junior Scottish Ministers, certain offices such as the Registrar General of Births, Deaths and Marriages for Scotland, the Keeper of the Registers of Scotland and the Keeper of the Records of Scotland, and their staff.

Scottish Constitutional Convention: the Scottish Constitutional Convention (SCC) was a body which was established in 1989 with the support of the Labour, Liberal Democrat, and several smaller parties, together with most of Scottish local authorities and representatives of a wide spectrum of Scottish civic life. In 1995 it published proposals, *Scotland's Parliament: Scotland's Right*, for a Scottish Parliament with powers over a wide range of domestic issues and limited tax raising powers.

Scottish Government: the members of the Scottish Government, namely the **First Minister**, the Scottish Ministers (currently termed **Cabinet Secretaries**), and the **Law Officers**. Prior to 2012, it was formally known as the Scottish Executive though it was frequently described as the Scottish Government before then. The term Scottish

Government is also commonly used to include the departments and civil servants of the **Scottish Administration**. The members of the Scottish Government are referred to collectively as the 'Scottish **Ministers**'.

Scottish Parliamentary Corporate Body (SPCB): the body which provides the Scottish Parliament with staff, services, and property.

secondary legislation: legislation normally made by Ministers which implements the details of policy already agreed in broad terms by an Act of Parliament or by an Act of the Scottish Parliament. It is also known as **subordinate** or **delegated legislation**. The most common forms are **statutory instruments** and **Orders in Council**. Statutory instruments made by Scottish Ministers are known as **Scottish statutory instruments**.

Sewel motions/Sewel Convention: under the Sewel Convention, the UK Government has undertaken that it will not normally legislate on devolved matters without the consent of the Scottish Parliament. A motion whereby the Scottish Parliament gives such consent is known as a Sewel motion, or a Legislative Consent Motion.

Smith Commission: a cross-party commission set up by the UK Government immediately after the Scottish independence referendum in September 2014. It reported shortly afterwards, making proposals for substantial further devolution of taxation and spending powers to the Scottish Parliament. Most of its recommendations were implemented by the Scotland Act 2016.

Standing Orders: the rules which govern the proceedings in the Parliament.

sub judice: currently subject to legal proceedings.

subordinate legislation: see **secondary legislation**.

ultra vires: outside the powers granted by legislation (for example, the powers of the Scottish Parliament as defined in the Scotland Act 1998).

Further Reading

Books and Articles

Aughey, Arthur, 'The Future of Britishness', in Robert Hazell (ed.), *Constitutional Futures Revisited: Britain's Constitution to 2020*, (2008).

Bogdanor, Vernon, *The New British Constitution*, (2009).

Bradley, Anthony W., Keith D. Ewing, and Christopher J. S. Knight, *Constitutional and Administrative Law* (16th edn, 2014).

Cairney, Paul, *The Scottish Political System Since Devolution*, (2011).

—, 'How Can the Scottish Parliament be Improved as a Legislature?', (2013) 1 *Scottish Parliamentary Review* 1.

The Rt Hon. The Lord Clyde and Denis J. Edwards, *Judicial Review*, (2000).

Devine, Tom, *The Scottish Nation*, (2012).

Devine, Tom and Jenny Wormald, *The Oxford Handbook of Modern Scottish History*, (2012).

Dimelow, Stephen, *The Interpretation of 'Constitutional Statutes'*, (2013) 129 LQR 498.

Dunion, Kevin, *Freedom of Information in Scotland in Practice*, (2011).

Hadfield, Brigid, 'Devolution: A National Conversation', in J. Jowell and D. Oliver (eds), *The Changing Constitution* (7th edn, 2011).

Hazell, Robert (ed.), *Constitutional Futures Revisited: Britain's Constitution to 2020*, (2008).

—(ed), *Devolution and the Future of the Union*, (2015).

Himsworth, Chris and Christine O'Neill, *Scotland's Constitution: Law and Practice*, (3rd edn, 2015).

Jowell, Jeffrey and Dawn Oliver (eds), *The Changing Constitution* (8th edn, 2015).

McFadden, Jean and Dale McFadzean, *Public Law Essentials* (2nd edn, 2016).

McHarg, Aileen and Tom Mullen (eds), *Public Law in Scotland* (2006).

Mackay, Donald (ed.), *Scotland: the Framework for Change* (1979).

Melton, James, Christine Stuart and Daniel Helen, *To codify or not to codify? Lessons from the United Kingdom's constitutional statutes* (2015).

Page, Alan, 'One Legal System Two Legislatures: Scottish Law-Making After Devolution', in A. McHarg and T. Mullen (eds*)*, *Public Law in Scotland* (2006).

—, *Constitutional Law of Scotland* (2015).

Page, Alan and Andrea Batey, 'Scotland's other Parliament: Westminster legislation about devolved matters in Scotland since devolution', *Public Law* (autumn 2002).

Paun, Akash and Robyn Munro, *Governing in an Ever Looser Union* (2015).

Reed, Robert and Jim Murdoch, *Human Rights Law in Scotland* (2012).

Sutherland, Elaine, Kay Goodall, Gavin Little and Fraser Davidson (eds), *Law Making and the Scottish Parliament: the Early Years* (2011).

Tierney, Stephen, 'Scotland and the Union State', in A. McHarg and T. Mullen (eds), *Public Law in Scotland* (2006).

—, 'The Three Hundred and Seven Year Itch: Scotland and the 2014 Independence Referendum', in M. Qvortrup (ed.), *The British Constitution: Continuity and Change* (2013).

Trench, Alan, 'Scotland and Wales: The Evolution of Devolution', in Robert Hazell (ed.), *Constitutional Futures Revisited: Britain's Constitution to 2020* (2008).

Turpin, Colin and Alan Tomkins, *British Government and the Constitution* (7th edn, 2011).

Blogs

Devolution Matters: http://devolutionmatters.wordpress.com/

EU Law Analysis: http://eulawanalysis.blogspot.co.uk/

European Futures: http://www.europeanfutures.ed.ac.uk/

Public Law for Everyone: http://www.publiclawforeveryone.wordpress.com

Scottish Constitutional Futures Forum: http://www.scottishconstitutionalfutures.org

UK Constitutional Law Group blog: http://ukconstitutionallaw.org/blog/

UK Supreme Court blog: http://ukscblog.com/

UCL Constitution Unit blog: http://constitution-unit.com/

Index